Managing SAP R/3 with Tivoli

Stefan Uelpenich

■ Poonam Dhawan ■ Stephane Gillardo ■ Masahiro Kubo
■ Jose Hernani Oliveira, Jr. ■ Thomas Serckx ■ Carsten Siegler
■ Theo Winkelmann

Prentice Hall PTR
Upper Saddle River, New Jersey 07458

Published by Prentice Hall PTR
Prentice-Hall, Inc.
Upper Saddle River, NJ 07458

Editorial/Production Supervision: Kathleen M. Caren
Acquisitions Editor: Michael M. Meehan
Editorial Assistant: Bart Blanken
Manufacturing Manager: Pat Brown
Marketing Manager: Bryan Gambrel
Cover Design Director: Jayne Conte
Cover Designer: Kiwi Design

Prentice Hall books are widely used by corporations and government agencies for training, marketing, and resale.
The publisher offers discounts on this book when ordered in bulk quantities. For more information, contact: Corporate Sales
Department, Phone: 800-382-3419; FAX: 201-236-7141; E-mail (Internet): corpsales@prenhall.com; or write:
Prentice Hall PTR, Corp. Sales Dept., One Lake Street, Upper Saddle River, NJ 07458.
Printed in the United States of America

10 9 8 7 6 5 4 3 2 1

ISBN 0-13-015037-1

Prentice-Hall International (UK) Limited, *London*
Prentice-Hall of Australia Pty. Limited, *Sydney*
Prentice-Hall Canada Inc., *Toronto*
Prentice-Hall Hispanoamericana, S.A., *Mexico*
Prentice-Hall of Private Limited, *New Delhi*
Prentice-Hall of Japan, Inc., *Tokyo*
Prentice-Hall (Singapore) Asia Pte. Ltd., *Singapore*
Editora Prentice-Hall do Brasil, Ltda., *Rio de Janeiro*

Contents

Figures

Tables

Foreword

As the new millennium approaches, Tivoli shines as the world's leading manufacturer of enterprise management software. Tivoli gives you the power to manage anything, anywhere.

Reading Tivoli's client list is similar to reading a Who's Who directory in financial services, telecommunications, transportation, manufacturing, electronics and computers, healthcare, retail, the service industries, the utilities business, and education.

Tivoli is building an industry, not just a company or product, around enterprise management. From a business perspective, this means that Tivoli helps businesses achieve greater returns on technology investments and optimize the use of existing staff and resources. This is in keeping with the Tivoli philosophy of unification and integration, which drives organizational efficiency and effectiveness. Tivoli aligns IT with business objectives.

A strong understanding of the Enterprise Resource Planning (ERP) market makes Tivoli the ideal accompaniment to SAP R/3. In addition to understanding the ERP market, Tivoli has a vision that includes solutions focused from a business, rather than from a pure information technology, perspective. The advantage provided by Tivoli's distinctive understanding of the ERP market combined with a cogent vision for the future proves, once again, that Tivoli is a pioneer in the world of technology.

By offering Tivoli Enterprise software products to manage SAP R/3, Tivoli successfully utilizes its application and systems management strategy to support the SAP R/3 client/server application system. Tivoli's management products for R/3 build on core Tivoli management applications and support the Tivoli approach to unified, comprehensive enterprise management. This approach allows R/3 to be managed as part of the enterprise and with the same tools that are used to manage the entire enterprise. Tivoli Enterprise software allows organizations to simplify the management of complex environments with offerings like the Tivoli solution for R/3, enabling continual operation of systems that drive customers' businesses.

At the core of Tivoli's management approach is Tivoli Enterprise, which provides a truly open and comprehensive foundation for the management of e-business. Tivoli Enterprise simplifies today's most complex e-business challenges.

As the Tivoli Enterprise name suggests, Tivoli not only creates products, but helps manage the entire enterprise. While other vendors worked on individual tools and tasks, Tivoli Enterprise was developed with a flexible architecture capable of working with any server, client, database, application, or user that provides the scalability and flexibility needed for true end-to-end enterprise IT management.

Leading the way once again Tivoli is focused on aligning IT with business goals to accelerate business growth and success.

The value of this book is in its detailed approach to managing SAP R/3 using the Tivoli Enterprise software products. By positioning the Tivoli application management strategy and providing specific examples, the expertise of the authors provides you with a unique perspective for managing an enterprise SAP R/3 installation.

Mike Turner
Vice President
Enterprise Business Unit
Tivoli Systems

Preface

As organizations replace and augment existing business applications with ERP systems such as SAP R/3, they need to manage a wide range of platforms, across the full set of management disciplines, including problem solving, change management, job schedules, output, help desk, software distribution, asset management, configuration management, performance management, event monitoring and correlation, user access, security, and service management.

Tivoli Systems offers a solution that is ideally suited to help companies achieve true global management and reduce the total cost of ownership of their SAP R/3 investment. The Tivoli R/3 management suite provides comprehensive application management, tailored to SAP R/3. Tivoli provides an exceptionally versatile management architecture, enabling thousands of diverse systems, applications, and users to be managed within a common framework. This allows a new level of automation and the ability to manage your entire I/T infrastructure through a single paradigm, with a minimal staff. With Tivoli, your I/T staff can be used more effectively to meet business goals, provide better service, and contribute to the corporate bottom line, instead of just continually "putting out fires."

In this book, we position the Tivoli application management and systems management strategy and then show in detail how to set up and use the Tivoli R/3 management suite to create an integrated R/3 management environment. This enables the reader to plan, design and successfully implement a comprehensive R/3 management solution based on Tivoli.

The Team That Wrote This Book

This book was produced by a team of specialists from around the world working at the IBM International Technical Support Organization, Raleigh Center.

This project was designed and managed by:

Stefan Uelpenich is a Senior ITSO Representative working as a project leader in the ITSO Tivoli Group, Austin. He applies his extensive field experience as an I/T architect and project leader to his work at the ITSO, where he writes extensively and consults worldwide on all areas of systems management. Before joining the ITSO, Stefan worked in IBM Germany's Professional Services organization as an Advisory I/T Architect for Systems Management, consulting major IBM customers. In this role, he architected the systems management solution for one of Germany's largest client/server networks. Having published 15 books on a wide area of topics in the field of systems management and Tivoli and being involved in numerous projects, Stefan is one of the leading experts in the field of systems management.

The other authors of this book are:

Dr. Masahiro Kubo is an Advisory I/T Specialist at the Technical Support Center in IBM Japan. He started working with Tivoli products when Tivoli merged with IBM and is now the technical lead for design and implementation of Tivoli systems management solutions. Recently, his customer engagement was to build a sophisticated management solution, where Tivoli acts as a manager of managers, managing multiple HP system management servers. His areas of expertise include knowledge of manufacturing industry solutions and SAP R/3 Basis. His writings relating to Tivoli are *The Vital Point of Introducing Tivoli, the Integrated System Control Package* published in ProVISION No.19 in October 1998 and *Thinking Way of Business System Management*, both of which received professional paper awards from IBM Japan.

Stephane Gillardo is an I/T Specialist working for IBM Global Services in the Service Delivery EMEA West group, located in La Gaude, France. He has been working with IBM for two years, and has expertise with all Tivoli core applications for the management of distributed systems. Stephane has been involved in Tivoli product evaluations and in projects for Tivoli solution deployments. His areas of expertise include Tivoli 3.6, and he was also one of the authors of another ITSO Tivoli book.

Thomas Serckx is an I/T Specialist working as a systems engineer at IBM Global Services in Belgium. He has been working for two years in the Service Delivery group, and his areas of expertise include Tivoli, networking, UNIX, and Windows NT. Now, as a member of the SAP/UNIX Systems Management team, Thomas is designing and deploying a Tivoli solution for the centralized management of the midrange servers of major IBM outsourced customers.

Carsten Siegler is a technical consultant working in IBM Global Services in Heidelberg, Germany. As a member of the SAP Systems Management team, he focuses on SAP R/3 systems management and SAP R/3 Basis. In his four years of experience, he has supported and designed SAP R/3 systems management solutions for the Tivoli Module for SAP R/3, SAP R/3 Backup, SAP R/3 Archiving and SAP R/3 Basis.

Jose Hernani Oliveira Jr. is an Advisory I/T Specialist working for IBM Global Services in the Strategic Outsourcing, Enterprise Automation group in

Sumare, Brazil. He has been with IBM for seven years and has held various positions as a systems analyst, technical support analyst and I/T specialist His areas of expertise include networking, operating systems, relational databases, and object technology. He is currently working in deploying Tivoli monitoring and automation products to outsourced SAP customers in Brazil.

Theo Winkelmann is an Advisory I/T Specialist, working as a technical consultant at IBM Global Services in South Africa. His areas of expertise include Tivoli, TCP/IP, UNIX, and Windows NT. In his current position, Theo consults major IBM accounts in South Africa and has been the lead architect for one of the largest Tivoli projects in Africa, managing close to 100000 desktop systems and involving all Tivoli core products. Theo has previously authored another ITSO Tivoli book.

Special thanks to Poonam Dhawan, Product Line Manager, Tivoli ERP Solutions, without whose guidance, direction and support this book would not have been possible.

Thanks to the following people for their invaluable contributions to this project:

Bill Sadek
International Technical Support Organization, Raleigh Center

Patrick Ancipink, Jon Goodman, Jay Kruemcke, David Moring
Tivoli Systems, Austin

Ellen Dickson, Terry Casstevens, Ron Cherveny, Todd Miller, Tom Songvichitr, Sandy Jenkins
Tivoli/SAP Solutions, Raleigh

Andy Kicklighter
Tivoli Systems, Santa Clara

Ingo Averdunk
Tivoli Professional Services

Frank Fischer
Tivoli/IBM Germany

Marcus Brewer, Tara Campbell
International Technical Support Organization, Austin Center

Kathryn Casamento, Linda Robinson, Shawn Walsh, Gail Christensen
Editing Team, International Technical Support Organization, Raleigh Center

Chapter 1. Maximizing the Value of Your R/3 Investment

Before we discuss how to manage SAP R/3 with Tivoli in detail, we briefly introduce the Enterprise Resource Planning (ERP) market and provide a high level overview of the management of ERP systems in general and of SAP R/3 in particular.

1.1 The Enterprise Resource Planning Market

During the past decade, information technology evolved from being a key component of business success into a critical element required for business strategy execution. The early 1990s gave birth to Enterprise Resource Planning (ERP) systems that integrated business functions, shared common data, and provided connectivity with a single interface.

Soon after, the ERP marketplace exploded. Packaged software, fueled by reliable hardware, modern databases, and huge information technology advances, offered tremendous business functionality to even the largest enterprises. Enterprise Resource Planning (ERP) systems emerged and have matured to become the core of successful information management.

An ERP system's greatest strength is its ability to integrate a company's business information. Companies need dynamic strategies to meet the challenges of today's fast-paced business world. The ability to respond nimbly to new customer needs and seize market opportunities as they arise is crucial. Managing core business processes in the context of enterprise resource planning is key to achieving and maintaining a competitive advantage in total quality, cost management and response time.

One of the premier ERP systems is SAP AG's R/3 system. SAP R/3 and its components are unmatched at integrating and improving business practices. For businesses of every size and industry, SAP R/3 products offer an unbeatable combination of functionality, flexibility, and technology, enabling companies to respond quickly to change. Faster response means you'll have more time to concentrate on strategically growing your business.

With the "enterprise" now being extended beyond the traditional boundaries of the organization to include customers and suppliers, the importance of well-managed, supply-chain-enhancing processes is heightened. New technologies offer extraordinary opportunities for business benefit, yet they can also embody complexity, apprehension and risk. Companies in pursuit of excellence must advantageously leverage complexity, convert uneasiness to resourcefulness and mitigate uncertainty.

Competition is more intense in today's information-driven economy than ever before. Speedy access to accurate, real-time information provides a basis for the critical decision making necessary to carry out business strategy. Therefore, competitive advantage and ultimate survival depends on the use of information systems and technology.

1.2 Managing R/3 Systems

Companies spend millions annually on R/3 software, services, and infrastructure. Corporate executives demand significant return on investment to achieve a competitive edge, offer unequaled customer service, and disarm the competition. R/3 solutions deliver agility and emphasize customer satisfaction, but are enabled by information technology. These IT resources must be managed effectively in order to maximize the R/3 investment.

R/3's open IT infrastructure supports various business activities and enables companies to adjust flexibly to change and progress. Therefore, companies depend on R/3 solutions to run critical business functions — from financial and human resource systems to supporting new e-commerce and supply-chain management.

The need to manage all of these I/T components as part of an overall Business System can be one of the greatest challenges associated with rolling out an R/3 system. To maximize the benefits of the R/3 investment and help end users reliably do their jobs, you have to manage a complex mixture of diverse resources and the connections between those resources that span the entire enterprise.

I/T managers typically face issues such as how to deploy client software to thousands of desktops, how to maintain the availability of the business systems, and how to identify and resolve problems — all in an environment where any failure can have an immediate impact on the company's bottom line.

To successfully manage this complex web of interdependencies and keep your business running in the most productive and efficient manner, you must:

- Ensure end-user productivity
- Increase the effectiveness of IT resources
- Easily accommodate change

Achieving these IT management goals in an R/3 environment is no easy task: You face the constant pressure to increase service levels without additional resources, find and retain skilled R/3 personnel, and support an ever-growing R/3 installation.

While R/3 offers excellent management capabilities, these capabilities are somewhat limited to the R/3 application itself. Although important, this just doesn't address the scope of management required. To effectively deal with the needs of this complex, enterprise-wide I/T environment, you need integrated tools that are open and flexible enough to handle management tasks affecting the enterprise as a whole, including the R/3 environment.

As organizations replace and augment existing business applications with R/3 systems, they need to manage a wide range of platforms, across the full set of management disciplines: problems, change, job schedules, output, help desk, software distribution, asset management, configuration management, performance management, event monitoring and correlation, user access, security, and service management.

Since the R/3 applications depend on information from numerous corporate systems, it is not enough to simply monitor the applications alone for "red alerts". What if a problem occurs in the middleware as data is translated from the mainframe to another server for use in an R/3 solution? Where does IS look when the sales force can't access product delivery information? Is it a problem with the R/3 solution? The integrated sales automation package? Or perhaps the problem is in the database feeding the R/3 application.

In the past, companies developed islands of management – separate organizations and tools that addressed once seemingly separate issues, such as network management, mainframe management, database management, LAN management, and desktop management. Yet with the increasing complexity of today's ERP environments, transforming systems management to a centralized, integrated approach has become a necessity for optimizing the use of information across an organization.

Tivoli Systems offers a solution that is ideally suited to help companies achieve true global management and reduce the total cost of ownership of their R/3 investment. Tivoli offers a complete set of management tools that address each layer of IT infrastructures — networks, systems, databases, middleware, and applications — under a single, integrated, and centralized monitoring and reporting environment. Using this multidisciplinary, "big picture" approach, companies can remain proactive in deploying and monitoring R/3 and the associated infrastructure components that may impact access to business critical data.

Tivoli's business systems approach to R/3 management maximizes the value of your SAP R/3 investment. Effective R/3 management increases the value of SAP in three key ways: by leveraging skills, by improving availability of SAP services, and by increasing user productivity.

In this book, we introduce the Tivoli solution for management of R/3 and explain in detail how this solution can be used to create an integrated R/3 management environment. We first analyze in detail the management requirements for an R/3 system and then show step-by-step how to set up a management environment based on the Tivoli Solution for R/3 that matches these requirements.

Chapter 2. Management Requirements for SAP R/3

In this chapter, we explain the management requirements for SAP R/3 and how they can be addressed by using the Tivoli management solution for R/3. We also discuss some of the planning considerations that have to take place before installing the necessary Tivoli components in our environment to manage the SAP R/3 installation.

2.1 Overview and Objective

It is important to understand the many components involved in building an SAP R/3 management solution before actually implementing the systems management products.

In this chapter, we first look at the challenges involved in managing an enterprise R/3 installation. We explain the benefits of using Tivoli to manage R/3, introduce the R/3 management solution provided by Tivoli and the R/3 system, and discuss its management tools.

Then we elaborate on how to define the requirements for the management of the R/3 installation, how to select the management products, and how to design an effective systems management solution for SAP R/3.

This chapter, however, can give you only some ideas to get started and cannot replace a thorough planning process for designing your R/3 management solution.

We strongly advise that all large-scale systems management deployments for R/3 be guided by an experienced I/T architect who understands the R/3 architecture and, more importantly, the overall systems management architecture of the environment.

2.2 Challenges in Managing an SAP R/3 Environment

Management of an R/3 system constitutes a challenge for the following main reasons:

- The R/3 installation is usually highly critical.
- R/3 installations are complex by nature and complex to manage.

The R/3 installation of an enterprise is highly critical because it runs the core of the company's business logic, such as the ordering system, sales, accounting, payroll, human resources, and so forth. Therefore, requirements are usually tough in regard to:

- Reliability
- Availability
- Security
- Accountability
- Performance

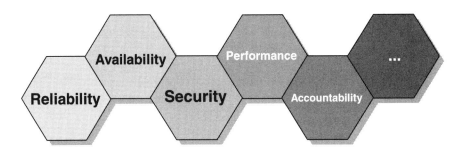

Figure 1. Requirements

The R/3 system must provide reliable service to the end user that is available at the desired times, usually 24 hours, 7 days a week. The security of the system must be guaranteed to protect the business data stored in the R/3 system, and the performance of the system must meet user requirements.

The R/3 application utilizes a complex network of components that comprise the R/3 application system. These components include the R/3 application itself, the operating systems and hardware on which the application components run, the RDBMS in which R/3 stores its data, and many others.

Hence, in order to achieve the goals for the above requirements, a number of components have to be managed in order to guarantee the desired service level. The major components are:

- The network
- Operating systems, including attributes such as memory utilization, paging space, and so on.
- Hardware devices, such as CPUs, printers, hard disks, and so forth.
- The RDBMS in which R/3 stores its data
- The R/3 application and its components themselves

When looking at the components and the requirements, you find there are many dependencies; for example, security of the R/3 system involves security of the network, the RDBMS setup and the operating system.

While managing each of these separate components themselves is not necessarily difficult or challenging, it is usually very challenging to create an integrated management solution.

For example, there are management tools to manage the network, tools to manage operating systems and even a number of tools to manage SAP R/3. However, a lot of the available tools constitute point products in their specific areas and do not integrate into an overall solution.

What we want is an integrated management of the system. To illustrate this, let's consider an example. An end user of the SAPGUI calls the help desk and reports a problem with the application, such as slow performance or application not available, for instance.

The help desk person now needs to determine the cause of the problem and help fix the problem. Since there are many possible reasons for a problem that can originate in all kinds of system components, the help desk person ideally needs a highly integrated and consolidated view of the system.

For instance, the network management system (for example, NetView) could have detected a node down event that is relevant for the problem just reported. While the network administrator is certainly aware of the problem, the help desk person also needs this information, perhaps consolidated so he/she can easily comprehend its impact. This simple example requires the network management system to be integrated with the help desk solution.

Similar causes for problems with the R/3 application could originate in the operating system on which the application runs, in hardware components, and so on. All relevant components need to be monitored so this information is available to determine the cause of problems.

Another important factor is to manage the R/3 application itself, which usually includes monitoring the application components, event management, operations management, and software distribution that enable a system administrator to include the R/3 application in the systems management process. The management module that manages the R/3 system must be highly integrated in the systems management solution so the management of R/3 can be effective and also uniform with the management of any other component in the system.

In this redbook, we explain Tivoli's consistent strategy for managing components, such as applications, in the enterprise. For SAP R/3, we explain the Tivoli management strategy and show in detail how the integrated Tivoli solution can provide comprehensive management of R/3 that is integrated with the overall systems management process.

2.3 The Benefits of Using Tivoli to Manage R/3

Managing an enterprise R/3 system is a complex and expensive task. The SAP R/3 systems will be around for quite some time, maybe 15-20 years. They will need to be fed and maintained.

This is where the Tivoli solution comes into place. Tivoli can significantly drive down the lifecycle cost of SAP R/3. Tivoli does that by providing a framework that allows R/3 to be managed within existing service levels and processes that hold cost down.

We show how R/3 can be managed within the context of the enterprise I/T system. You will see that R/3 can be managed by Tivoli using the same paradigm that is used for any other component in the I/T system. At the same time, dedicated Tivoli solutions for the management for R/3, such as Tivoli Manager for R/3 and Tivoli Maestro Extended Agent for R/3, provide management functions specific to R/3.

By integrating management of R/3 with the enterprise management platform provided by Tivoli, the management of the R/3 system becomes more effective, accountable and secure. Costs for maintaining the R/3 systems go down significantly as a number of management tasks can be standardized and streamlined using Tivoli, thus allowing you to shift these tasks from expensive R/3 specialists to a general I/T help desk.

We show a number of examples of how R/3 can be managed using Tivoli in this book, including software distribution of SAPGUI, monitoring of R/3 as part of the I/T system, managing R/3 jobs and output, and more.

The Tivoli SAP solution can complement the SAP system in many ways that help to minimize the impact of SAP operations on the overall business.

2.4 Tivoli Enterprise Software

We give only a brief overview of Tivoli here. A comprehensive introduction to Tivoli can be found in the book *An Introduction to Tivoli's TME 10*, ISBN 0-13-899717-9.

Tivoli provides a suite of enterprise management software (Tivoli Enterprise Software) that is based on the Tivoli Framework. This framework provides a wide array of services that can be used by systems management applications that reside on top of this framework.

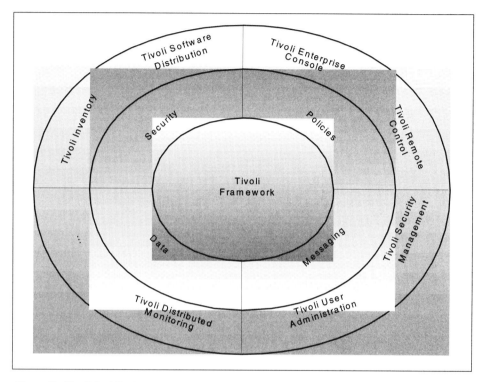

Figure 2. Tivoli Architecture

Tivoli provides a set of key applications that reside on top of the Tivoli Framework and that address core functions of systems management. These core applications are:

- Tivoli Distributed Monitoring
- Tivoli Enterprise Console
- Tivoli Software Distribution
- Tivoli User Administration
- Tivoli Security Management
- Tivoli Inventory
- Tivoli Remote Control

Besides these core applications, management functionality for specific components can easily be integrated with the Tivoli Framework and the Tivoli core applications. This management functionality is provided by software that is based on the Tivoli Framework and/or the Tivoli core applications. Tivoli Manager for R/3 is such a software module.

2.5 The Tivoli Management Solution for SAP R/3

In this section, we provide an overview of the Tivoli management solution for R/3 and the Tivoli components involved. For each component, we offer a brief introduction of what part this component plays in the management of R/3. Later on in this book, we describe the components in more detail.

2.5.1 Tivoli Manager for R/3

We give a brief overview of the Tivoli Manager for R/3 functions in this section because we explore all the functions available in detail later in this book.

Tivoli Manager for R/3 is a key component in the management of R/3 systems with Tivoli. It should, however, be noticed that this product is one of the many Tivoli components that can be used to implement an enterprisewide management solution for R/3 systems.

While the other Tivoli management components refer to more general areas of systems management, the Tivoli Manager for R/3 deals with specifics of the management of the R/3 system, while at the same time leveraging the Tivoli core applications.

Tivoli Manager for R/3 provides management for the R/3 component in the areas of:

- Availability management
- Task automation
- Deployment
- Secure delegation

For availability management, the Tivoli Manager for R/3 utilizes Tivoli Distributed Monitoring and Tivoli Enterprise Console. An event adapter is provided that sits on top of the R/3 MIB that is provided with data from CCMS. The event adapter then transforms the events into TEC events.

Using a similar concept, Tivoli Distributed Monitoring is used to provide synchronous monitoring of the R/3 system. For that purpose, Tivoli Manager for R/3 provides dedicated R/3 monitoring collections.

Tivoli Manager for R/3 provides a number of tasks to operate the R/3 system from the Tivoli Desktop. This allows for secure and easy execution for certain R/3 tasks from anywhere in the network. Since Tivoli authorization is used for running tasks, this also provides robust security, for example, by using dedicated TMR roles.

A typical challenge in the management of R/3 installations is the deployment of the SAP graphical user interface (SAPGUI) to a large number of desktops. This task can be automated by using Tivoli Software Distribution and the tools for creating file packages for SAP R/3 that come with Tivoli Manager for R/3.

Since Tivoli Manager for R/3 runs on the Tivoli Framework, all security capabilities can be leveraged for the management for R/3, such as policy regions, TMR roles and resource roles. Specifically, the Tivoli Framework allows for secure delegation of management tasks. For example, routine tasks can be handed to junior administrators by giving them exactly the authorization level required.

2.5.2 Tivoli Global Enterprise Manager

Tivoli Global Enterprise Manager (GEM) is the industry's first solution for unifying the management of cross-platform business applications that run businesses and make them competitive. Tivoli GEM allows you to manage strategic applications from a unique business systems perspective, focusing your IT resources on keeping these systems healthy and productive. With Tivoli GEM, you can graphically monitor, control, and configure applications residing in distributed and host (S/390) environments and utilize the concept of business systems management to organize related components and give business context to management decisions.

While at the moment Tivoli Manager for R/3 1.5 does not provide GEM instrumentation, the next version of the product will provide this instrumentation.

The following figure gives you an idea of what that GEM integration will look like:

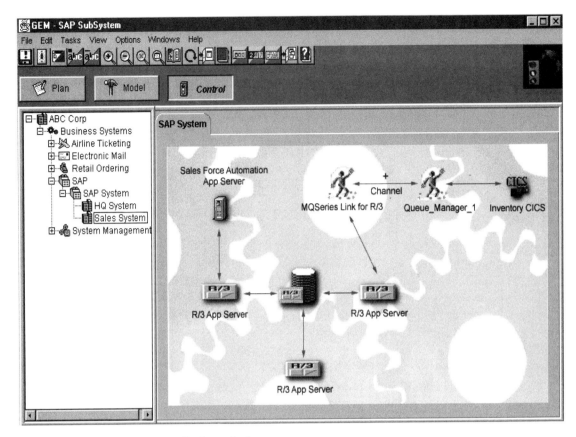

Figure 3. SAP R/3 Managed as a Business System

2.5.3 Tivoli Distributed Monitoring

Tivoli Distributed Monitoring is the Tivoli application for monitoring systems and applications. Tivoli Distributed Monitoring is tightly integrated with the Tivoli Framework and provides monitoring capabilities for a wide range of systems and components. The strength of Tivoli Distributed Monitoring is that monitoring collections for components can easily be added, thus allowing you to monitor any kind of component.

The Tivoli Manager for R/3, for example, provides its own monitoring collections for Tivoli Distributed Monitoring that allow the administrator to monitor specific attributes of an R/3 system using Tivoli Distributed Monitoring.

2.5.4 Tivoli Enterprise Console

Tivoli Enterprise Console (TEC) provides a central event display and correlation for the enterprise, regardless from which source the events are originating. Unlike traditional SNMP managers, TEC uses event adapters that can convert any kind of event stream into TEC events that can then be processed by TEC.

Event adapters are available for a wide range of systems and applications. For example, there are adapters for NetView, Windows NT, etc.

The Tivoli Manager for R/3 provides its own adapter that can convert events from R/3 to TEC events.

The major strength of TEC is that events from any kind of system can be displayed, and more importantly correlated, in one place. This allows, for example, correlating a network event that comes from NetView with an application event coming from R/3, and triggering an action as a result of the correlation.

2.5.5 Tivoli Software Distribution

Tivoli Software Distribution provides a simple and reliable service to distribute software in the enterprise across platforms and networks. Tivoli Software Distribution has features such as fan-out and bandwidth optimization. Software is grouped in so-called file packages that Tivoli Software Distribution can then automatically distribute to the desired targets.

Many applications require distribution of application components or data across the network. This function can be provided by Tivoli Software Distribution. For example, the Tivoli Manager for R/3 provides utilities that assist in the creation of file packages for R/3 so the SAPGUI component can be automatically deployed to a large number of presentation clients.

2.5.6 Tivoli Workload Scheduler (Maestro)

Tivoli Workload Scheduler, also known as Maestro, is the Tivoli product for enterprise-wide job scheduling. Tivoli Workload Scheduler is an application with full functionality in scheduling purposes and is available on several platforms. It can be integrated with Tivoli using the Tivoli Plus for Maestro product. This product allows managing the Tivoli Workload Scheduler (Maestro) application from the Tivoli Desktop.

For integration of SAP R/3 in enterprisewide scheduling, there is an interface available called SAP R/3 Extended Agent. With this interface, it is possible to manage SAP R/3 jobs with the external job scheduler, Maestro. Later on in this book, we describe in more detail the functionality and the components of Tivoli Workload Scheduler in combination with SAP R/3.

2.5.7 Tivoli Output Management

Tivoli Output Management, formerly known as Destiny, is the Tivoli product for enterprisewide output control. The output environment is an ever-changing and diverse environment containing, for example, different printing devices (PostScript, PCL, encapsulated PostScript, plotters, line printers), different printer cartridge fonts in printing devices, facsimile machines, Web servers, different mail gateways (X400, PROFS, cc:Mail, Lotus Notes, Microsoft Exchange, Microsoft MS Mail, Microsoft OutLook, SMTP), and the global differences in paper sizes in the distribution centers. Companies are starting to look at enterprise output managers for coordination, routing paths, delivery, and, above all, security of documents. Tivoli Output Manager is positioned to do just that with an easy-to-use user interface and rule engine to deliver documents reliably across the enterprise.

Enterprise applications such as SAP R/3 rely on the output environment to deliver the critical daily, weekly and month-end reports to a single end user or groups of management teams. It is the responsibility of the enterprise output manager to orchestrate and deliver these reports according to the business rules that have been defined by the process engineers.

Tivoli Output Manager can do the following:

- Centralize output management
- Controlled access of output resources
- Routed output resources
- Reliable and secure output channels
- Automated delivery channels

2.5.8 Tivoli Database Management Products

An important part of the management of R/3 systems is the management of RDBMS systems because R/3 uses an RDBMS to store its data. Hence, to provide management of the system, not only do the application, networks and operating systems need to be managed but also the RDBMS servers.

The Tivoli database management products allow for the seamless management of RDBMS components with Tivoli. Similar to the Tivoli Manager for R/3, they use the Tivoli Framework and core applications to manage a certain application, in this case RDBMS servers.

Since the Tivoli database management products are based on Tivoli, management follows the same procedure as management for any other component

Tivoli database management products are available for a wide range of RDBMS servers, including Oracle, Sybase, DB2, MS SQL Server, and Informix.

2.5.9 Tivoli Service Desk

Tivoli Service Desk is Tivoli's solution for enterprise help desk implementations. Tivoli Service Desk is integrated with other Tivoli applications. For example, events in Tivoli Enterprise Console can be used to generate problem records in Tivoli Service Desk.

Becuase SAP R/3 can be managed by these Tivoli components, including Tivoli Enterprise Console and Tivoli Distributed Monitoring (through Tivoli Manager for R/3) problem management for the R/3 system can be seamlessly integrated with the enterprise problem management process.

We do not discuss Tivoli Service Desk in detail in this book. A detailed discussion of Tivoli Service Desk can be found in the book *Problem Management Using Tivoli Service Desk and TEC*, SG24-5301.

2.5.10 Tivoli Adstar Distributed Storage Manager (Tivoli ADSM)

ADSM is Tivoli's enterprise backup/restore and archive/retrieve solution that is available on a wide range of platforms. ADSM provides integration of several databases and applications, such as DB/2, Oracle, Lotus Notes, SAP R/3, and so forth.

The ADSM connection to SAP R/3 allows the customer to back up his/her SAP R/3 database and archive his/her SAP R/3 application data with one utility.

2.5.11 Tivoli Framework

The Tivoli Framework is the backbone of the Tivoli solution and the basis for all Tivoli systems management applications. Consequently, the Tivoli Manager for R/3 and the other Tivoli components used to manage R/3 use and require the Tivoli Framework.

The Tivoli Framework provides the basic systems management services, such as communications, presentation, security, and so on. that all Tivoli systems management applications use, thus ensuring consistency and integration.

All Tivoli systems management tasks, regardless of the application or component that is to be managed, are performed using the Tivoli Desktop, which provides a user interface consistent throughout Tivoli management applications.

2.5.12 Tivoli NetView

Tivoli NetView is Tivoli's network management solution that is focused on managing IP-based networks. NetView displays the nodes in the network on a map representing the network topology and the status of network nodes.

In case something happens in the network, NetView generates SNMP traps that are displayed in a central event window and which can trigger actions or correlations. In that regard, NetView is similar to TEC. However, NetView is exclusively focused on processing SNMP events, usually events related to the network.

NetView events, however, can be forwarded to TEC, which allows correlation with events from other sources, for example, such as from the R/3 system. A simple example could be that TEC receives an event indicating that the R/3 application server is down and also receives an event from NetView before indicating that the network node on which the application server is running is down.

A correlation rule can then find the dependency between the two events and take appropriate action.

2.6 SAP R/3 Management Tools

We only give a brief overview of SAP R/3 in this section. For more detailed coverage of SAP R/3, refer to the appropriate R/3 materials.

SAP R/3 is a client/server application system used for Enterprise Resource Planning (ERP). R/3 has many different modules to model all parts of the enterprise business and can manage data from finance, sales, accounting, manufacturing, human resources, and other business departments.

A major value of R/3 is that it provides a framework for the customer to integrate business data and business processes. R/3 can act as a catalyst for change as it not only allows the customer to automate business processes using information technology but also can be used to drive changes to the business processes themselves.

R/3 runs on many different platforms, including Windows NT and all major UNIX operating systems. R/3 has a multitier architecture with the following main components:

- Database Server
- Application Server(s)
- Presentation Clients

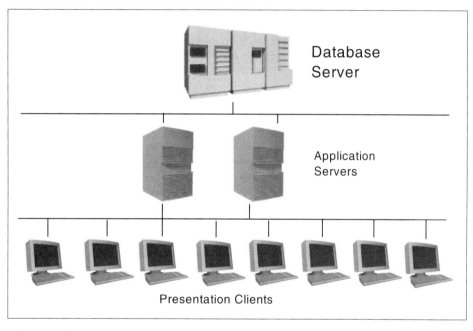

Figure 4. SAP R/3 Components

Typically, there is one database server in an R/3 system. The database server stores data in a Relational Database Management System (RDBMS), such as DB2, Oracle, Informix, ADABAS, or Microsoft SQL Server. These database servers can also run on different platforms, such as Oracle on Windows NT and UNIX, DB2 on Windows NT, UNIX or OS/390 and many others. The communications protocol used between the three main components of the R/3 system is TCP/IP.

The users log in from their presentation clients to the applications server, where the actual R/3 application is running. The application servers in turn communicate with the database server. Application servers can also run on

Windows NT and all major UNIX platforms. The database server and application server can physically run on the same machine.

The presentation client, often referred to as SAPGUI, runs on Windows platforms, UNIX platforms and OS/2. The following figure shows an example of the initial login window of the SAPGUI on Windows 95:

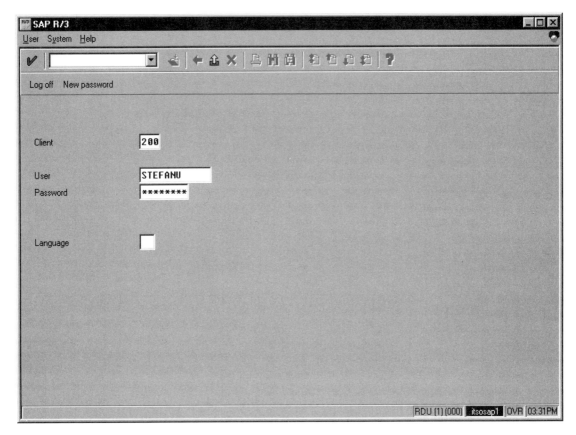

Figure 5. SAPGUI Initial Login Window

An R/3 system is comprised of the database server and one or more application servers as well as the presentation clients. The R/3 system is identified by a three-character system identifier (SID), such as DEV, TST, and so on. The SID logically groups the database server and the application servers; that is, it identifies the R/3 as a whole.

Instances are assigned to the application servers in the R/3 system (remember, there can be one or more application servers per R/3 system). One of the instances is designated as the central instance.

The R/3 system contains a built-in component for systems management called Computing Center Management System (CCMS). CCMS provides functions for monitoring, system optimization, logging, and so on.

CCMS can be accessed from the SAPGUI. For example, the following figure shows an example of the CCMS Alert Monitor.

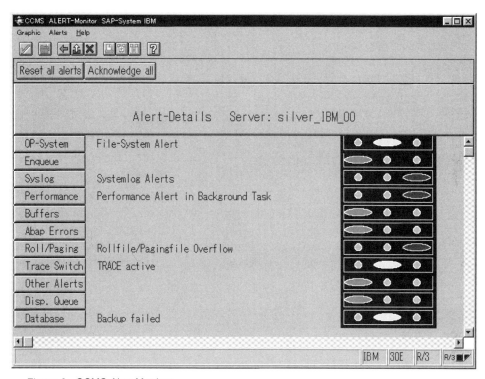

Figure 6. CCMS Alert Monitor

CCMS is, however, intended mainly for controlling and managing R/3 systems and does not provide for scaling to a large-scale systems management solution for R/3 systems. This is where the Tivoli solution comes into place. The Tivoli Manager for R/3 uses the features provided by CCMS and adds many additional features and also allows scaling systems management of the R/3 system to an enterprise level while at the same time integrating with the systems management of other components. The features provided by the Tivoli solution discussed in full detail in this book.

2.7 Defining Management Requirements for SAP R/3

Before thinking of implementing a management solution for SAP R/3, the management requirements for the SAP R/3 system must be clear. While some of these requirements may be obvious and quite precise, others may be more complex and more difficult to describe precisely.

This is why it is very important to structure the requirements in a form that allows for proper selection of adequate tools and for designing an effective overall solution.

Let's start by looking at a few typical management requirements for an R/3 management solution:

- An administrator must be notified when an exception at the R/3 system occurs, and if possible, the problem must be corrected automatically.
- Software updates in the R/3 system, especially for the many SAPGUI clients, must be automated and must be able to be triggered from one central location.
- It must be possible to perform synchronous monitoring and asynchronous monitoring of the R/3 system and all relevant components. That is, constant checking of critical system parameters must be possible as well as triggering a notification when an unexpected event occurs.
- The SAP R/3 system must be available to the end users 24 hours a day, 7 days a week.
- The availability of all components that are critical for the R/3 system must be ensured by the management solution.
- A help desk operator must be assisted by the management solution so calls related to R/3 can be resolved efficiently, even when components other than the R/3 system are involved.
- The management solution must be consistent with the management solution that is employed for other applications, databases, systems, or networks.

These are just a few example requirements, but you can see that they differ in quality. While some requirements, such as automatic software distribution or monitoring of the R/3 system, are relatively precise and easy to match with a product, others require a view of the entire IT system.

In the following sections, we provide some help on structuring the requirements.

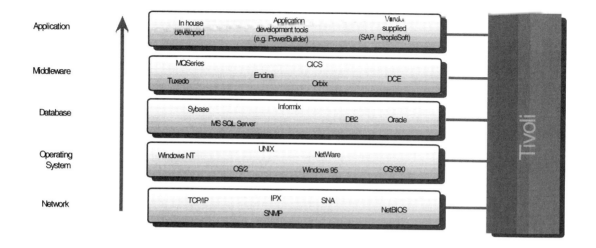

Application	In house developed	Application development tools (e.g. PowerBuilder)	Vendor supplied (SAP, PeopleSoft)
Middleware	MQSeries / Tuxedo	CICS / Encina / Orbix	DCE
Database	Sybase / MS SQL Server	Informix / DB2	Oracle
Operating System	Windows NT / OS/2	UNIX / Windows 95 / NetWare	OS/390
Network	TCP/IP / SNMP	IPX / SNA	NetBIOS

Figure 7. Management Layers

First of all, it is important to understand that an application such as SAP R/3 relies on many components of the IT system. Therefore, for an effective management of the R/3 system, most of these components must be covered by the proposed management solution. For example, since R/3 relies on a relational database system, management of this RDBMS must be covered as well as management of the R/3 application itself.

Other components that usually must be covered are management of the operating system, paging space, memory, and the network.

While for almost any component in the IT system you can find a management product in the marketplace, most of these tools provide only a very specific management solution for a specific area (point products). A comprehensive management solution, however, especially for a complex application system such as R/3, must allow for integration of all the specific component management functions.

This function is provided by the Tivoli Framework. This framework allows you to unify the management processes for all applications, systems, databases, and networks by providing a common set of services and a unified graphical user interface for management. The Tivoli Framework also allows you to scale the management solution to the enterprise level.

Thus, no matter what specific components will be included in the management solution for R/3, the base will be the Tivoli Framework implementation. One issue that needs to be resolved here is the design of the framework infrastructure, such as the TMR design. Since the Tivoli Framework is the basis for the systems management for all components in the IT system, the design of the framework infrastructure will most likely be based on general requirements, such as on branch office structures or department structures and not on the specific requirements for managing R/3.

However, before selecting and implementing the Tivoli management products, the Tivoli Framework structure has to be adjusted with the specific requirements for the management of R/3. For example, it needs to be determined which systems in the R/3 installation need to be Tivoli Managed Nodes, and so forth.

Once the basic Tivoli Framework infrastructure is defined, the Tivoli components need to be selected that are to become part of the management solution. The components that are relevant for management for R/3 are listed in more detail in 2.8, "Selecting the Necessary Tivoli Components" on page 23.

While some components are mandatory (for example, usually the Tivoli core applications such as Tivoli Software Distribution, Tivoli Distributed Monitoring and Tivoli Enterprise Console), other components can be either optional or required only at a later stage.

To illustrate this, let's look at an example. For the immediate management of the R/3 system, it is decided to first implement the Tivoli Manager for R/3, which is the obvious choice, since this Tivoli component deals directly with the management of the R/3 component.

The Tivoli Manager for R/3 requires the Tivoli Framework, so the design for the framework layout needs to be in place. Further, the Tivoli Manager for R/3 requires some of the Tivoli core applications, namely Tivoli Software Distribution, Tivoli Distributed Monitoring and Tivoli Enterprise Console.

In the next step, the management for R/3 could be unified with the management of other components. For example, the Tivoli database management products could be included to manage the RDBMS that is used by R/3. Other components, though not directly related to R/3, are also relevant for the management of the R/3 system, such as management of the network, which can be performed using Tivoli NetView.

It is also important to understand that Tivoli components that are currently not based on the Tivoli Framework can add to the value of the R/3 management solution, two of which we explain in detail in this book: Tivoli Output

Management (formerly known as Destiny) and Tivoli Workload Scheduler (formerly known as Maestro). Since these products do not require the Tivoli Framework, but define their own topology requirements, a design for these topologies needs to take place.

When defining requirements, it can also be found that the requirements are based on the different levels of the management solution. For example, a requirement on the lowest level could be to monitor the availability of the R/3 application processes on all of the R/3 production systems.

On the next level, this requirement could be extended to require that once an R/3 application process goes down, a TEC event is sent to Tivoli Enterprise Console, where it can be correlated with other events to determine the root cause of the problem. While the first requirement can easily be implemented by just using Tivoli Distributed Monitoring and Tivoli Enterprise Console, the second case requires more integration with other components, for example Tivoli NetView.

We can reach even more abstraction and automation by generating trouble tickets in Tivoli Service Desk for certain problems that were reported to TEC. The service desk personnel can then use an existing knowledge base to fix problems.

Due to the nature of these levels, in most cases it is appropriate to create an initial design where all levels are considered and then employ an incremental approach for the implementation. That is, start with the component specific management tasks and then increase integration with other components step by step.

2.8 Selecting the Necessary Tivoli Components

The main purpose of this section is to give an overview of all Tivoli components that can be useful for the management of a complex R/3 system. This overview is presented in the form of a table. This table will help you in a first evaluation of which products you might want to consider for your overall solution.

Table 1. Tivoli Products for the Management of SAP R/3

Product Name	Description	Requires	Benefit for Managing R/3
Tivoli Manager for R/3	Tivoli product to manage R/3 system	Tivoli Framework Tivoli Software Distribution Tivoli Enterprise Console Tivoli Distributed Monitoring	Manage all aspects of R/3 system
Tivoli Distributed Monitoring	Tivoli application for synchronous monitoring	Tivoli Framework	Monitor R/3 applications (through Tivoli Manager for R/3) and other components, such as RDBMS (through Tivoli database management products), operating systems, etc.
Tivoli Enterprise Console	Tivoli application for asynchronous monitoring/event management	Tivoli Framework	Monitor R/3 (through Tivoli Manager for R/3) and other components
Tivoli Global Enterprise Manager	Allows managing applications from the perspective of a business system	Tivoli Framework and core applications	Manage R/3 as part of a business system (not yet supported; support will be in Tivoli Manager for R/3 Version 2.0)
Tivoli Workload Scheduler (Maestro)	Tivoli product for enterprisewide job scheduling	n/a	Manage R/3 job scheduling
Tivoli Maestro Extended Agent for R/3	R/3-specific extension for Maestro	Tivoli Job Scheduler (Maestro)	Manage R/3 job scheduling

Product Name	Description	Requires	Benefit for Managing R/3
Tivoli Plus for Maestro	Integrates Maestro with Tivoli Framework	Tivoli Framework Tivoli Software Distribution Tivoli Enterprise Console Tivoli Distributed Monitoring	Integrate Maestro with Tivoli management solution
Tivoli Database Management Products (DB2, Oracle, Sybase, Informix, MS SQL Server)	Tivoli products to manage RDBMS serves	Tivoli Framework Tivoli Software Distribution Tivoli Enterprise Console Tivoli Distributed Monitoring	Manage the RDBMS that is used by the R/3 system
Tivoli Manager for MQ Series	Provides complete management for IBM MQ Series middleware	Tivoli Framework Tivoli Software Distribution Tivoli Enterprise Console Tivoli Distributed Monitoring	Manage IBM MQ Series, the leading message-oriented middleware for R/3
Tivoli Software Distribution	Tivoli application for electronic software distribution	Tivoli Framework	Deploy SAPGUI clients (through Tivoli Manager for R/3)
Tivoli Service Desk	Tivoli product for help desk	n/a	Integrate R/3 management with corporate help desk
Tivoli Security Management	Provides cross-platform ability to manage user groups, roles, resources and system policies	Tivoli Framework	Manage security on the platforms R/3 runs on
Tivoli Output Management (Destiny)	Tivoli product for enterprisewide output management	n/a	Manage R/3 output, such as print jobs

Product Name	Description	Requires	Benefit for Managing R/3
Tivoli ADSM	Tivoli product for enterprisewide backup and restore	n/a	Backup and restore R/3 data, for example, on-line backup of database
Tivoli Module Builder	Toolkit for creating application management modules	Tivoli Framework Tivoli Distributed Monitoring Tivoli Software Distribution Tivoli Enterprise Console	Quickly build management for any in-house application that interfaces to R/3
Tivoli NetView	Tivoli product for network management	Tivoli Framework	Manage the network infrastructure (TCP/IP) used by R/3 system
Tivoli Integration Pack for NetView (TIPN)	Integrates Tivoli NetView with Tivoli Framework applications	Tivoli Framework Tivoli Enterprise Console Tivoli Inventory	Integrate network management with Tivoli
Tivoli Framework	Provides basic management infrastructure for all Tivoli applications	n/a	Provide scalability, security and other generic services

2.9 Designing a Management Solution for R/3

Designing a systems management solution for the enterprise R/3 system is usually a very complex task. Therefore, we can give only a few suggestions here for the main points to consider.

The management solution for SAP R/3 is usually comprised of several different parts, depending on the management level. For example, the following points have to be considered:

- Implementing effective management of the R/3 system and other relevant components
- Integrating the management solution for R/3 with the management solution for other components

- Implementing the processes that are described, for example in the service level agreements (SLAs)

It is important to understand that management of the R/3 system is to some extent specific to the R/3 system, but also has a lot of interfaces with the overall management solution.

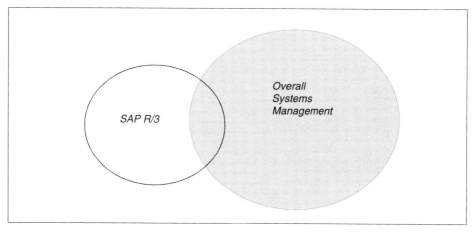

Figure 8. Management of SAP R/3 within the Overall Systems Management

We consider for our discussion only the part of the R/3 system that is relevant to the systems management solution, which is on the one hand the systems management for the R/3 system and on the other hand the actual interfaces between the R/3 system and the systems management system, for example, CCMS.

A main focus has to be on the overall systems management solution since the R/3 management solution is an integral part of that solution. From a practical approach, that means the following:

- Assuming that the underlying Tivoli infrastructure is already in place, this infrastructure is reused and adjusted for the management of R/3. For example, the existing TMR topology needs to be reviewed as to whether it is feasible for the R/3 management and possibly adjusted.

- For the Tivoli core applications, the specific management requirements for R/3 have to be reflected, which are mainly monitoring, operating and deployment requirements. This task is significantly simplified by the Tivoli Manager for R/3, which supplies standard monitors, TEC rules, file packages, and task libraries for the management of R/3. However, it is still required that the administrator defines, for example, the specific monitors to use. Also, when integrating with other management components, further planning has to take place. For example, in most cases it is desirable that a TEC event from Tivoli Manager for R/3 is correlated, for example, with a TEC event from NetView to determine the root cause of a problem. To achieve this, the overall management system has to be adjusted and tailored for the management of R/3.

- Besides the more technical implementation of the systems management solution, it is also important that the corporate management policies are reflected in the physical implementation of the management system. While this is not specific to R/3 management, the specific requirements for R/3 management have to be integrated in the management processes. The system management processes can then be implemented using the appropriate tools, for example using Tivoli Service Desk.

It is beyond the scope of this book to discuss the various design techniques for creating an enterprise systems management solution, such as design methodologies. The reader is encouraged, however, to review and employ these techniques when designing a management solution for R/3.

In this book, we supply the reader with all information necessary to implement the various Tivoli components that can be involved in creating a comprehensive management solution for R/3. This knowledge, combined with the generic techniques, tools and procedures that can be employed to design and implement a Tivoli systems management solution, enable the reader to design and implement a comprehensive and effective systems management solution for SAP R/3.

Chapter 3. Setting Up the SAP R/3 Management Environment

In this chapter we describe how to set up the environment in which we manage our SAP R/3 installation, that is the installation and configuration of the R/3 system itself, as well as the necessary Tivoli components.

We describe in detail how to set up the R/3 systems, Tivoli Manager for R/3, Tivoli Workload Scheduler, Tivoli Output Management and other relevant components.

3.1 Overview and Objective

The environment is implemented to reflect a typical business design; more than one SAP R/3 system per Tivoli Management Region with the possibility to have SAPGUI clients outside the Tivoli Management Region. We also wanted to see the implications with connected Tivoli Management Regions and the functionality/behavior of the Tivoli Manager for R/3 in an interconnected design.

We performed the following steps to set up our environment:

- Installing Tivoli Manager for R/3
- Configuring R/3 for use with Tivoli Manager for R/3
- Configuring Tivoli Manager for R/3
- Configuring Tivoli Enterprise Console
- Configuring the R/3 clients using Tivoli Manager for R/3
- Installing Tivoli Workload Scheduler (Maestro)
- Configuring Tivoli Workload Scheduler (Maestro)
- Installing Maestro Extended Agent for R/3
- Configuring R/3 for use with Extended Agent for R/3
- Installing Tivoli Plus for Maestro
- Configuring Tivoli Plus for Maestro
- Installing Tivoli Output Management
- Configuring Tivoli Output Management

For information on installing the dependent platform for Tivoli Manager for R/3, such as Tivoli Framework, Tivoli Enterprise Console, Tivoli Software

Distribution and Tivoli Distributed Monitoring refer to the appropriate product manuals.

3.2 Overview of Our SAP R/3 Environment

To reflect a typical business environment and to show the possibilities of managing SAP R/3, we set up our environment in the following way: two SAP R/3 systems in the Tivoli Management region, one system located in the ITSO building in Raleigh and the second system located in Heidelberg, Germany.

The system in Raleigh has besides the central instance, another application server on a separate machine. The database is running on the same machine as the central instance.

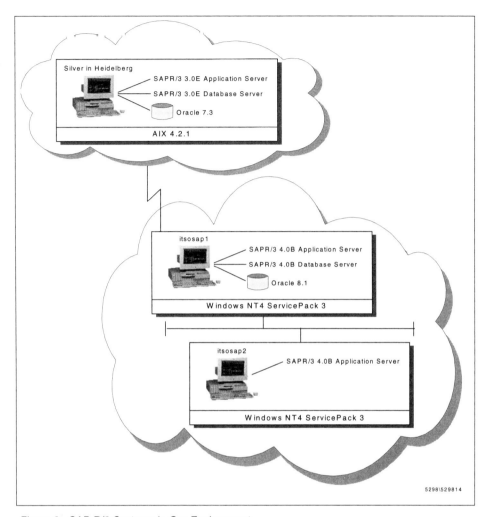

Figure 9. SAP R/3 Systems in Our Environment

The system in Heidelberg is a central system, which means that database and application server are installed on the same machine.

3.3 Overview of Our Tivoli Environment

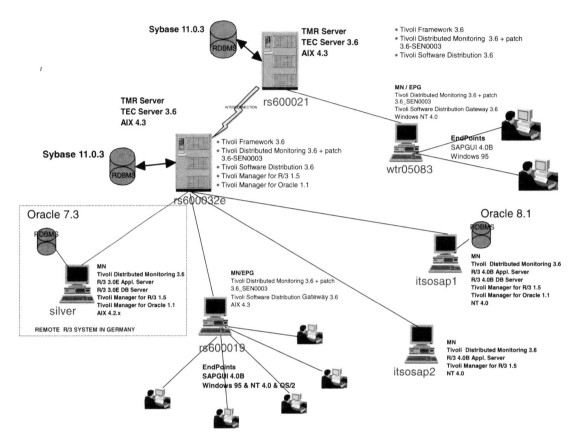

Figure 10. Tivoli/SAP Management Environment

Our environment consists of seven machines that are part of the Tivoli
Management Environment (they have the Tivoli Management Framework
installed) and another five machines configured as Tivoli Management Agents
(TMAs). The following list contains a detailed description of all the machines
and products in our environment.

> **Note**
>
> It should be noticed that in a production environment the majority of the systems will be Tivoli Management Agents, that is they will only act as clients in the Tivoli Management Environment. Only machines running SAP R/3 database or application servers, the TEC and TMR server and other systems performing management functions will be actual Tivoli Managed Nodes running the full Tivoli Management Framework.

- rs600019

    This machine is configured as the endpoint gateway for the *rs600032e-region*. All endpoints are configured during installation to use rs600019 as the preferred gateway. The machine rs600019 will be responsible for all the up and down method invocations on the endpoints, for example, the software distribution of the SAPGUI to the endpoints in the *rs600032e-region*. The products installed on this machine are:

    - AIX 4.3

    - Tivoli Framework 3.6

    - Tivoli Distributed Monitoring 3.6

    - Tivoli Distributed Monitoring Patch 3.6-003

    - Tivoli Software Distribution Gateway 3.6

- rs600021

    The main objective of rs600021 is to investigate the interconnected features of the Tivoli Manager for R/3. The machine rs600021 is installed as a separate Tivoli Management Region server with the ability to do profile and software distributions to the *rs600021-region* and its subscribers. One can also refer to this region as the *focal TMR* or the *manager-of-managers*. The products installed on this machine are:

    - AIX 4.3

    - Sybase Version 11

    - Tivoli Framework 3.6

    - Tivoli Enterprise Console 3.6

    - Tivoli Enterprise Console Server 3.6

    - Tivoli Software Distribution 3.6

    - Tivoli Software Distribution Gateway 3.6

    - Tivoli Distributed Monitoring 3.6

- Tivoli Distributed Monitoring Patch 3.6-003

```
┌──────────── An output of wlookup -ar ProductInfo on rs600021 ────────────┐
│ Courier              1987273457.1.678#TMF_Install::ProductInfo#          │
│ CourierGw            1987273457.1.731#TMF_Install::ProductInfo#          │
│ NTMonitors           1987273457.1.736#TMF_Install::ProductInfo#          │
│ Sentry2.0.2          1987273457.1.586#TMF_Install::ProductInfo#          │
│ TEC_CONSOLE          1987273457.1.575#TMF_Install::ProductInfo#          │
│ TEC_SERVER           1987273457.1.530#TMF_Install::ProductInfo#          │
│ TecMonitors          1987273457.1.732#TMF_Install::ProductInfo#          │
│ TmeMonitors          1987273457.1.734#TMF_Install::ProductInfo#          │
│ UniversalMonitors    1987273457.1.766#TMF_Install::ProductInfo#          │
│ UnixMonitors         1987273457.1.764#TMF_Install::ProductInfo#          │
└──────────────────────────────────────────────────────────────────────────┘
```

```
┌──────────── An output of wlookup -ar PatchInfo on rs600021 ────────────┐
│ 3.6-SEN-0003         1987273457.1.773#TMF_Install::PatchInfo#          │
└──────────────────────────────────────────────────────────────────────────┘
```

- rs600032e

  The machine rs600032e is the chosen machine to be the Tivoli Management Region server for both SAP R/3 systems. This machine will be connected via a two-way connection to rs600021 with exchange of the following resources: Profile Managers, EventServer and Administrators. The products on rs600032e are:

  - AIX 4.3
  - Sybase Version 11
  - Tivoli Framework 3.6
  - Tivoli Enterprise Console 3.6
  - Tivoli Enterprise Console Server 3.6
  - Tivoli Software Distribution 3.6
  - Tivoli Software Distribution Gateway 3.6
  - Tivoli Distributed Monitoring 3.6
  - Tivoli Distributed Monitoring Patch 3.6-003
  - Tivoli Manager for Oracle Framework 1.1
  - Tivoli Manager for Oracle Distributed Monitoring 1.1
  - Tivoli Plus for Maestro 2.0

```
┌─────── An output of wlookup -ar ProductInfo on rs600032e ───────┐
│ ARMEP_36           1306805911.1.689#TMF_Install::ProductInfo#   │
│ ARMMON_36          1306805911.1.684#TMF_Install::ProductInfo#   │
│ ARM_36             1306805911.1.683#TMF_Install::ProductInfo#   │
│ Courier            1306805911.1.690#TMF_Install::ProductInfo#   │
│ CourierGw          1306805911.1.1049#TMF_Install::ProductInfo#  │
│ NTMonitors         1306805911.1.627#TMF_Install::ProductInfo#   │
│ NetWareMonitors    1306805911.1.655#TMF_Install::ProductInfo#   │
│ OS2Monitors        1306805911.1.665#TMF_Install::ProductInfo#   │
│ OS400Monitors      1306805911.1.667#TMF_Install::ProductInfo#   │
│ OracleFramework    1306805911.1.798#TMF_Install::ProductInfo#   │
│ OracleSentry       1306805911.1.875#TMF_Install::ProductInfo#   │
│ SNMPMonitors       1306805911.1.661#TMF_Install::ProductInfo#   │
│ Sentry2.0.2        1306805911.1.530#TMF_Install::ProductInfo#   │
│ TEC_CONSOLE        1306805911.1.787#TMF_Install::ProductInfo#   │
│ TEC_SERVER         1306805911.1.742#TMF_Install::ProductInfo#   │
│ TecMonitors        1306805911.1.623#TMF_Install::ProductInfo#   │
│ TmeMonitors        1306805911.1.625#TMF_Install::ProductInfo#   │
│ UniversalMonitors  1306805911.1.659#TMF_Install::ProductInfo#   │
│ UnixMonitors       1306805911.1.657#TMF_Install::ProductInfo#   │
└─────────────────────────────────────────────────────────────────┘
```

```
┌─────── An output of wlookup -ar PatchInfo on rs600032e ───────┐
│ 3.6-SEN-0003       1306805911.1.887#TMF_Install::PatchInfo#   │
└───────────────────────────────────────────────────────────────┘
```

- silver

  The machine silver is located in Heidelberg, Germany. The WAN link is judged as 128 kbps or faster from the ITSO building to Heidelberg. This machine has all the products for a full SAP R/3 system locally installed on it. The database that silver uses is Oracle 7.3. Here is full list of software and versions installed on silver:

  - AIX 4.2.1

  - SAP R/3 3.0E

  - Oracle 7.3

  - Tivoli Framework 3.6

  - Tivoli Distributed Monitoring 3.6

  - Tivoli Distributed Monitoring Patch 3.6-003

  - Tivoli Manager for Oracle Framework 1.1

  - Tivoli Manager for Oracle Distributed Monitoring 1.1

  - Tivoli Workload Scheduler (Maestro) 6.0 (Fault-Tolerant Agent)

- Tivoli Maestro SAP R/3 Extended Agent
- wtr05083

  This machine is configured as the endpoint gateway for the *rs600021-region*. All endpoints are configured during installation to use rs600021 as the preferred gateway. The machine rs600021 will be responsible for all the up and down method invocations on the endpoints, for example, the software distribution of the SAPGUI to the endpoints in the *rs600021-region*. The products installed on this machine are:
  - Microsoft Windows NT 4.0
  - Tivoli Framework 3.6
  - Tivoli Software Distribution Gateway 3.6

- wtr05274

  This is a Windows NT Managed Node used for Maestro.

  The products on this machine are:
  - Windows NT 4.0 with Service Pack 3
  - TEC Windows NT event adapter
  - Tivoli Framework 3.6
  - Tivoli Distributed Monitoring 3.6 with
  - Universal Monitoring Collection
  - Tivoli Workload Scheduler (Maestro) 6.0
  - Tivoli Plus for Maestro 2.0

- itsosap1

  This is the second SAP R/3 server for the *rs600032e-region*. This machine also has all the SAP R/3 components locally installed, SAP R/3 Application Server and SAP R/3 Database Server, and uses Oracle 8.1 as the RDBMS.
  - Microsoft Windows NT 4.0
  - SAP R/3 4.0B
  - Oracle 8.1
  - Tivoli Framework 3.6
  - Tivoli Distributed Monitoring 3.6
  - Tivoli Distributed Monitoring Patch 3.6-003
  - Tivoli Manager for Oracle Framework 1.1

- Tivoli Manager for Oracle Distributed Monitoring 1.1

- itsosap2

  This is the second SAP R/3 Application Server for the R/3 system installed on the itsosap1 machine. This machine only has the SAP R/3 Application Server installed.

  - Microsoft Windows NT 4.0
  - SAP R/3 4.0B
  - Tivoli Framework 3.6
  - Tivoli Distributed Monitoring 3.6
  - Tivoli Distributed Monitoring Patch 3.6-003
  - Tivoli Manager for Oracle Framework 1.1

3.4 The SAP R/3 Systems in Our Environment

The SAP R/3 systems are installed and configured the following way:

The Raleigh System:

Table 2. Raleigh System

SID	RDU
SAP Release	4.0B
Database	Oracle 8.1

running on the following machines:

Table 3. Configuration of Raleigh System

	Database & Central Instance	Application Server
Hostname	itsosap1	itsosap2
Platform	Windows NT	Windows NT
Release	4.0 service pack 3	4.0 service pack 3

The Heidelberg System:

Table 4. Heidelberg System

SID	IBM
SAP Release	3.0E

SID	IBM
Database	Oracle 7.3.3

running on the following machines:

Table 5. Configuration of Heidelberg System

	Database & Central Instance	Application Server
Hostname	silver	none
Platform	AIX	none
Release	4.2.1	

3.5 Tivoli Output Management (Destiny) in Our Environment

In 3.9, "Installing and Configuring Tivoli Output Management (Destiny)" on page 113 we show how to set up Tivoli Output Management (Destiny) for use with our R/3 installation.

The installation and configuration will be performed as shown in the following figure.

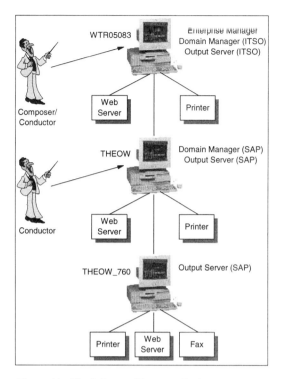

Figure 11. Tivoli Output Manager Environment

Tivoli Output Manager consists of the following components:

- Enterprise Server
- Domain Manager Server
- Output Server
- Direct Client
- Composer
- Conductor

3.5.1 Enterprise Server

The Enterprise Server is responsible for the structure, security and scheduling of the output network. There is only one Enterprise Server in an output network and all modifications are controlled and distributed from this entity. The Enterprise Server platform is restricted to Windows NT in Version 1.1.0.

The objects that are maintained and synchronized by the Enterprise Server throughout the output network are:

- Domains
- Lists
- Users
- Calendars
- Groups
- Nodes
- Destinations

The Enterprise Server also includes a Domain Manager Server and an Output Server. The Enterprise Server creates a database (UED) a domain manager server database (SCD) and an output server database (NEWS) either in a JET database included with the Microsoft platform or Microsoft SQL Server. Our installation makes use of the JET database and the structure after the Enterprise Server installation.

3.5.2 Domain Manager Server

The Domain Manager Server maintains the domain structure. Every domain you add to the Enterprise Server requires another Domain Manager Server. This server synchronize the SCD database with the enterprise to keep the domain structure up to date. This node can also provide domain logons for Administrator and can localize traffic over slow network links. The Domain Manager Server includes an Output Server. The databases maintained by the Domain Manager Server are SCD and NEWS. The objects maintained by the Domain Manager Server are:

- Stationery
- Banners
- Gloms
- Watchers
- Filters
- Handles
- Queues
- Mappers
- Destinations

These objects are specific for the domain that the Domain Manager Server supports.

3.5.3 Output Server

The Output Server database contains a copy of the information in the Enterprise Configuration database, the Destiny configuration database, as well as real-time information about jobs specific to that server. This allows the Output Server to operate independently and continue processing in the event of a network failure.

Destiny clients connect to the Output Server to submit output jobs from their remote nodes.

3.5.4 Direct Client

Destiny Direct Client is the end-user interface into the Destiny output network. This allows the user to choose destinations and Destiny output defined by the Destiny administrator. The Direct Client acts like a printer under Windows 95 and Windows NT but has the advantage that is independent of an output device such as PostScript or PCL. This gives the Destiny network the ability to reprocess that data into all kinds of formats and destinations if it needs to.

3.5.5 Composer

Composer is the Java utility for creating, modifying and maintaining the Destiny network. All the new definitions for the Destiny network are done via Composer and it interacts directly with the Enterprise Server of the Destiny network.

3.5.6 Conductor

Conductor is the Java utility for monitoring and status updates of the Destiny network. It shows you all the information for the queues, destinations, etc. of the Destiny Network. Conductor interacts with the Domain Manager Server and the Output Server depending on which operation you are monitoring.

3.6 Installing and Configuring Tivoli Manager for R/3

The first product we install and configure is Tivoli Manager for R/3. In this section we explain in detail how to prepare the R/3 systems and how to install and configure Tivoli Manager for R/3.

3.6.1 Installing Tivoli Manager for R/3

Tivoli Manager for R/3 must be installed on each TMR server, TEC server and R/3 database or application servers.

The installation must be performed as root user. The authorization role required for user root is the install_product role. The setting of the authorization role for the root user is made via the Tivoli Desktop.

Before installing the Tivoli Manager for R/3, it is recommended to take a backup of the Tivoli database.

To install the module, follow these steps:

- Log on to the TMR server as user root@ *TMR_Hostname* (and not as simple root user). This is a prerequisite for the installation. Then, launch the Tivoli Desktop by running the `tivoli` command.

- In the Tivoli Desktop main window select **Desktop** from the menu bar and the **Install->Install Product...** from the pull-down menu.

- In the Install Product window click the **Select Media** button to set the right path where the code will be installed from, and click the **Select & Close** button.

- Back in the Install Product window, select the **Tivoli Manager for R/3 (Version 1.5)** entry from the Select Product to Install section as shown in Figure 12 on page 43. Select also the clients on which the code must be installed. Remember that clients are the TMR server, the TEC server and all the R/3 database and applications servers.

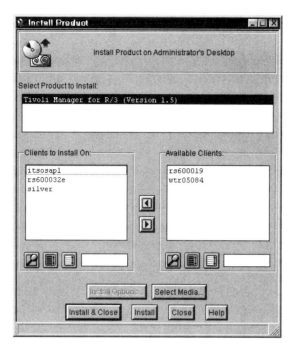

Figure 12. Installing Tivoli Manager for R/3: Install Product Window

- Once the settings are correct, click the **Install & Close** button to start the installation. Dependencies for this product will be checked and the directories where the code will be installed are mentioned in the Product Install window. If the information contained in this window is correct, then click the **Continue Install** button.

- When the installation is completed successfully, a message is displayed in the Product Install window. Do not forget to take a new backup of the Tivoli database, after the Tivoli Manager for R/3 installation.

A new policy region named AMS Module for R/3 is added to the administrator's Tivoli Desktop. This new object contains two task libraries, as shown in Figure 13 on page 44. The AMS Module for R/3 Tasks library provides a set of tasks for supporting internal processing of R/3 events. The AMS Module for R/3 Utilities task library provides the product-wide configuration tasks.

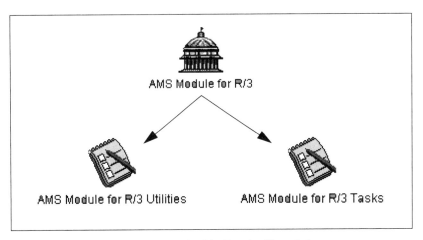

Figure 13. Installing Tivoli Manager for R/3: Result of Installation

3.6.2 Configuring the Tivoli Manager for R/3

After installing the code on the TMR server, the TEC event server, each R/3 application and database server, some configuration must be performed before customizing and using the product.

The configuration consists of the following steps:

1. Configuring each R/3 system

   - Creating an SAP user
   - Creating a development class
   - Copying the transport files
   - Importing the function modules
   - Configuring an RFC user

2. Configuring the Tivoli Manager for R/3 for each R/3 system

   - Configuring Tivoli for an R/3 system
   - Configuring roles
   - Configuring the application servers
   - Configuring the database servers
   - Configuring the SAPGUI servers
   - Configuring the RFC
   - Configuring the environment

3. Configuring the TEC server and TEC consoles

- Configuring the TEC event server
- Configuring the TEC event consoles

The following sections will explain each configuration step, highlighting points that are not clearly described in the user's guide. We advise here the reader to have the user's guide and the release notes of Tivoli Manager for R/3 at hand for further complementary investigation.

3.6.3 Configuring Each R/3 System

Some actions have to be performed on each R/3 system in order to allow Tivoli to interact and communicate with the SAP systems. These actions should be performed by the SAP administrators of the different systems but we document them here briefly in order to allow a Tivoli administrator with only basic SAP knowledge to perform them.

The following steps must be repeated for each R/3 system that is to be managed.

3.6.3.1 Creating an SAP User

In the case that you don't already have an SAP user who has the authority to create a development class, you have to create one. The default SAP users SAP* and DDIC don't have this authority. We recommend creating a new user named TIVOLI (for example) who is a copy of the SAP* user. This dialog user could be used later by the Tivoli administrator for other actions, such as checking the import or configuring other R/3-related Tivoli products (Maestro for example).

> **Note**
>
> Typically, your R/3 Basis administrator will have IDs already set up that have the desired authorization. We describe how to set up a user here in order to provide the complete sequence of steps necessary to configure Tivoli Manager for R/3.

The following is the procedure for a 4.0B R/3 system:

- Via a SAPGUI, log on to the R/3 system as SAP*.
- Issue the transaction su01.
- In the User field, type SAP* and click the **Copy** icon.
- Enter TIVOLI in the To field of the Copy Users window.

- Enter the initial password in the Logon data folder (you will be asked to change it at the first logon).

- Make sure it is a Dialog user in the Logon data folder and that it has SAP_ALL as authorization profile in the Profiles folder.

- Save your entries and log off.

3.6.3.2 Creating the Development Class

The R/3 hierarchy is structured in the following way: a development class structures function groups, ABAPs, data elements and tables; a function group structures function modules. We must here create a development class (ZTV1) that will structure the two function groups (ZTV1, ZTV2), the two tables (ZTTC180, ZTIVOLI), the data element (ZTVDATA) and the program (ZTIV1INC) that will be imported in the subsequent step (see Figure 17 on page 50).

- Via a SAPGUI, log on to the system as the previously created user (TIVOLI).

- Issue the sm31 transaction.

- Enter TDEVC in the Table field and click the **Maintain** icon.

- In the following window, click the **New entries** icon.

- Enter ZTV1 in the Development class field and Tivoli Objects in the Short text field.

- The Person responsible field already contains the user ID of your session (TIVOLI).

- Save your entries and log off.

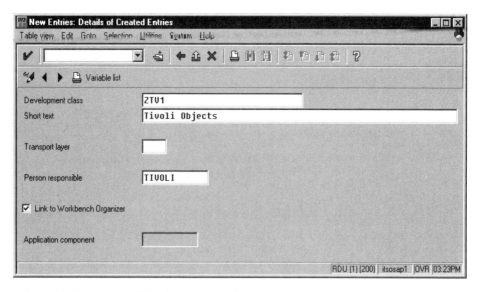

Figure 14. Creating the ZTV1 Development Class

3.6.3.3 Copying the Transport Files

On the application server that will be used to execute the import, copy the data and cofiles files from $BINDIR/../generic_unix/TME/SAP/2.2C/abap to /usr/sap/trans/data and /usr/sap/trans/cofiles respectively. The cofiles files contain the configuration parameters for the transport and the data file contain the real data that is imported.

The files to be copied depend on the release of the R/3 system. In our case, these are R900057.TV1 and K900057.TV1 for our 3.0E system and R900095.TV1 and K900095.TV1 for our 4.0B system. You can find this information in the Tivoli Manager for R/3 release notes.

3.6.3.4 Importing the Function Modules

Check first if the transport system is already configured and functioning. Go to the /usr/sap/trans/bin directory and verify the existence and content of the TPPARAM file there (configuration file for transports). If the file is missing, the transport system is probably not yet configured (newly installed R/3 system). Locate the sample configuration file, copy it to /usr/sap/trans/bin, rename it to TPPARAM and adapt the content.

- Verify that there are no other imports waiting in the transport buffer by entering `tp showbuffer <SID>`, with the SID corresponding to your R/3 system.

- If some imports are waiting, contact the SAP administrator of the system. In the other case, add the correction to the buffer by entering `tp addtobuffer <SID>K9xxxxx <SID>`.

- Verify it is now in the buffer by typing `tp showbuffer <SID>`.

- Import the function modules by typing `tp import <SID>K9xxxxx <SID> u4`. The u4 option is only specified for R/3 releases prior to 4.0A.

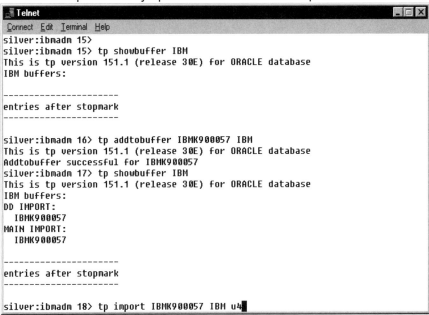

```
Telnet                                                      _ □ ×
Connect  Edit  Terminal  Help
silver:ibmadm 15>
silver:ibmadm 15> tp showbuffer IBM
This is tp version 151.1 (release 30E) for ORACLE database
IBM buffers:

----------------------
entries after stopmark
----------------------

silver:ibmadm 16> tp addtobuffer IBMK900057 IBM
This is tp version 151.1 (release 30E) for ORACLE database
Addtobuffer successful for IBMK900057
silver:ibmadm 17> tp showbuffer IBM
This is tp version 151.1 (release 30E) for ORACLE database
IBM buffers:
DD IMPORT:
  IBMK900057
MAIN IMPORT:
  IBMK900057

----------------------
entries after stopmark
----------------------

silver:ibmadm 18> tp import IBMK900057 IBM u4█
```

Figure 15. Importing the Function Modules

Afterwards, check in the R/3 system that the objects are active. Depending on the R/3 release, they might have not been activated and you will have to do it.

- Via a SAPGUI, log on to the R/3 system and perform the se12 transaction.

- Enter `ZTTC180` in the Objects name field and click the **Display** icon.

- Check if the status is Active and Saved.

- If not, click the **Activate** icon (depending on the R/3 release, a developer key maybe required) and save your entries.

- Go back to the previous window and perform the same steps for the ZTIVOLI table.

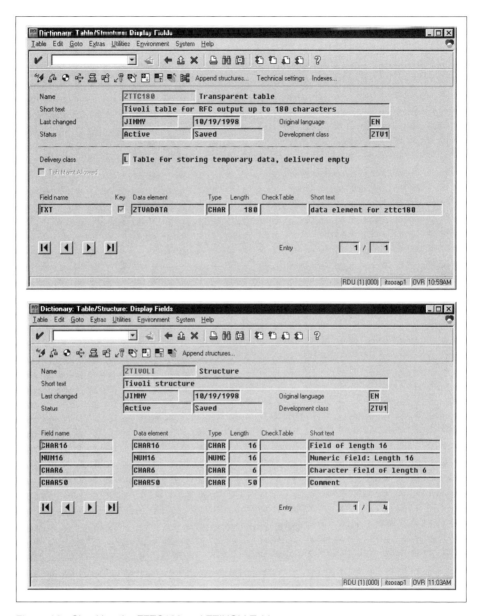

Figure 16. Checking the ZTTC180 and ZTIVOLI Tables

In Figure 17 on page 50 (obtained through the se80 transaction and then display development class ZTV1), you can see how the imported objects are structured in the R/3 system:

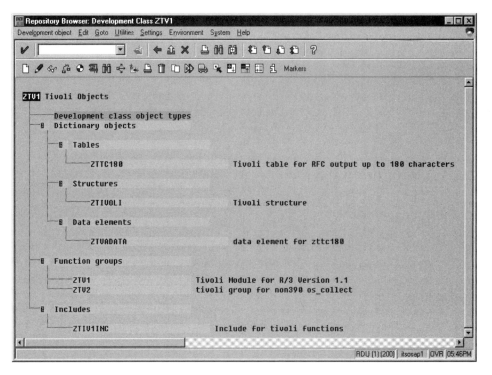

Figure 17. Imported Objects Structure

3.6.3.5 Configuring an RFC User

We have chosen to create a new user for the RFC interface access in order to have a CPIC-only user for this with the minimal set of authorizations, keeping the user we created before (for the development class creation) to log on to the R/3 system via the SAPGUI (dialog user).

- Via a SAPGUI, log on to the system as TIVOLI (or SAP*).

- Issue the su01 transaction.

- Enter TME (for example) in the User field and click on the **Create** icon.

- Enter Tivoli RFC user in the Last name field of the Address folder.

- Change from Dialog to CPIC in the Logon data folder and enter a password.

- In the Profiles folder, add the S_A.SYSTEM authorization profile.

- Save your entries and log off.

> **Note**
>
> New users are normally forced to change their password on the first login. Therefore, if you make the user a CPIC user, he/she will never have the chance to modify the password. As an alternative to the procedure described above, you can make the user a dialog user first and then change the properties to CPIC once you have validated the permissions and changed the password.

3.6.4 Configuring the Tivoli Manager for R/3 for Each R/3 System

Each R/3 system must be registered to the Tivoli Manager for R/3 through the execution of predefined tasks and jobs.

The following steps must be repeated for each R/3 system that is to be managed.

3.6.4.1 Configuring Tivoli for an R/3 System

In this scenario a Tivoli job is executed that creates, for a given R/3 system, Tivoli objects, such as policy regions, profile managers, task libraries, etc. Some of the tasks and jobs that are created will be used during the subsequent configuration steps.

If you want to have a look at the script corresponding to the job, it resides in the $BINDIR/../generic_unix/TME/SAP/sh directory on the TMR server and it is named sap_create_system.sh. During the installation process, when the task and the corresponding job are created, this script is copied and renamed in another directory.

> **Note**
>
> Knowing the script location will allow you to modify the scripts if you want to. Tivoli, however, does not recommend changing the scripts provided by Tivoli Manager for R/3, as the results may be unpredictable.

- In the Tivoli desktop, double-click the **AMS Module for R/3** policy region.
- In this policy region, double-click the **AMS Module for R/3 Utilities** task library.
- In this task library, double-click the **Configure TME for an R/3 System** job.

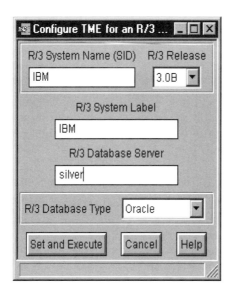

Figure 18. Entering Parameters for the Configure TME for an R/3 System Job

- Enter then the SID of the R/3 system in the R/3 System Name (SID) field and select the R/3 release (3.0B for the 3.0B and later releases; 2.2C for the others).

> **Note**
>
> The R/3 Release field refers to the level of the SAPGUI that you want distributed by Tivoli Manager for R/3, not to the actual release level of the R/3 system being managed.

- Enter the SID of the R/3 system in the System Label field if you don't have another R/3 system to be managed that has the same SID. If you have other systems with the same SID, enter here an alias that identifies the system without ambiguity.
- Enter the name of the managed node that is running the system database in the R/3 Database Server field and select the database type.
- Click the **Set and Execute** button and you will get an output window that will give you the job status.
- Be sure the job ended successfully as shown in the figure before going further.

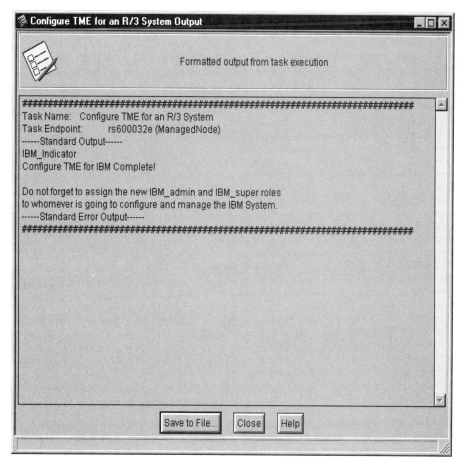

Figure 19. Configure TME for an R/3 System Job Status

3.6.4.2 Configuring Roles

Two new resource roles have been created through the previous jobs: <SystemLabel>_super and <SystemLabel>_admin. A Tivoli administrator named <SystemLabel> Admin has also been created. We assign these resource roles to our main Tivoli administrator as TMR roles and then continue working with this administrator instead of using a new one.

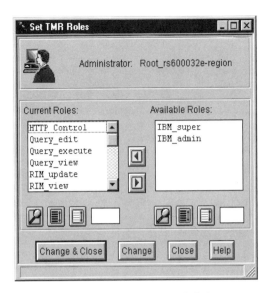

Figure 20. Assigning the New TMR Roles

In the above example, <SystemLabel> is IBM. Make sure to restart the Tivoli desktop after assigning the new roles.

3.6.4.3 Configuring the Application Servers

The script corresponding to the task that will be used here is located on the TMR server in the $BINDIR/../generic_unix/TME/SAP/<SystemLabel>/sh and it is named sap_create_server.sh. This task allows you to configure several application servers at the same time if they have the same instance number. Repeat the following procedure for each instance number of the R/3 system.

- In the AMS Module for R/3 policy region, double-click the **<SystemLabel>** policy region.

- Open the <SystemLabel> Utilities task library.

- Double-click the **Configure TME for a <SystemLabel> Server** task.

- In the Execute Task window, increase the timeout to 500 and select the **Display on Desktop** check box.

- In the Available Task Endpoints list, select the managed nodes that are application servers of the R/3 system with the same instance number and move them to the Selected Task Endpoints list.

- Click the **Execute & Dismiss** button.

- In the resulting window enter the instance number in the System Number field (this entry is only used in order to create the Tivoli object name corresponding to each application server, ManagedNode_SID_instance, but no real checking is performed).

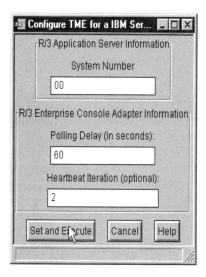

Figure 21. Configuring an Application Server

- Increase the polling delay to 60, enter a heartbeat iteration of 2 (this gives a heartbeat interval of 2 minutes in this case) and then click the **Set and Execute** button.

Note

We set the heartbeat in this example for demonstration purposes. In a production environment care should be taken when setting this parameter, as the heartbeat creates load on the Tivoli Enterprise Console. Therefore, in a production environment it should first be determined if the heartbeat is needed and what delay and iteration work best in the specific environment.

- Verify in the task status window that you received no errors.

3.6.4.4 Configuring the Database Server

The corresponding script is located on the TMR server in the $BINDIR/../generic_unix/TME/SAP/<SystemLabel>/sh and it is named sap_create_db.sh.

- Open then the <SystemLabel> Utilities task library.

- Double-click the **Configure TME for a <SystemLabel> Database** task.

- In the Execute Task window, increase the timeout to 500 and select the **Display on Desktop** check box.

- In the Available Task Endpoints list, select the managed node that is running the database and move it to the Selected Task Endpoints list.

- Click the **Execute & Dismiss** button.

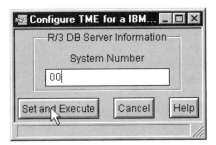

Figure 22. Configuring the Database Server

- Enter the instance number in the System Number field and then click on the **Set and Execute** button (if you have more than one instance number in your R/3 system, you should enter the central instance number, for example; this number is only used to create the Tivoli object name corresponding to the database object, ManagedNode_SID_instance_DB).

- Verify in the task status window that you received no errors.

3.6.4.5 Configuring the SAPGUI Servers

This task is used to manage SAPGUI servers. The script corresponding to the job that will be used here is located on the TMR server in the $BINDIR/../generic_unix/TME/SAP/<SystemLabel>/sh and it is named sap_create_client.sh. SAPGUI servers are named "client servers" in the Tivoli Manager for R/3 terminology.

- In the AMS Module for R/3 policy region, double-click the **<SystemLabel>** policy region.

- Open then the <SystemLabel> Utilities task library.

- Double-click the **Configure TME for a <SystemLabel> Client** task.

- In the Execute Task window, increase the timeout to 500 and select the **Display on Desktop** check box.

- In the Available Task Endpoints list, select the managed nodes that will be your SAPGUI servers for the R/3 system and move them to the Selected Task Endpoints list.

- Click the **Execute & Dismiss** button.

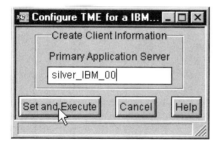

Figure 23. Configuring a SAPGUI Server

- Enter the name of the primary application server and then click the **Set and Execute** button.

- Verify in the task status window that you received no errors.

3.6.4.6 Configuring the RFC

The Tivoli Manager for R/3 uses RFC to log on to each R/3 managed system in order to run some tasks and monitors. For this access, it uses the previously defined RFC user. This user is here defined to the Tivoli Manager for R/3 through the following job. The corresponding script is located on the TMR server in the $BINDIR/../generic_unix/TME/SAP/<SystemLabel>/sh and it is named sap_config_rfc.sh.

- Open the <SystemLabel> Utilities task library.

- Double-click the **Configure_<SystemLabel>_Remote_Function** job.

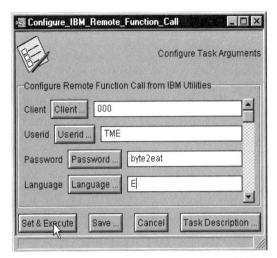

Figure 24. Configuring the Remote Function Call

- In the resulting window, enter the 3-digit client number associated with the RFC user ID, enter the RFC user name (TME), its password and the language used.
- Click the **Set and Execute** button.
- Verify in the task status window that you received no errors.

We recommend that you test if the RFC is correctly configured, executing the wr3rfc command for each application server of each R/3 system:

- On the TMR server (or any Managed Node where the module is installed), copy the wr3rfc program from $BINDIR/TME/SAP/2.2C to $BINDIR/../generic_unix/TME/SAP/<SID>/rfc.
- For each Managed Node running an application server, execute the following command:

  ```
  wr3rfc -u userid -c client -p password -l language -d SID -h ManagedNode
  -s InstanceNumber Z_TV1_BUFFER_NAMES
  ```

  Z_TV1_BUFFER_NAMES is a parameters file that is used by the called function modules previously imported in the R/3 system.

- You should get an output list (see the Figure 25 on page 59). This means that you communicate properly with the R/3 system.
- Execute

  ```
  wr3rfc -d SID -h ManagedNode -s InstanceNumber Z_TV1_BUFFER_NAMES
  ```

- You should get the same output list. It means that your logon information is properly configured in the Manager for R/3.

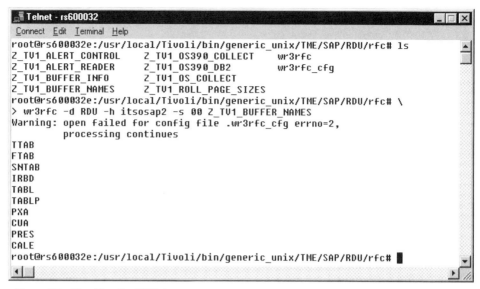

```
Telnet - rs600032
Connect  Edit  Terminal  Help
root@rs600032e:/usr/local/Tivoli/bin/generic_unix/TME/SAP/RDU/rfc# ls
Z_TV1_ALERT_CONTROL    Z_TV1_OS390_COLLECT    wr3rfc
Z_TV1_ALERT_READER     Z_TV1_OS390_DB2        wr3rfc_cfg
Z_TV1_BUFFER_INFO      Z_TV1_OS_COLLECT
Z_TV1_BUFFER_NAMES     Z_TV1_ROLL_PAGE_SIZES
root@rs600032e:/usr/local/Tivoli/bin/generic_unix/TME/SAP/RDU/rfc# \
> wr3rfc -d RDU -h itsosap2 -s 00 Z_TV1_BUFFER_NAMES
Warning: open failed for config file .wr3rfc_cfg errno=2,
         processing continues
TTAB
FTAB
SNTAB
IRBD
TABL
TABLP
PXA
CUA
PRES
CALE
root@rs600032e:/usr/local/Tivoli/bin/generic_unix/TME/SAP/RDU/rfc#
```

Figure 25. Checking the RFC Access

3.6.4.7 Configuring the Environment

If your database is running on Windows NT and if you plan to use the start/stop database facility of the Tivoli Manager for R/3, you must create two scripts containing the specific database commands that will start and stop the database. These two scripts, named sap_start_db_exit.sh and sap_stop_db_exit.sh, must reside in the %BINDIR%\..\generic_unix\TME\SAP directory on the Windows NT database server. When called through the start/stop task, two parameters will be provided to them. The first one is the database type and the second one is the SID. The scripts must return an exit code of zero for a successful completion and a non-zero exit code for an unsuccessful completion.

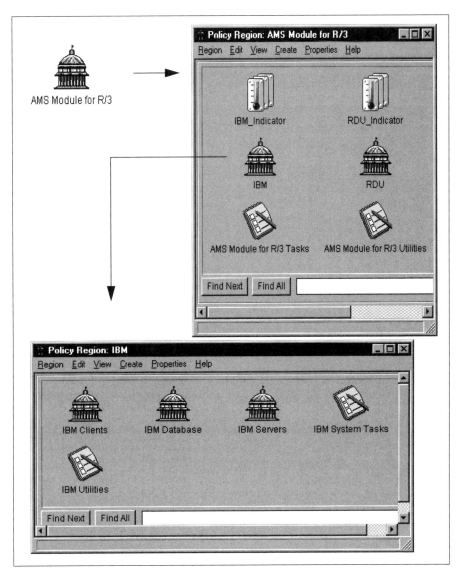

Figure 26. Tivoli Manager Configuration (Part 1)

Figure 26 on page 60 and Figure 27 on page 61 show the main created objects on the Tivoli desktop after the Tivoli Manager for R/3 configuration steps.

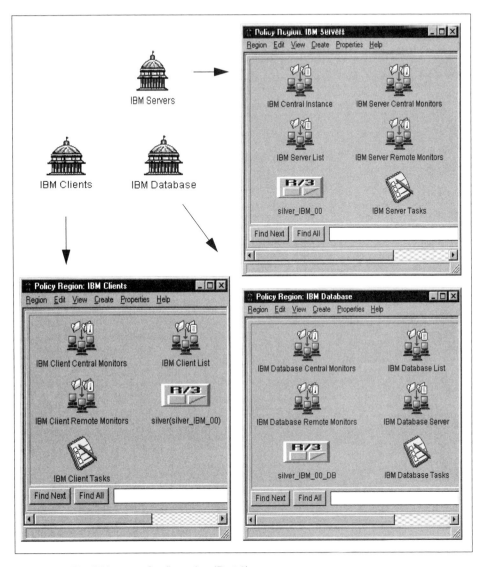

Figure 27. Tivoli Manager Configuration (Part 2)

3.6.5 Configuring the TEC Server and TEC Consoles

Tivoli Manager of R/3 will monitor the R/3 systems through event adapters running on each application server and a set of Tivoli Distributed Monitoring monitors distributed to each application and database server (remote monitors) and to the TMR server (central monitors). The TEC server will receive events directly from the adapters and from the Tivoli Distributed Monitoring engines. In order to handle them, new event classes and rules must be imported into TEC. The following job will import them, creating a new rule base or extending an already existing one. The script corresponding to the job that will be used here is located on the TMR server in the $BINDIR/../generic_unix/TME/SAP/sh and it is named sap_event_config.sh.

Note

The Configure Event Server for R/3 task updates your existing rule base if you specify no rule base to clone, or creates a new rule base from an existing rule base.

- In the AMS Module for R/3 policy region, double-click the **AMS Module for R/3 Utilities** task library.
- Double-click the **Configure EventServer for R/3** job.
- In the resulting window, enter the name of the new rule base you want to create or the name of the already existing one that you want to modify (in the second case, enter the name of the rule base you want to clone and the path to its directory; in the first case, erase these entries).
- If you want the TEC server to forward events directly to another TEC server, enter the name of this other event server in the Managed Node Name to Forward Events field.
- Click the **Set and Execute** button.
- Verify in the task status window that you received no errors.

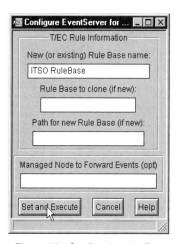

Figure 28. Configuring the Event Server

> **Note**
>
> In our case, the rule base name contained a space and it generated errors during the job execution. The script corresponding to the job had a problem when compiling and loading the rule base. So we modified it ($BINDIR/../generic_unix/TAS/TASK_LIBRARY/bin/<TME region number>/AMS_Module_f_nrfdyoaa), adding double quotes around the argument of both wcomprules and wloadrb commands and ran the task again.

3.6.5.1 Configuring TEC Consoles

An event group or an event source consists of a filter on all events contained in the TEC database. This step creates an event group for each R/3 system that is to be managed in order to see the events per SAP system. It also creates an event source for all adapter events (WR3MIB). The script corresponding to the job that will be used here is located on the TMR server in the $BINDIR/../generic_unix/TME/SAP/<SystemLabel>/sh and it is named sap_tec_config.sh. Repeat the following procedure for each R/3 system.

The following steps must be repeated for each R/3 system that is to be managed.

- Open the <SystemLabel> Utilities task library.

- Double-click the **Configure <SystemLabel> Event Console** job.

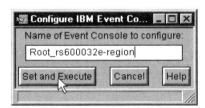

Figure 29. Configuring the Event Console

- In the resulting window, enter the name of the event console to which the new event group will be added.

- Click the **Set and Execute** button.

- Verify in the task status window that you received no errors.

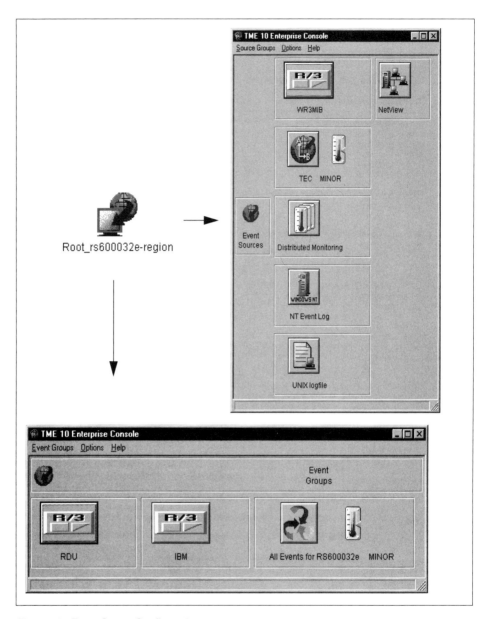

Figure 30. Event Server Configuration

Figure 30 on page 64 shows you the created objects in the event console.

3.6.6 Configuration of the R/3 Clients

In this section we are going to use the first functionality of Tivoli Manager for R/3, which is automatic deployment of R/3 SAPGUI clients.

In order to complete the configuration of our environment, we deploy SAPGUI to all PCs in our environment as shown in Figure 10 on page 32.

An R/3 client is a UNIX or Windows 95/NT machine running the SAP R/3 presentation graphical user interface (SAPGUI) code. Once this code is installed on the target machine, a configuration is needed to define a specific SAPGUI for a specific R/3 application server. This configuration is a part of the SAP R/3 installation, which we're not going to cover here. For information about it, refer to the R/3 manuals.

Two phases are required to correctly set up a client. The first one consists of building a file package that contains the R/3 SAPGUI code, and which will be distributed to all the clients. The second phase is the process of distributing this file package, launched by using Tivoli Software Distribution.

To configure such a file package, two methods are available. The configuration can be done using either a reference installation or an R/3 native installation.

The distribution of the file package is done via Tivoli Software Distribution, whatever configuration method is used.

3.6.6.1 Configuring a R/3 Client using a Reference installation
This method proposes first to install and configure a SAPGUI locally on a node, using the R/3 CD-ROM, to create a reference client machine for the distribution of the code to other future clients. We performed this installation on a Windows NT running the Tivoli Management Agent (TMA).

Note

The first client installation required by the reference installation method is a basic R/3 client installation, using the R/3 Presentation CD-ROM. As the purpose of this chapter is not to give the procedure of such a basic R/3 installation, refer to R/3 manuals for details.

Once the local installation is completed, you have to transfer the R/3 client directories and files from the PC client to the TMR server, to a specific directory. For example, we have created a directory named /REF/NT/ on our AIX TMR server, as repository for the R/3 client code for Windows NT. This transfer can be made using ftp. Directories and files copied are listed below, in Figure 31 on page 66 (just remember that /REF/NT/ is the repository directory):

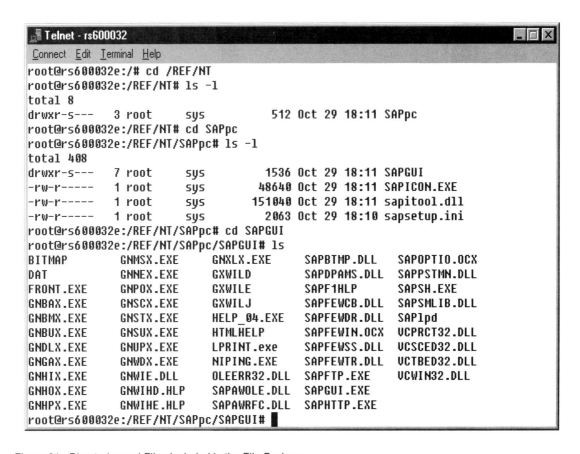

```
 Telnet - rs600032                                              _ □ ×
Connect  Edit  Terminal  Help
root@rs600032e:/# cd /REF/NT
root@rs600032e:/REF/NT# ls -l
total 8
drwxr-s---   3 root    sys          512 Oct 29 18:11 SAPpc
root@rs600032e:/REF/NT# cd SAPpc
root@rs600032e:/REF/NT/SAPpc# ls -l
total 408
drwxr-s---   7 root    sys         1536 Oct 29 18:11 SAPGUI
-rw-r-----   1 root    sys        48640 Oct 29 18:11 SAPICON.EXE
-rw-r-----   1 root    sys       151040 Oct 29 18:11 sapitool.dll
-rw-r-----   1 root    sys         2063 Oct 29 18:10 sapsetup.ini
root@rs600032e:/REF/NT/SAPpc# cd SAPGUI
root@rs600032e:/REF/NT/SAPpc/SAPGUI# ls
BITMAP        GNMSX.EXE     GNXLX.EXE     SAPBTMP.DLL    SAPOPTIO.OCX
DAT           GNNEX.EXE     GXWILD        SAPDPAMS.DLL   SAPPSTMN.DLL
FRONT.EXE     GNPOX.EXE     GXWILE        SAPF1HLP       SAPSH.EXE
GNBAX.EXE     GNSCX.EXE     GXWILJ        SAPFEWCB.DLL   SAPSMLIB.DLL
GNBMX.EXE     GNSTX.EXE     HELP_04.EXE   SAPFEWDR.DLL   SAPlpd
GNBUX.EXE     GNSUX.EXE     HTMLHELP      SAPFEWIN.OCX   VCPRCT32.DLL
GNDLX.EXE     GNUPX.EXE     LPRINT.exe    SAPFEWSS.DLL   VCSCED32.DLL
GNGAX.EXE     GNWDX.EXE     NIPING.EXE    SAPFEWTR.DLL   VCTBED32.DLL
GNHIX.EXE     GNWIE.DLL     OLEERR32.DLL  SAPFTP.EXE     VCWIN32.DLL
GNHOX.EXE     GNWIHD.HLP    SAPAWOLE.DLL  SAPGUI.EXE
GNHPX.EXE     GNWIHE.HLP    SAPAWRFC.DLL  SAPHTTP.EXE
root@rs600032e:/REF/NT/SAPpc/SAPGUI# █
```

Figure 31. Directories and Files Included in the File Package

This method for the transfer can be applied either between a UNIX TMR server and a Windows PC TMA, or between a Windows NT TMR server and a UNIX TMA.

If your TMR server and your future SAPGUI clients are running on the same platform, you just have to install the SAPGUI on the TMR server, instead of using ftp to transfer the code.

Now the SAPGUI's code repository has been created, you have to configure the task that will put the code into a Tivoli Software Distribution File Package, ready to be distributed to other machines.

By default, the file package created by the reference installation process *does not* support a TMA as a target machine. Indeed, the job provided by tho Tivoli Manager for R/3 Version 1.5 creates a file package, including Tivoli Framework programs and DLL files, that only support Managed Nodes or PC Managed Nodes, but not TMAs. This is caused by the fact that Tivoli Manager for R/3 1.5 was available before the version of the Tivoli Management Framework that introduced the concept of a TMA. Support for TMAs, however, can be accomplished with a very minor change that we describe in this book.

If you try to distribute the default-created file package to a TMA target, you will get an error message at the end of the software distribution, saying that the process failed for the subscriber you have specified. The result will be an incomplete configuration of the SAPGUI target machine: the SAPGUI icon to access the R/3 server you have specified is not created. More details about the distribution failure are given in the log file you have specified in the file package. Here is the typical log file content you should have in such a case:

```
File Package:  "DEBUG"
Operation:     install  (m=5)
Finished:      Mon Nov  2 14:10:21 1998
--------
Source messages:
cmd (ls -d /REF/NT/*)
--------
wtr05084:FAILED (fatal error)
temp script: nt_before: C:/Program Files/Tivoli/lcf/dat/1/Tiv99.BAT
size=-1, nest_level=0
starting program: C:/Program Files/Tivoli/lcf/dat/1/Tiv99.BAT
'C:/Program Files/Tivoli/lcf/dat/1/Tiv99.BAT' script complete: status = 0
C:/SAPpc: creating path
starting program: C:/SAPpc/POSTC.BAT
script stderr: [The name specified is not recognized as an^M
internal or external command, operable program or batch file.^M
]
'C:/SAPpc/POSTC.BAT' script complete: status = 1
after script failure
after script failure
FATAL.
================
~
"sap_ci.log" 22 lines, 707 characters
```

The program POSTC.BAT, that calls the program POST.BAT, returns a status code 1 after the script execution. This failure occurred because the program POST.BAT contains the wrong wrunui program and three wrong dll files, to run successfully on a TMA. The right program and dll files are mentioned below, and can be copied manually, to bypass the problem:

```
$BINDIR/../lcf_bundle/lib/w32-ix86/tools/wrunuiep.exe
$BINDIR/../lcf_bundle/w32-ix86/libdes.dll
$BINDIR/../lcf_bundle/w32-ix86/libcpl.dll
$BINDIR/../lcf_bundle/w32-ix86/libmrt.dll
```

The following is the location of the wrunui.exe executable and the necessary dll as provided by the Tivoli Manager for R/3 Version 1.5:

```
$BINDIR/../generic_unix/TME/SAP/win32/wrunui.exe
$BINDIR/../generic_unix/TME/SAPwin32/libtmf.dll
```

Use the following procedure to configure the task and to get the result as it should be.

- Log on as root on the TMR server. Check that you have the super role to run the subsequent tasks.

- From the Tivoli Desktop, double-click on the **AMS Module for R/3** policy region.

- Double-click on the R/3 system policy region icon, corresponding to the SID of the R/3 system you want to configure a client for. For us, this policy region is RDU. Open the task library RDU Utilities.

- In the task library, edit the appropriate job for a reference installation, by right-clicking on the job icon. The job's name is Configure RDU Client Install.

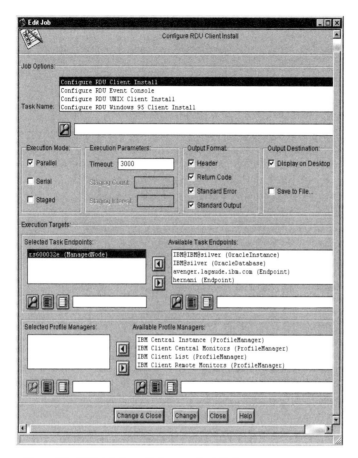

Figure 32. Edit Job for a Reference Installation

By default, the name of the task executed by the job is highlighted in the Task Name scrolling menu: Configure RDU Client Install.

The other default settings are correct, except for the Execution Parameter Timeout, that we recommend you to set to a higher number, for example, 600. Check also that the Display on Desktop option is selected for the Output Destination.

Check that the TMR server is selected as task endpoint, as the task must be executed on it. In our case, the TMR server name is rs600032e (Managed Node).

Once all settings are correct, click on the **Change & Close** button.

- Double-click on the job icon. A dialog box is displayed that allows you to set some parameters to perform the execution (see Figure 33 on page 70).

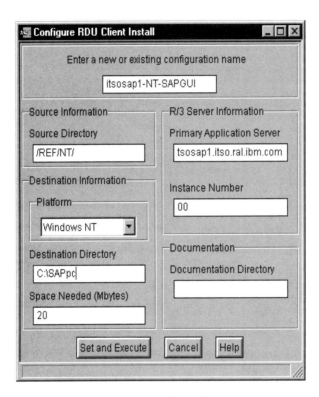

Figure 33. Settings for the Job's Execution

The Configuration Name you will specify will be an identifier of the current configuration. It will be, for example, the name of the profile manager created by the job's execution.

The Source Information field must be filled with the path where the client code is stored: for us, this is /REF/NT/, on the TMR server, as explained before.

In the Destination Information section, you have to specify the platform your target clients have, the directory where to distribute the code (we recommend also that you install the code in an SAPpc directory) and the required disk space (20 MB is the recommended size).

Then, some information about the R/3 server for which the clients will be configured is required. This information contains the Primary Application server name and the Instance Number.

Then, click on **Execute & Close** to run the job. A window is displayed when the execution is finished, saying the job's execution was completed successfully.

The job has executed a task running a script that creates a Tivoli Software Distribution file package. In our example, this file package contains the SAPGUI code for a Windows NT R/3 client. This file package is included in a profile, itself added in a profile manager, as shown in Figure 34 on page 71. Both are created during the job's execution.The name of the profile manager is the one you associated with the file package when you ran the configuration task.

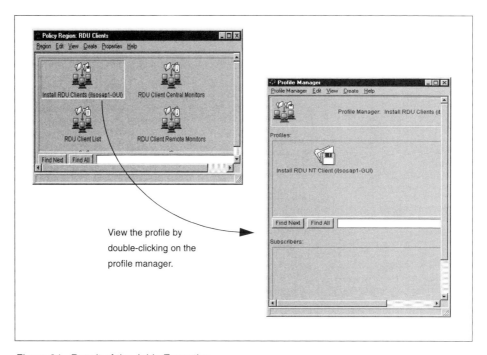

Figure 34. Result of the Job's Execution

You can edit the Tivoli Software Distribution profile to see the content of the file package, by double-clicking on it (see Figure 35 on page 72).

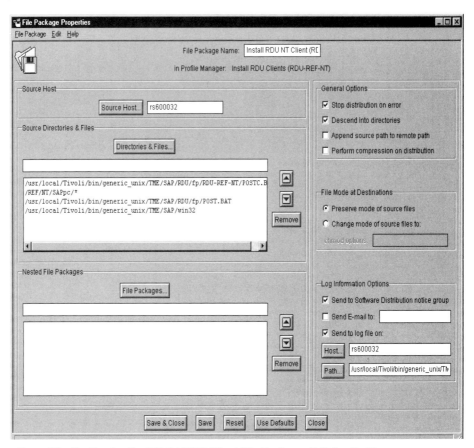

Figure 35. Configuring the R/3 SAPGUI Client File Package: Edit the Profile

You can verify that the package contains the R/3 client code for NT, located in the /REF/NT/ directory on the node rs600032e, which is the TMR server.

Distributing this file package to the target machine will create on it an SAPGUI icon in the Start Menu, to access the R/3 system specified during the configuration of the job.

3.6.6.2 Configuring a R/3 Client Using a Native R/3 Installation

This method assumes that the R/3 SAPGUI CD-ROM image is available on the target machine.This image can be the CD-ROM itself, inserted in a target machine, or a mount of it on all the other target machines. Via this method, the code is installed directly on the targets, from the CD-ROM image, using R/3 install tools and procedures.

Compared to the reference installation method, the R/3 native installation method avoids copying the SAPGUI code to the TMR server. The second advantage of such a method is the fully automatic icon customizing for the SAPGUI on the target machines.

First of all, be sure that the SAPGUI CD-ROM image is available on the target machines. Then, you have to configure the task that will extract the code from the image and put it into a Tivoli Software Distribution file package, ready to be distributed to other machines, whatever the platform of the targets is, as the Tivoli Manager for R/3 provides tasks for UNIX, Windows NT and 95 clients.

To configure the task, use the following steps.

- Log on as root to the TMR server. Check that you have the super role to run the followings tasks;

- From the Tivoli Desktop, double-click on the **AMS Module for R/3** policy region.

- Then, double-click on the R/3 system policy region icon, corresponding to SID of the R/3 system you want to configure a client for. For us, this policy region is RDU. Open the task library RDU Utilities.

- In the task library, edit the appropriate job for an R/3 native installation, according to the platform of your target. In this example, we are performing an R/3 native installation on a Windows NT target machine. In this case, the job's name is Configure RDU NT Client Install, as shown in Figure 36 on page 74.

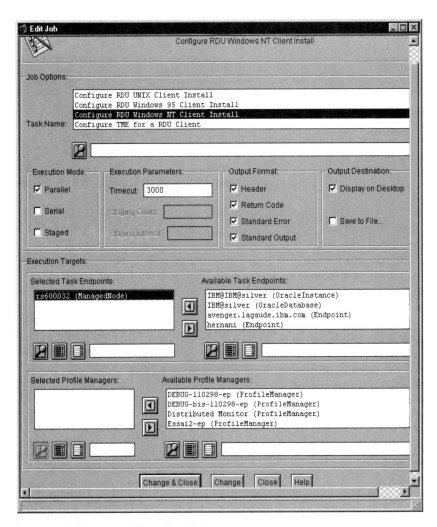

Figure 36. Edit Job for a Native Installation

By default, the name of the task executed by the job is highlighted in the Task Name scrolling menu: Configure RDU NT Client Install.

The other default settings are correct, except for the Execution Parameter Timeout, which we recommend setting to 600. Check also that the Display on Desktop option is selected for the Output Destination.

Check that the TMR server is specified as the task endpoint, as the task will be executed on it. In our case, the TMR server is rs600032e (Managed Node).

Once all settings are correct, click on the **Change & Close** button.

- Double-click on the job icon. A dialog box is displayed, which allows you to cot some parameters to perform the execution (see Figure 37 on page 75).

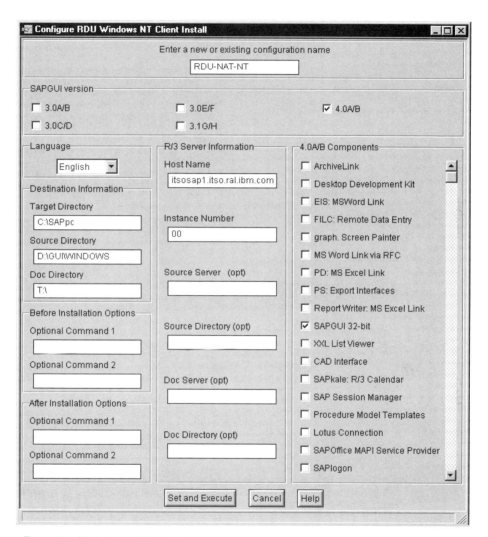

Figure 37. Native Installation Job

The Configuration Name you will specify will be an identifier of the current configuration. It will be, for example, the name of the profile manager created by the job's execution.

The Source Information fields must be filled in as explained below. We give the settings only for mandatory fields. For the optional fields, refer to the R/3 manuals for information.

- SAPGUI version: indicates the level of SAPGUI being installed on the target. For us, we have selected the 4.0B version.

- Language: enter the language you want to use, chosen from the R/3 supported languages list.

- Destination Information: fill in the fields for the destination directory on the target machine, where the code is going to be copied (we recommend that you install it into a SAPpc directory) this is the source directory where the image is stored. It is either the CD-ROM drive itself, or a mount point if the CD-ROM is shared with other target machines. In both cases, the source path must end with WINDOWS, for example D:\GUI\WINDOWS. Do not specify the subdirectory WIN32, for instance, because only a part of the code would be installed. The third attribute you have to set in this section is the path where the documentation will be copied.

- R/3 Server Information: enter the hostname of the server name and its Instance Number.

- 4.0B Components: by default, the 32-bit option is set. For the other parameters, refer to the R/3 manuals for details.

Click on **Execute & Close** to run the job. A window is displayed when the execution is finished, saying the job's execution was completed successfully.

The job has executed a task running a script that creates a Tivoli Software Distribution file package. This file package contains a set of R/3 installation tools and commands to install the SAPGUI for Windows NT on the NT targets, from the SAPGUI CD-ROM image. This set of R/3 tools and commands has been copied from the Tivoli Manager for R/3 directories, on the TMR server.

This file package is included in a profile, itself added in a profile manager, as shown in Figure 38 on page 77. Both have been created during the job's execution. The name of the profile manager is the one you associated with the file package when you ran the configuration task.

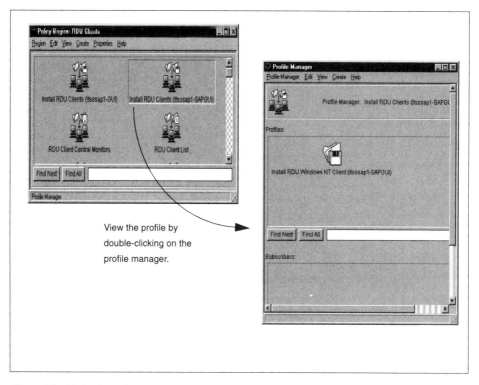

Figure 38. Native Installation Result

You can edit the Tivoli Software Distribution profile to see the content of the file package, by double-clicking on it (see Figure 39 on page 78).

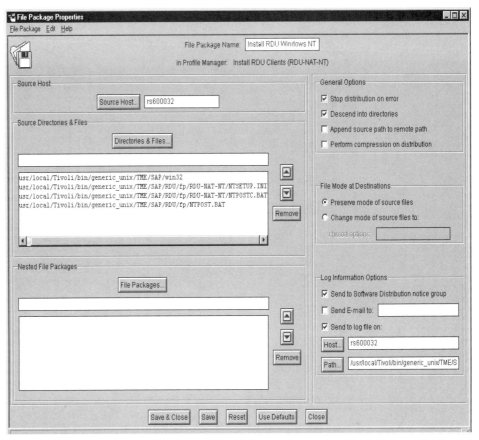

Figure 39. Configuring the R/3 SAPGUI Client Native Installation Profile

You can verify that the package contains the set of R/3 tools and commands to install the SAPGUI on a Windows NT target. You can also see that this set is located in the Tivoli Manager for R/3 directories, on the node rs600032e which is the TMR server.

Distributing this file package to the target machine will create on it a SAPGUI icon in the Start Menu, to access the R/3 system specified during the configuration of the job.

3.7 Installing and Configuring Tivoli Manager for Oracle

We only give a brief overview about Tivoli Manager for Oracle in this section, as this product, as well as the other Tivoli database management products, is described in detail in the book *Managing RDBMS Servers with Tivoli*, IBM Form SG24-5240.

The reason for installing Tivoli Manager for Oracle in our environment is that we want to be able to manage the RDBMS that SAP R/3 uses as well as the SAP application itself. Although CCMS and Tivoli Manager for R/3 give us some functions to manage the RDBMS used by SAP, the Tivoli Manager for Oracle gives us a lot more functionality in managing the RDBMS itself.

Hence, if you use a different RDBMS with your R/3 installation, you can use the other Tivoli database management products, such as Tivoli Manager for Sybase, Tivoli Manager for DB2, Tivoli Manager for Informix and Tivoli Manager for MS SQL.

In our environment, we install Tivoli Manager for Oracle 1.1 on silver and itsosap1, as these are our two RDBMS servers. The silver system is running Oracle 7 on AIX, while the itsosap1 system is running Oracle 8 on Windows NT.

After installing Tivoli Manager for Oracle on these two systems, we have to assign the new TMR roles added by Tivoli Manager for Oracle to our administrators and set the managed resources for the policy region where we want to register our databases. This procedure is described in detail in *Managing RDBMS Servers with Tivoli*, SG24-5240.

After registering our two RDBMS servers, we can manage them with Tivoli.

3.8 Installing and Configuring Tivoli Maestro

In this section we describe how to set up Tivoli Workload Scheduler (Maestro) and the Maestro Extended Agent for R/3 that allows you to manage R/3 jobs from Maestro. We also explain the necessary configuration steps for the R/3 system.

3.8.1 Installing Tivoli Maestro Master and FTA (Fault-Tolerant Agent)

Tivoli Maestro for NT is installed on host wtr05274, one of the Windows NT servers, as Maestro Master/Domain Manager. At least one Master/Domain Manager must be installed in the environment. In this case, SAP R/3 resides on silver in Germany and the Master/Domain was chosen to be at the local site in Raleigh. All of the Maestro scheduling is done at this site; thus a centralized administration management policy was adopted.

The installation must be performed using the Administrator user account. During the installation process, the Maestro installer will create a Maestro account, which has Windows NT user rights to:

- Act as part of the operating system
- Log on as batch job
- Log on as a service
- Replace a process token

The above role assignment is done by the Maestro Version 6.0 installer. To start the installation of Tivoli Maestro for NT, do the following:

- Make sure that the current Windows NT user doesn't have the same name as the Maestro account (the default is maestro) because the installer would not update the current user's password resulting in installation failure. If you are to make use of the current user, make sure you know what the current password is or reset the password in advance.
- Log on to the TMR server as user Administrator and launch the installer of Tivoli Maestro for NT by running the `setup.exe` program from the Tivoli Maestro CD-ROM.

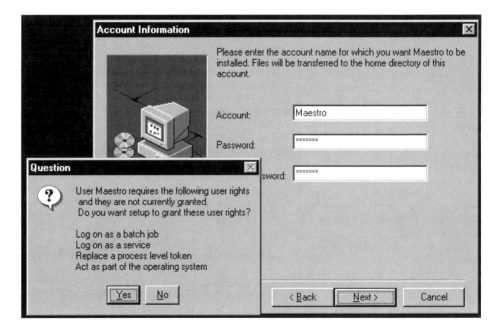

Figure 40. Installing Tivoli Maestro: Creating Maestro NT Account

- After launching the installer, you are prompted to specify the Windows NT account for Tivoli Maestro. The default name is maestro, which we accept.

- The next panel will ask you to select the Maestro internal database type: Expanded database, which supports more than eight characters for Maestro object names, or Non-expanded database type, for compatible use with Maestro 5.x. Here, Non-expanded database was selected because it might be necessary to connect Maestro 5.0 to another machine.

- The next panel is an important one. In this panel we must specify the names of the company, CPU, Master/Domain CPU and Product Group. CPU is the Maestro object that names the computer. In our case, as shown in the figure, This CPU is ITSOMSTR, Master CPU is ITSOMSTR and the Product Group is DEFAULT, respectively. The product group is the Tivoli Maestro concept of managing a Tivoli product installation; however, we will not describe it in detail. In Master/Domain server, This CPU and Master CPU names are identical. Keep in mind that the name of Master CPU is necessary in installing a fault-tolerant agent.

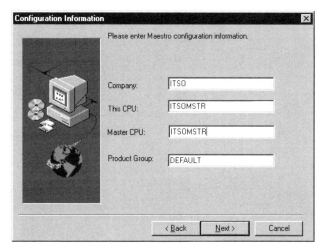

Figure 41. Maestro Configuration Information Window

- The installer opens the Tivoli Maestro Netman installer window, as it has not been previously installed. Netman is in charge of the communication between Tivoli Maestro Master and FTA.

- The next panel shows the TCP port number. The default is 31111 which we accept.

- Then back in the Maestro installer window, it requests the validation code. Specify it now, or you can set it later using the `psetcode -v` command.

- After the installation, you must reboot the system.

- You will have product directories by default: c:\win32app\maestro for Maestro and c:\win32app\unison if not otherwise specified.

- Make sure that the Maestro services are correctly installed.

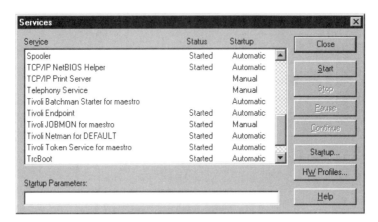

Figure 42. Maestro NT Services Batchman, JOBMAN, Netman, Token Services

3.8.1.1 After Installation Procedure for Maestro Master/Domain

After finishing the Tivoli Maestro installer program, follow the procedure below.

- The Windows NT path environment must be configured to point to the Maestro home directory and product binary directory, in our case, c:\win32app\maestro and c:\win32app\maestro\bin, respectively.

- Log in as maestro.

- Launch the Tivoli Maestro composer program from the Start menu.

- Confirm the CPU definition for the computer. Maestro installer should create the same name for CPU as for the Master CPU specified during the installation process. In our case, this is ITSOMSTR.

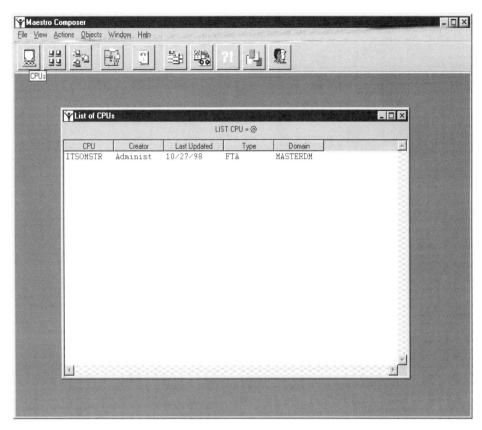

Figure 43. Tivoli Maestro SHOWCPUs Display

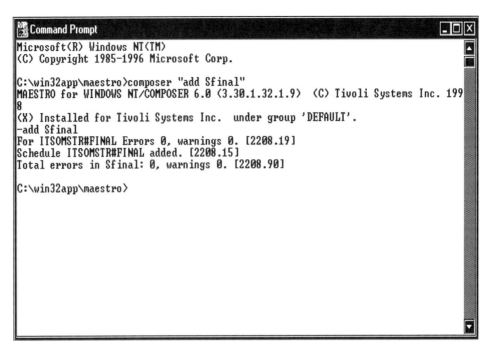

```
Command Prompt                                                    [_][□][X]
Microsoft(R) Windows NT(TM)
(C) Copyright 1985-1996 Microsoft Corp.

C:\win32app\maestro>composer "add Sfinal"
MAESTRO for WINDOWS NT/COMPOSER 6.0 (3.30.1.32.1.9)  (C) Tivoli Systems Inc. 199
8
(X) Installed for Tivoli Systems Inc.  under group 'DEFAULT'.
-add Sfinal
For ITSOMSTR#FINAL Errors 0, warnings 0. [2208.19]
Schedule ITSOMSTR#FINAL added. [2208.15]
Total errors in Sfinal: 0, warnings 0. [2208.90]

C:\win32app\maestro>
```

Figure 44. Scheduling Final (Staging Maestro Database to be in Effect)

- Add the final schedule to reflect the current scheduling and definition in effect. At the command prompt, enter the following command: composer "add Sfinal". The schedule defined in the file named Sfinal was added.

- At the command prompt, to run the Jnextday job, enter Jnextday.

- Verify that the Maestro is alive. At the command prompt, enter the conman status command. You should get the reply Batchman LIVES. This can be achieved by launching Console Manager from the Start menu and selecting **Status** from the View menu.

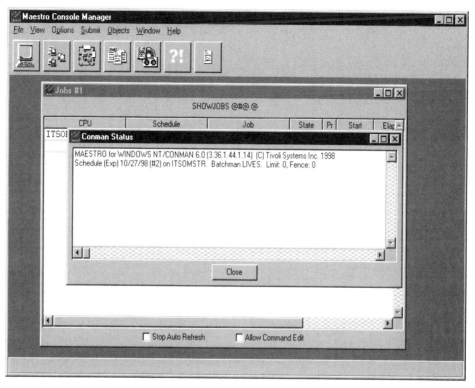

Figure 45. Confirm the Installation

• Click the **CPUs...** button in the tool bar. The SHOWCPUs display will appear as shown in Figure 46 on page 86. Your Master computer should be displayed with following status:

```
Jobman Init YES
Jobman running YES
```

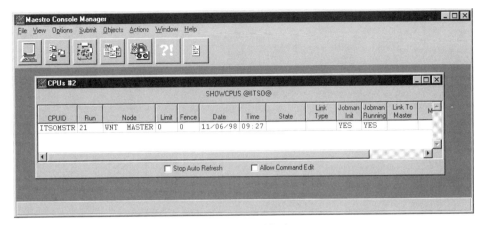

Figure 46. Maestro Console Manager SHOWCPUs Display

- Raise the job limit on the CPU to allow jobs to execute in SHOWCPU display. Select **LIMIT** from the Actions menu. Enter 10 in the Limit field in the next dialog.

3.8.1.2 Installing and Configuring Fault-Tolerant Agent for UNIX

For controlling the SAP R/3 system with Tivoli Maestro, the Maestro product must be installed on the same box as SAP R/3. Here, we install FTA on silver.

Follow the procedure below:

- Create the group unison and the user maestro (on AIX you can use SMIT to do this). The home directory must be specified. This will be the installation directory for Tivoli Maestro. In our case, this is /usr/lib/maestro.
- Log in as root. Copy the file MAESTRO.TAR from CD to *maestro home*.
- Change directory to *maestro home*.
- Extract the software by typing `tar -xvf MAESTRO.TAR`
- Execute the customize script:

  `/bin/sh customize -new -thiscpu silver -master ITSOMSTR`
- Add *maestrohome* and *maestrohome*/bin to the PATH in the profile for the user.
- Start Maestro with the command `maestrohome/StartUp` for Netman or `maestrohome/bin/conman start`.
- The next task is to create a new CPU for silver. As we adopted the management policy of central administration, all the Maestro administrative work afterward is done from the Maestro Master/Domain on

wtr05724. Launch the Maestro composer from the Start menu. Click the **CPUs...** button in tool bar. Select **New** from the Actions menu. You can add silver's CPU as shown in Figure 47 on page 87. Node is the hostname or IP address. In the Maestro Options section click on **Fault Tolerant Agent**, **AUTO Link**, **Resolve Dependencies** and **Full Status.**

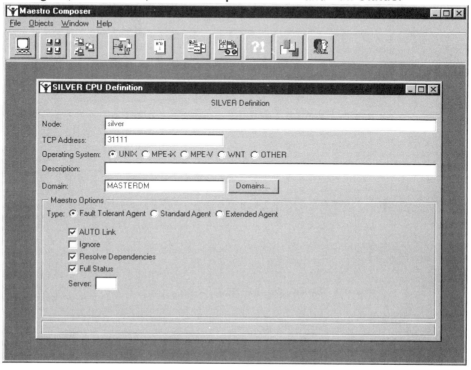

Figure 47. Maestro Silver CPU Definition Window

- At the command prompt, to run the Jnextday job, enter `Jnextday`, reflecting the change done for silver.

- The SHOWCPU display shows SILVER working. Confirm that the State is LINKED, link type TCP/IP, Jobman init YES and Jobman running YES, respectively. You may need a real job to be scheduled for the view like this because Maestro contacts the other CPUs when necessary.

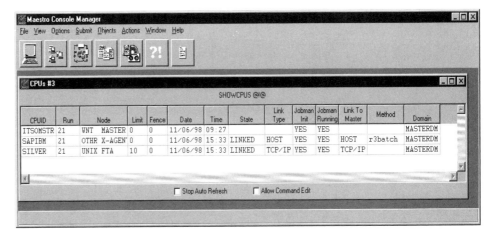

Figure 48. Maestro SHOWCPUs for silver

3.8.2 Installing and Configuring Tivoli Maestro Extended Agent 3.0

In this section we cover the installation and configuration of Maestro Extended Agent for R/3 and the necessary steps that need to be performed on the R/3 system.

3.8.2.1 Preparation in R/3

Before we start to install Tivoli Maestro Extended agent, the following setup in SAP R/3 is required:

- Creation of a R/3 user profile for Maestro. A new profile ZMAESTRO is created by the R/3 Maintain Profiles transaction, for R/3 authorization. Please refer to Figure 49 on page 89.

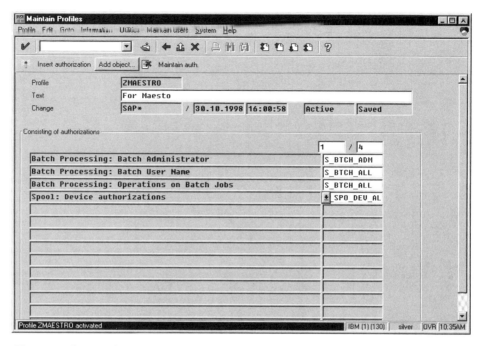

Figure 49. Create R/3 User Profile ZMAESTRO

- Creation of R/3 user. A new user MAESTRO is created in R/3. This user has the ZMAESTRO authorization profile. User type CPIC was specified. Either CPIC or Dialog is acceptable; however, care should be taken if you assign a user type of Dialog. The password change is required for the first login after user creation. The first temporary password should be input and it is up to you to log in and change the password. In the next stage, input of this password is required.

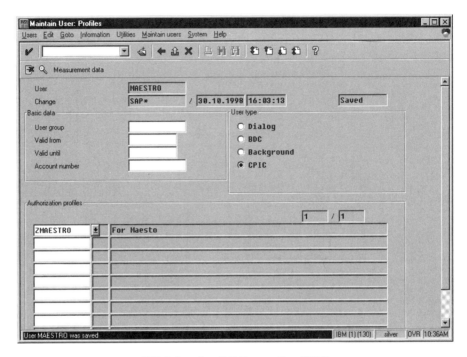

Figure 50. R/3 User MAESTRO Creation (R/3 Transaction SU01)

3.8.2.2 Initial Setup Program r3setup

Tivoli Maestro Extended agent must be installed on the system where SAP R/3 is running. After installing FTA on silver, follow the procedure below:

- Log in as root. Copy the install file SAP.TAR from CD-ROM to *maestro home*.

- Change directory to *maestro home*.

- Extract the software by typing `tar -xvf SAP.TAR`

- Execute the r3setup script. This script copies binaries and transport files K900031.IXK and R900031.IXK, and then creates the r3options file, which has an entry for each instance of R/3:

  ```
  /bin/sh r3setup -new
  ```

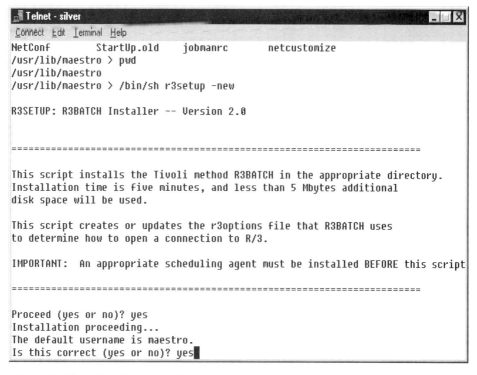

```
Telnet - silver
Connect  Edit  Terminal  Help
NetConf        StartUp.old    jobmanrc      netcustomize
/usr/lib/maestro > pwd
/usr/lib/maestro
/usr/lib/maestro > /bin/sh r3setup -new

R3SETUP: R3BATCH Installer -- Version 2.0


========================================================================

This script installs the Tivoli method R3BATCH in the appropriate directory.
Installation time is five minutes, and less than 5 Mbytes additional
disk space will be used.

This script creates or updates the r3options file that R3BATCH uses
to determine how to open a connection to R/3.

IMPORTANT:  An appropriate scheduling agent must be installed BEFORE this script

========================================================================

Proceed (yes or no)? yes
Installation proceeding...
The default username is maestro.
Is this correct (yes or no)? yes
```

Figure 51. Executing the r3setup Command

```
What is the host CPU name for this R/3 system? SAPIBM
What is the host name of your R/3 application server? silver
Ping silver: (xxxxxxxxx).....
.....
Do you wish to specify a separate R/3 gateway host (yes/no) no
What is your three-character R/3 system id? IBM
What is your two-digit R/3 instance number? 00
What is your three-digit R/3 client number? 130
What is your R/3 user id for RFC calls? maestro
What is the password for your R/3 rfc user id? xxxx
Your password is being encrypted.....
.....
If you wish to change the intervals from the defaults(30/300),
edit the r3options file after this script completes.

What is your R/3 interface audit level(only for R/3 version 3.1G or higher) 0? 0
...
+++ New r3option file entry is:
```

Figure 52. Output from r3setup Command

3.8.2.3 Import Function Modules

On the R/3 server, silver, which will be used to execute the import, copy the data and cofiles from maestrohome to /usr/sap/trans/data and /usr/sap/trans/cofiles respectively. The cofiles contain the configuration parameters for the transport and the data files contain the real data that is imported.

On the application server that will be used to execute the import, copy the file R900031.IXK and the file K900031.IXK from *maestrohome* to /usr/sap/trans/data and /usr/sap/trans/cofiles respectively.

```
cp R900031.IXK /usr/sap/trans/data/R900031.IBM
cp K900031.IXK /usr/sap/trans/cofiles/K900031.IBM
```

The files to be copied may depend on the release of the R/3 system. In our case, these are the files above.You can find the information in the Tivoli Maestro SAP R/3 Extended Agent supplement and release note.

Check first if the transport system is already configured and functioning. Go to the /usr/sap/trans/bin directory and verify the existence and contents of the TPPARAM file there (configuration file for transports). If the file is missing, the transport system is probably not yet configured (newly installed R/3 system). Locate the sample configuration file, copy it to /usr/sap/trans/bin, rename it to TPPARAM, and adapt the content.

Although it is not mentioned in the Tivoli Maestro SAP R/3 Extended Agent supplement and release note, we created a development class YMA3.

Verify that there are no other imports waiting in the transport buffer by entering `tp showbuffer <SID>`, where SID is the identifier of your R/3 system. If some imports are waiting, contact the SAP administrator of the system. In the other case, add the correction to the buffer by entering `tp addtobuffer <SID>K9xxxxx <SID>`.

- Verify the buffer by typing `tp show buffer IBM` and then enter `tp addtobuffer IBM900031 IBM`.
- Verify the buffer by typing `tp show buffer IBM`.

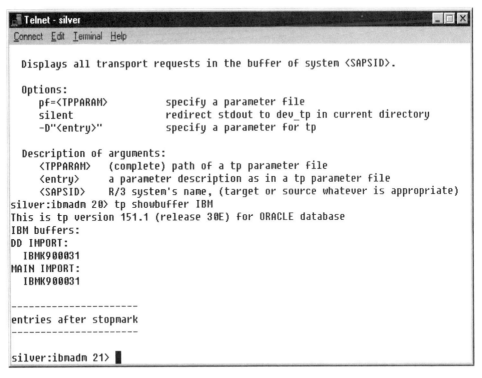

```
Telnet - silver                                                    _ □ X
Connect  Edit  Terminal  Help

 Displays all transport requests in the buffer of system <SAPSID>.

 Options:
    pf=<TPPARAM>          specify a parameter file
    silent               redirect stdout to dev_tp in current directory
    -D"<entry>"          specify a parameter for tp

 Description of arguments:
    <TPPARAM>   (complete) path of a tp parameter file
    <entry>     a parameter description as in a tp parameter file
    <SAPSID>    R/3 system's name, (target or source whatever is appropriate)
silver:ibmadm 20> tp showbuffer IBM
This is tp version 151.1 (release 30E) for ORACLE database
IBM buffers:
DD IMPORT:
  IBMK900031
MAIN IMPORT:
  IBMK900031

---------------------
entries after stopmark
---------------------

silver:ibmadm 21> █
```

Figure 53. Showing Transport Requests

- Verify the contents by typing `tp tst IBMK900031 IBM`.

- Perform the import by typing `tp import IBMK900031 IBM client=130`. In the previous tp tst command the results showed return code 04, thus the 'client=130' option was added according to the release notes.

```
    IBMK900031
MAIN IMPORT:
    IBMK900031

---------------------
entries after stopmark
---------------------

silver:ibmadm 21> tp tst IBMK900031 IBM
This is tp version 151.1 (release 30E) for ORACLE database
This is /usr/sap/IBM/SYS/exe/run/R3trans version 5.30.3 (release 30E - 04.09.96
/usr/sap/IBM/SYS/exe/run/R3trans finished (0004).
silver:ibmadm 22> tp import IBMK900031 IBM client=130
This is tp version 151.1 (release 30E) for ORACLE database
This is /usr/sap/IBM/SYS/exe/run/R3trans version 5.30.3 (release 30E - 04.09.96
/usr/sap/IBM/SYS/exe/run/R3trans finished (0004).
sapparam(1c): No Profile used.
sapparam(1c): No Profile used.
sapparam(1c): No Profile used.
This is /usr/sap/IBM/SYS/exe/run/R3trans version 5.30.3 (release 30E - 04.09.96
/usr/sap/IBM/SYS/exe/run/R3trans finished (0004).
sapparam(1c): No Profile used.
sapparam(1c): No Profile used.
sapparam(1c): No Profile used.
silver:ibmadm 23>
```

Figure 54. Import Function Modules

Finally, make sure that the function modules that Tivoli Maestro provides
were correctly imported. In the ABAP/4 Development Workbench, you can
click the **Object Browser** button, put YMA3 in the Development Class input
box, click the **Display** button and get the list of the installed modules as
shown in Figure 55 on page 95.

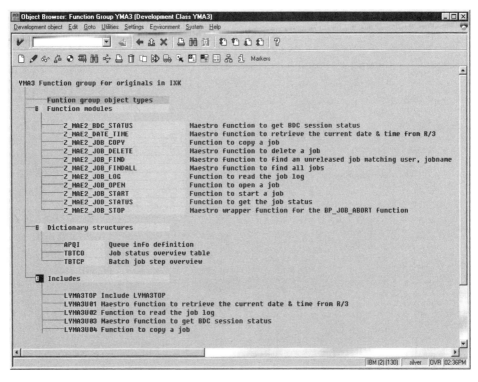

Figure 55. Tivoli Maestro R/3 Function Modules List

3.8.3 Creating Jobs for Tivoli Maestro in SAP R/3

Before we proceed with Tivoli Maestro Extended Agent CPU in Maestro Master, let us explain the way to create jobs in SAP R/3. Because the scheduling functions are now to be done by Tivoli Maestro, we don't have to specify these items in R/3 scheduling; however, it is still up to R/3 to define the jobs running in R/3. Tivoli Maestro only picks up a job created in R/3.

- In the SM36 Define Background Job transaction, specify your Job name, Job class and Target host. Here, the Job name is MAESTRO_1.

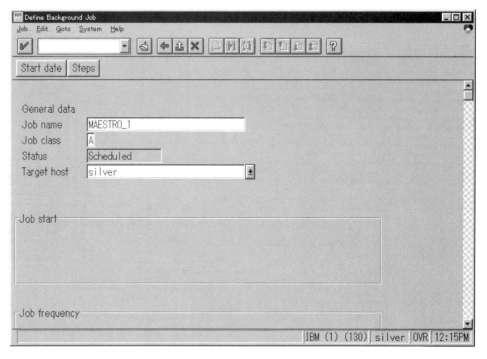

Figure 56. Background Job Definition in R/3 (SM36)

- Specify the step. In Figure 57 on page 97, click the **ABAP/4** button and input the Name of the program. Click the save icon to save the step definition.

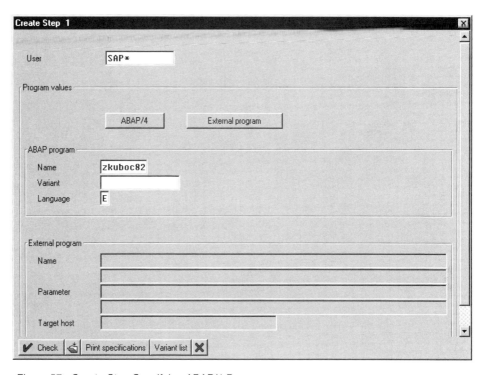

Figure 57. Create Step Specifying ABAP/4 Program

- Don't specify the start date information. Leave it empty as shown in Figure 58 on page 98.

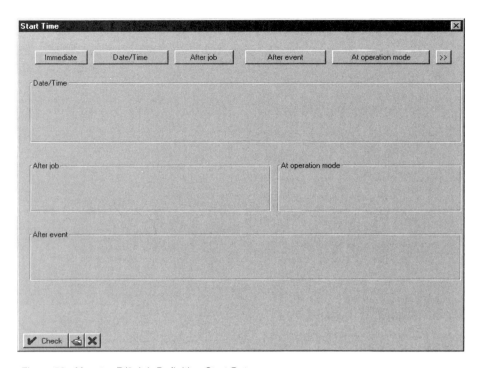

Figure 58. Maestro R/3 Job Definition Start Date

- To verify if the R/3 job is correctly defined, enter your job's name in the SM37 Select Background Jobs Transaction. Don't forget to check the **Jobs without start date** check box.

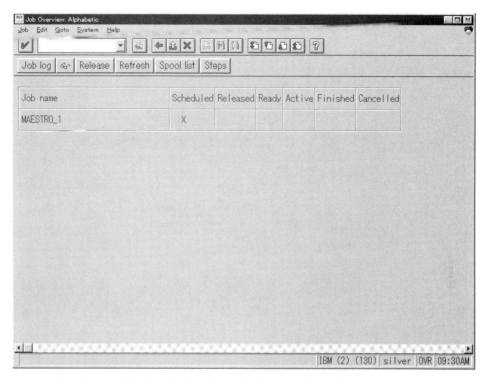

Figure 59. Maestro R/3 Job Definition: Status is Shown as Scheduled

- Executing the SM37 transaction shows that the status of job MAESTRO_1 is scheduled.

3.8.3.1 Tivoli Maestro SAP R/3 Extended Agent CPU Definition

Next, the Tivoli Maestro Extended Agent CPU must be defined in the Maestro Master machine as shown in Figure 60 on page 100. Remember that we adopted the central administration policy.

- Launch the Maestro composer from Start menu. Click the **CPUs...** button in the tool bar. Select **New** from the Actions menu. You can input the SAP R/3 Extended Agent CPU name as specified in the r3setup program previously. Here, it is SAPIBM. The Node name is the hostname (in this case the Extended Agent host, silver), or we can specify the IP address of the host. In the Operating System section we check **OTHER**. In the Maestro Options section we check **Extended Agent** and **AUTO Link**. In the Host CPU: field we enter `silver` and in the Access: field we enter `r3batch`. Be careful that r3batch is not installed locally but is installed on the remote node silver. Thus, even choosing the **Methods...** button, you cannot find our method r3batch. You can find the r3batch method in the directory *maestrohome/*methods on silver. To finish select **Save** from the File menu.

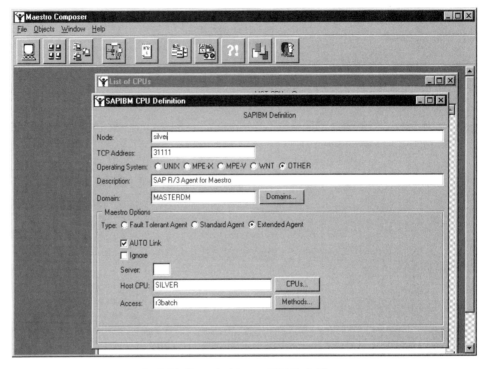

Figure 60. Tivoli Maestro SAP R/3 Extended Agent CPU Definition

Now, you are ready to start scheduling Jobs in R/3. Remember that we already defined an R/3 Job, MAESTRO_1.

- Log in as maestro.
- Launch the Tivoli Maestro composer program from the Start menu.
- First, we create a job in the SHOWJOBS display. Click the jobs icon in the tool bar. Select **New Jobs...** from the Action menu. You will see the New Job window.

Figure 61. Maestro Composer New Job Window

- Click the **CPUs...** button and you are prompted to select a CPU from the choice list. Enter the Job Name. Here, we enter SAP_1.

- You can see the SAPIBM#SAP_1 Job Definition window. Click the **Retrieve** button, and you are prompted to specify the R/3 Job Name and user filter criteria in the Retrieve R3 Job List window.

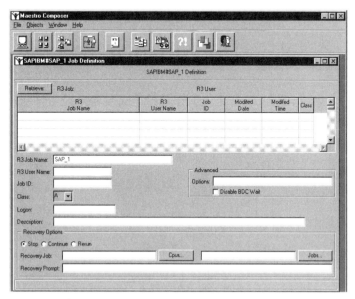

Figure 62. SAPIBM#SAP_1 Job Definition Window

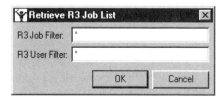

Figure 63. Retrieve R3 Job List Window

- Click the **OK** button in the Retrieve R3 Job List Window, and you will find that R3 Job Name List in SAPIBM#SAP_1 Job Definition window is filled with R3 Jobs, which was done by the Maestro r3batch method. Select one of the R3 jobs; here it is MAESTRO_1. In the Logon: field specify the Maestro user on silver. Here it is maestro. You can optionally input Recovery Options or Advanced options in this dialog. When finished, select **Save** from the File menu.

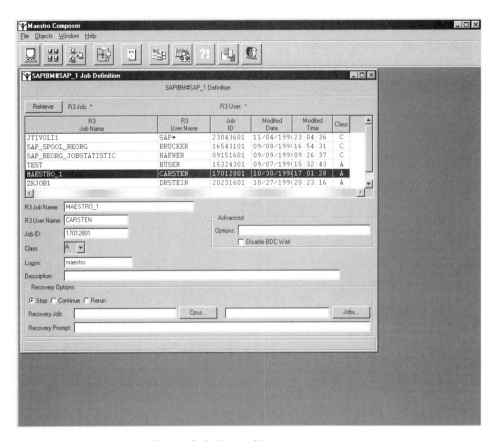

Figure 64. Final Display of R3 Job Definition by Maestro

- Next, you must specify when the SAP_1 job is to be run in the SHOWSCHEDULEs display. Click the schedules icon in the tool bar. Select **New...** from the Action menu. You will see the New Schedule window. You are prompted to specify the name of the CPU and the Schedule. Here, the CPU name is ITSOMSTR, which is the Maestro master, and the schedule name is SAPJOB1.

- You will see the ITSOMSTR#SAPJOB1 Schedule Definition window. In this window you make your schedule condition. Here we checked Everyday at 09:40 and set the priority to HIGH.

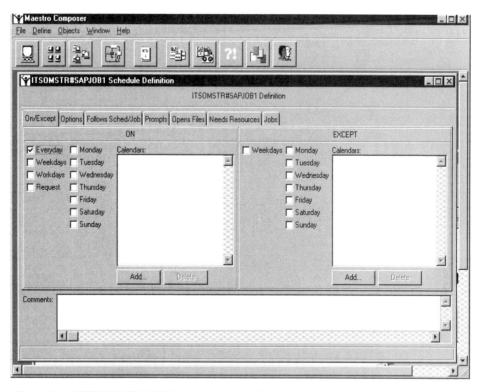

Figure 65. ITSOMSTR#SAPJOB1 Schedule Definition

- At the command prompt, to run the Jnextday job, enter `Jnextday`.
- We see in the CPUs Window in the Maestro Console Manager that SAPIBM is running.

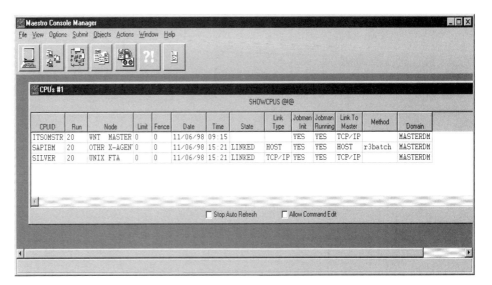

Figure 66. Maestro Console Manager: CPUs Display

- Finally you will find the scheduled job (SAPIBM#)SAP_1 completing in the SHOWJOBS display in the console manager.

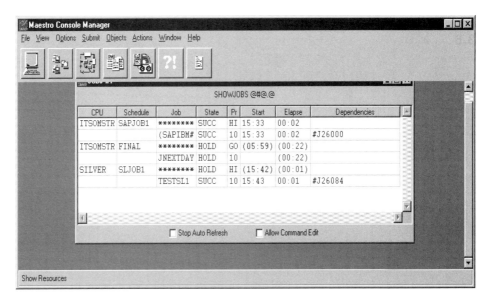

Figure 67. Maestro Console Manager: SHOWJOBs Display

- We find two copies of MAESTRO_1 in the Job Overview Display (SM37) (Figure 68 on page 105), one of which is the original job and the other is the one created by Maestro in runtime. The original job is used as a template job, so that we don't have to define the same jobs everyday.

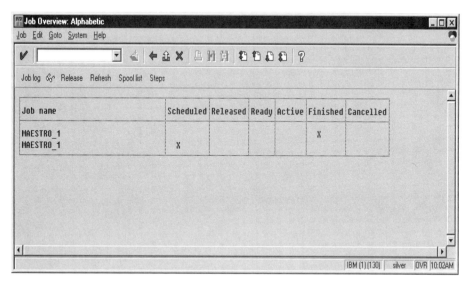

Figure 68. R/3 Job Overview Alphabetic Window

3.8.4 Installing and Configuring Tivoli Plus for Maestro

In this section we show how to install and configure Tivoli Plus for Maestro. We only give a short description of how to install and configure Tivoli Plus for Maestro and don't explain this product in full detail. Using the Tivoli Plus for Maestro module, the Maestro application can be managed across a multi-platform network with both PCs and UNIX systems. Though this does not immediately affect the management of R/3, it further integrates the management environment by integrating Maestro with the Tivoli Framework, while Maestro itself is integrated with R/3 through the Extended Agent for R/3.

In our environment, Tivoli Plus for Maestro is installed on host wtr05274 (the Maestro Master/Domain Manager) and on host rs600032 (the TMR Server and also the TEC Server).

To install Tivoli Plus for Maestro, follow the procedure below:

- Log on as root and copy the file MAESTRO.TAR from CD-ROM to a temporary directory.

- Extract the software by typing `tar -xvf TIVOLIPLUS20.TAR`.
- Next, start Tivoli Desktop on the TMR Server and select **Desktop** from the menu bar and then **Install->Install Product..** from the pull-down menu. The Install Product window will appear as shown in Figure 69 on page 106.

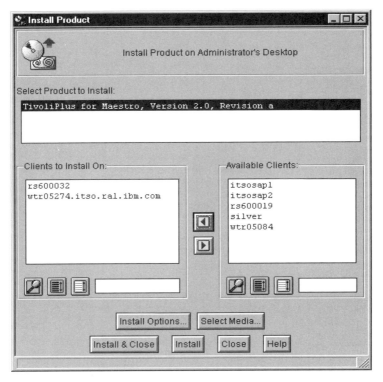

Figure 69. Install Product Window for Tivoli Plus for Maestro

- Click the **Select Media...** button and select the source of the install image, which is the temporary directory into which you extracted the code from the CD-ROM.
- Select **TivoliPlus for Maestro 2.0, Revision a**.
- The Install Options dialog will appear. Just fill in the information regarding your Maestro installation, for example, the Maestro user name (as it was defined in the Maestro Master installation) and the Maestro installation directory (same as above). In our case, the options set can be seen in Figure 70 on page 107.

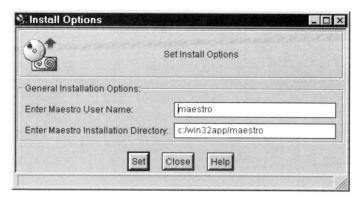

Figure 70. Set Install Options for Tivoli Plus for Maestro

- Click **Set** to complete setting the installation options.

- Click the **Install** button to continue the Installation process. You will see the Product Install window showing the list of operations that take place when installing the software, and if there are any warnings about configuration problems you can correct before installing the product. Click the **Continue Install** button and when the installation is complete, look at the completion message at the bottom of the Product Install window to make sure everything went fine with the installation.

3.8.4.1 Configuring TEC and Logfile Adapter

After installing Tivoli Plus for Maestro, you must configure Tivoli Enterprise Console to be used with it, in order to manage events coming from Maestro. You must also configure the logfile adapter on the Maestro Server to relay event notifications from Maestro to Tivoli.

Follow the procedure below:

- Start by running the job Setup EventServer for Maestro as shown in Figure 73 on page 109.

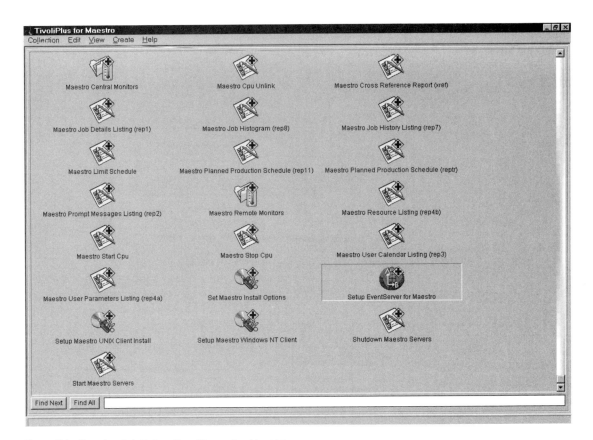

Figure 71. Running Job Setup EventServer for Maestro

- After that, you will be prompted with the Setup EventServer for Maestro window where you can either create a new rule base to add the Tivoli Plus for Maestro event classes rules or add them to your existing rule base. In our environment, we decided just to add to our existing rule base, as shown in Figure 72 on page 109.

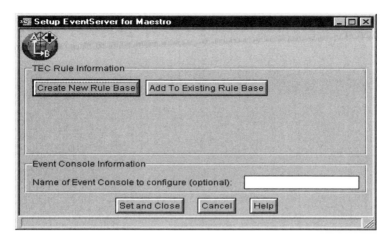

Figure 72. Adding To Existing Rule Base Options Window

- Then select **Set and Close** to run the job and the completion window can be seen in Figure 73 on page 109.

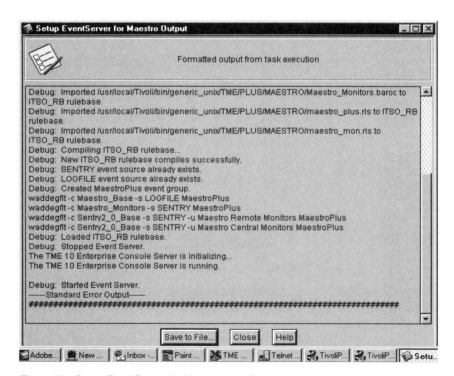

Figure 73. Setup EventServer for Maestro Job Completion

> **Important**
>
> This job sets up TEC:
>
> - Recognize and accept Maestro events.
> - Respond to Maestro events according to its predefined rules.
> - Notify the system administrator of the events received and the action taken.

- At this point you can see the event classes and rules inserted into your EventServer rule base by this procedure. As an example, see Figure 74 on page 110.

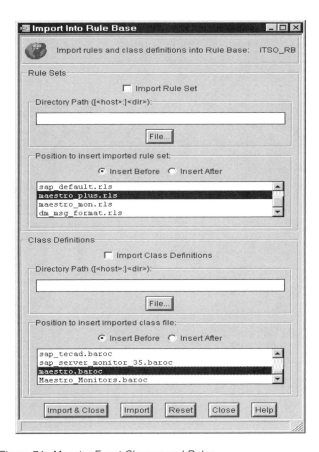

Figure 74. Maestro Event Classes and Rules

- Next, to configure the logfile adapter, begin by running the job Configure Logfile Adapter as shown in Figure 76 on page 112.

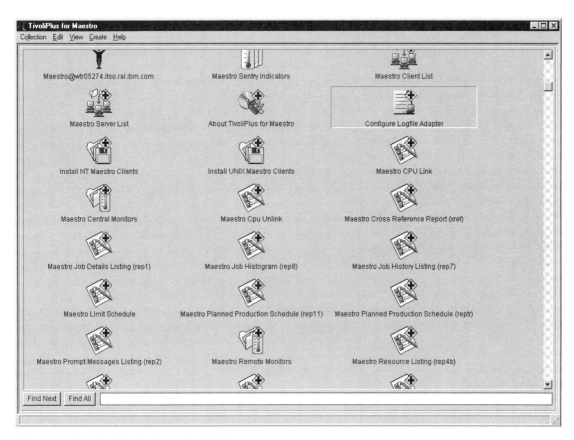

Figure 75. Running Job Configure Logfile Adapter

- After running the job you can see a sample completion window in Figure 76 on page 112.

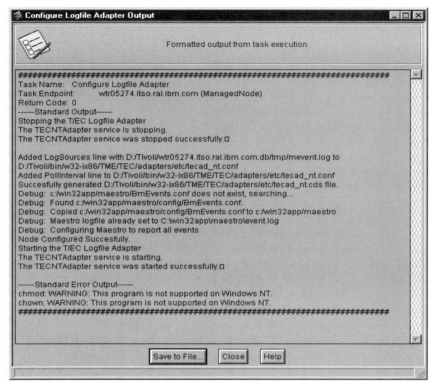

```
Configure Logfile Adapter Output                                    _ □ ×

                            Formatted output from task execution

##################################################################################
Task Name:   Configure Logfile Adapter
Task Endpoint:       wtr05274.itso.ral.ibm.com (ManagedNode)
Return Code: 0
------Standard Output------
Stopping the T/EC Logfile Adapter
The TECNTAdapter service is stopping.
The TECNTAdapter service was stopped successfully.□

Added LogSources line with D:/Tivoli/wtr05274.itso.ral.ibm.com.db/tmp/mevent.log to
D:/Tivoli/bin/w32-ix86/TME/TEC/adapters/etc/tecad_nt.conf
Added PollInterval line to D:/Tivoli/bin/w32-ix86/TME/TEC/adapters/etc/tecad_nt.conf
Succesfully generated D:/Tivoli/bin/w32-ix86/TME/TEC/adapters/etc/tecad_nt.cds file.
Debug:  c:/win32app/maestro/BmEvents.conf does not exist, searching...
Debug:  Found c:/win32app/maestro/config/BmEvents.conf.
Debug:  Copied c:/win32app/maestro/config/BmEvents.conf to c:/win32app/maestro
Debug:  Maestro logfile already set to C:\win32app\maestro\event.log
Debug:  Configuring Maestro to report all events
Node Configured Succesfully.
Starting the T/EC Logfile Adapter
The TECNTAdapter service is starting.
The TECNTAdapter service was started successfully.□

------Standard Error Output------
chmod: WARNING: This program is not supported on Windows NT.
chown: WARNING: This program is not supported on Windows NT.
##################################################################################

              Save to File...      Close      Help
```

Figure 76. Configure Logfile Adapter Job Completion

- After running this job, you must stop and restart Maestro by running the following commands on the Maestro Master CPU:

```
conman stop
conman start
```

┌─ **Important** ───

This job does the following:

- Configures the logfile adapter to read events from the Maestro log file.
- Configures Maestro to send events to the log file.

└───

3.9 Installing and Configuring Tivoli Output Management (Destiny)

Each type of Destiny Server is installed separately in the Destiny network. The Destiny Network consist out of three components, as discussed earlier:

- Enterprise Server
- Domain Manager Server
- Output Server

The Destiny components don't use Windows NT long file names so you should use the standard 8.3 DOS format file names.

3.9.1 Considerations Before Installation

Before installing the Destiny servers it is a good idea to have a Destiny Enterprise model designed. You may find the installation will proceed easier if the following decisions have been answered before installation.

- Which Windows NT Server node will host the Enterprise Server?
- How many Destiny domains will be created and what will they be called?
- How many Destiny Output Servers will be created and to which Destiny domains will they belong?

The Destiny Enterprise Server also includes a Domain Manager Server and an Output Server. When the Enterprise Server is installed it will create its database (UED), a Domain Manager Server database (SCD), and an Output Server database (NEWS). Each Destiny Domain Manager Server also includes an Output Server. When the Domain Manager Server is installed, it will create its own database (SCD) and an Output Server database (NEWS). Each Destiny Output Server will create its own database (NEWS).

Jet databases must be compressed from time to time. When database records are deleted, the space the database occupies is not reclaimed. This will cause the file to grow and will take up hard drive space. By compacting the database, you can reclaim used space. No users can be connected to a database that you are attempting to compact. Before compacting the databases, make sure Spoolman and Conductor are not running.

The following steps are used to compact Jet databases:

- From the Start menu, choose **Settings**, **Control Panels**, then choose **ODBC**.
- Select the **System DSN** tab and double-click on the database you want to compress.

- Click the **Compact** button.
- Choose the Database Name to compact from.
- Choose the Database Name to compact to.
- Click **OK** to compact the database and exit from the dialog box.

See Figure 77 on page 114 for the successful completion of the above steps.

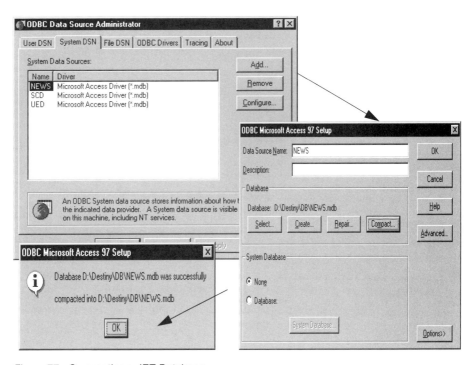

Figure 77. Compacting a JET Database

3.9.2 Destiny Installation Steps

Install the Enterprise Server first, then install each distributed Domain Manager Server, and then install each distributed Output Server. Use these same instructions for installing each type of server. In certain steps you will need to follow the specifics for the type of server being installed.

- Log in as Administrator. If you are installing to another machine in your domain, you must be logged on as the domain Administrator.
- Insert the Destiny CD-ROM disk into your CD-ROM drive.

- From the Start menu, select **Run...**. The Run dialog box appears. In the command line we enter: D:\Destiny\Win32\setup where D is the drive letter of your CD-ROM drive. Click the **OK** button to continue.

- This will start the Destiny installation program.

- A welcome window is displayed prompting you to close all other applications while installing Destiny. Click the **Next>** button to continue.

- The Software Agreement window is displayed. Click the **Yes** button.

- The next window gives you an option list of all the components that you can install. We select all components and click the **Next>** button.

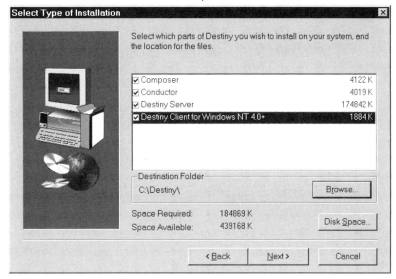

Figure 78. Destiny Installable Components

- When installing Destiny Server you must have either Microsoft SQL Server installed or have enough space (about 400 MB) for the JET database. The next window asks you for your database preference (Figure 79 on page 116). Click on **Next>**. Once done with the database selection you must now enter parameters for the platform you choose. JET database only requires a path name for creating UED, SCD or NEWS as in Figure 79 on page 116. For MS SQL configuration please refer to the Destiny Administrator's Guide. Click on **Next>** when done.

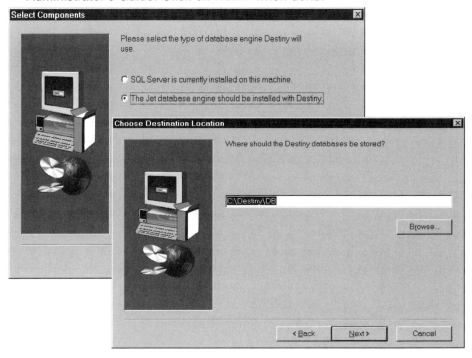

Figure 79. Database Selection and Location

- The next window is the core selection of the Destiny infrastructure. Our installation requires the Enterprise Server on wtr05083. Only one Enterprise Server is required per domain setup. We installed this component onto wtr05083 and the domain name is ITSO. The Enterprise Server does not require network functionality but when installing Domain Manager Server or the Output Server make sure that your TCP/IP channels between Enterprise Server and the component that you are installing is in place. See Figure 80 on page 117 for the specific window.

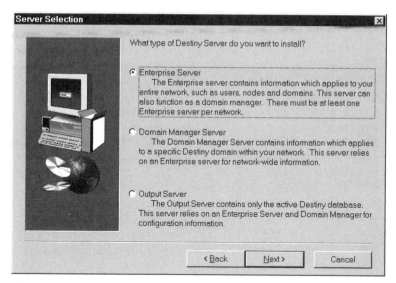

Figure 80. Server Components for Destiny Network

- The next window asks for the *domain information*. This information provides the structure for the Destiny network and determines which Output Server connects to which Domain Manager Server and so forth. Three parameters must be supplied:

  - Domain. This is the domain structure into which you are installing the specific component of Figure 80 on page 117. This entity is controlled by the Enterprise Server but also has distributed attributes controlled by the entity itself.

  - Node. This is a short naming standard for the description of the functionality of the node. The naming standard that we have used is *DOMAIN_DESTINY COMPONENT*, for example *ITSO_MGR* is the Enterprise Manager for the ITSO domain; *SAP_OUT* is the Output Server for the SAP domain. There is a limitation to the amount of characters (16) and type of characters.

  - Network Node. This is the name of the node given to it by the Administrator. Be very careful that it does not contain dashes (-) and specify it in capitals. Sometime the node must be in capitals and sometimes not, so be consistent and use capitals everywhere. To get this information of a Windows NT machine, type `net config workstation`. The output return is similar to Figure 81 on page 118. It is very important to use the above command because of the discrepancies between the Windows NT name, IP name, DNS name and NetBIOS name of an NT workstation. The `net config` workstation command returns always the name that would be used if all else fails and this is displayed as the Computer name in Figure 81 on page 118.

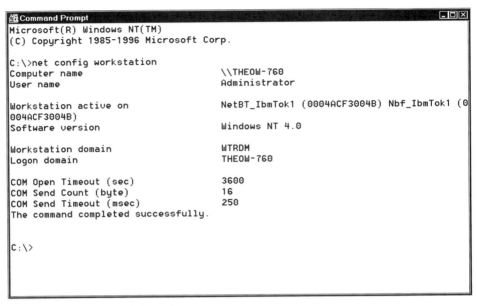

```
Command Prompt                                                          _ □ ×
Microsoft(R) Windows NT(TM)
(C) Copyright 1985-1996 Microsoft Corp.

C:\>net config workstation
Computer name                        \\THEOW-760
User name                            Administrator

Workstation active on                NetBT_IbmTok1 (0004ACF3004B) Nbf_IbmTok1 (0
004ACF3004B)
Software version                     Windows NT 4.0

Workstation domain                   WTRDM
Logon domain                         THEOW-760

COM Open Timeout (sec)               3600
COM Send Count (byte)                16
COM Send Timeout (msec)              250
The command completed successfully.


C:\>
```

Figure 81. Node Name Information

With the name of the machine known you can now fill in all the information for the domain structure of the component you are installing (Figure 82 on page 119). This figure has dependencies if you are installing Enterprise Server, Domain Manager Server and Output Server. If you are installing another Domain Manager Server then the Enterprise Server must be reachable within the Domain already defined. The same is valid for Output Servers or extending the structure of any given domain. Click on **Next>** when done.

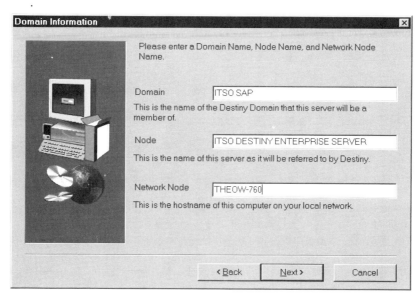

Figure 82. Domain Information for Destiny Domain Structure

- The next window prompts you for a port number. We strongly advise you to leave it running on the suggested port 32222 but other factors like enterprise security might play a role here. Destiny uses mainly this port for communication between all the servers, either for pushing output jobs through the channels or changing the structure of the output network. Destiny also uses other ports, such as 32223 for notifications, etc. Figure 83 on page 120 shows the field where a port value could be defined. Here is an output of the TCP/IP connections between an enterprise server and output server.

```
┌─ netstat -n during a push operation ──────────────────────
│  TCP    9.24.106.44:1326      9.24.106.59:139      ESTABLISHED
│  TCP    9.24.106.44:32222     9.24.106.59:1090     ESTABLISHED
│  TCP    127.0.0.1:1025        127.0.0.1:1026       ESTABLISHED
│  TCP    127.0.0.1:1026        127.0.0.1:1025       ESTABLISHED
└────────────────────────────────────────────────────────────
```

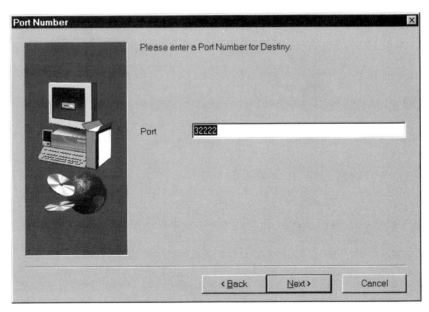

Figure 83. Destiny Port Selection

- With every installation we encountered a `Read Only File Detected` message. Click on the **Don't display this message again** checkbox and then on **Yes**. Figure 84 on page 120 shows you this window.

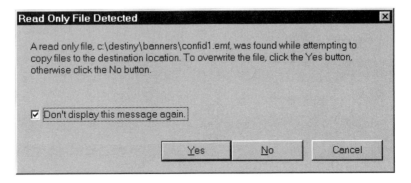

Figure 84. Read Only Message During Installation

- If you are installing Destiny Client for Windows NT 4.0 you will get the window shown in Figure 85. There are two ways to get output into the Destiny network: intercepting printer spoolers on Windows NT and UNIX, or creating a Destiny printer in Windows NT and letting users print through this device. The advantage of the second option is that the output format is device independent. The format of spooler catchers are already generated for the specific output device and to re-route the data to another output device requires re-formatting of the data or an intelligent driver for removal of only the data from the already formatted text.

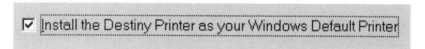

Figure 85. Destiny Printer

- After a successful installation these are the objects on the machine's desktop:

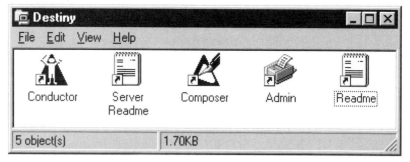

Figure 86. Destiny Icons

The Destiny Netman service can be found in the Windows NT Services window as shown in the following figure.

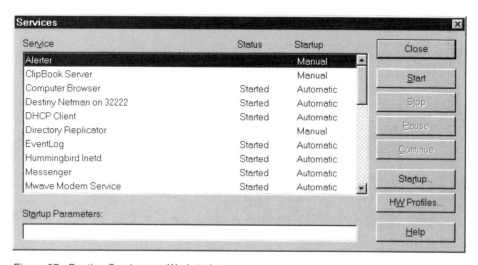

Figure 87. Destiny Services on Workstation

3.9.3 Testing the Destiny Installation

Destiny comes with an out-of-the-box demo to test the installation. If this does not work, then something went wrong during the installation or the database creation.

This demo monitors the path C:\Destiny\Demo\Incoming where C: is the installation drive for any new files. When the watcher, the Destiny object which monitors for files in a specific directory, finds a new file it will copy the file to C:\Destiny\Demo\Web\Docs and update the html index file: index.htm in C:\Destiny\Demo\Web. This file can be viewed by any browser or be part of a Web server for dynamic publishing. Figure 88 shows you the flow of the demo that comes with the installation of Destiny's Enterprise Server component.

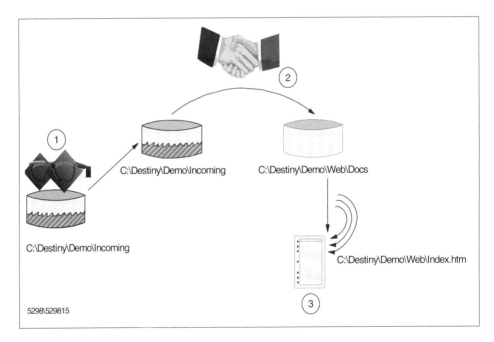

Figure 88. Destiny Demo

3.9.3.1 Activation of Destiny Demo

The Destiny demo will work after you follow these steps:

- Push the Enterprise Configuration and the Domain Configuration to every domain.

- Start the Spoolman process on the Enterprise Server.

To activate the demo you must have Composer and Conductor installed on your machine. The first action is performed by using Composer. To start Composer, click on **Start**, **Program**, **Destiny**, **Composer**. This will bring up the Composer window as shown in Figure 89.

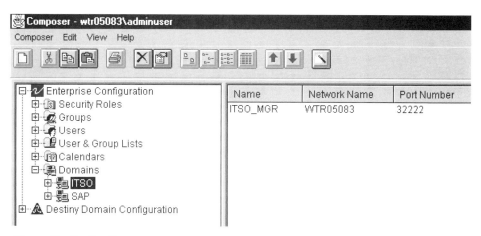

Figure 89. Destiny Composer

Click on **Enterprise Configuration**, **Domain**, and then click on the domain name. In our example the domain name is ITSO and not SAP because after a fresh install of the Enterprise Server only that particular domain is available. Once you have selected the domain for configuration update, select **Composer**, **Push**, **All** as shown in Figure 90. This action will synchronize the SCDs to the Enterprise UED database. The Windows NT service that handles this configuration update is Destiny Netman on 32222, as we left the port on its default value, 3222, during the installation process.

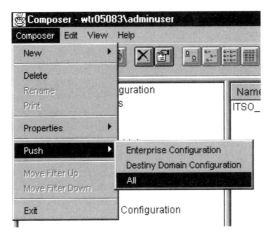

Figure 90. Push Configuration

The following boxes show you an output of all the trace files as an explanation of what happened during the *push* process.

Command: notepad c:\destiny\stdlist*1998.11.11*\compserv

```
Connected to database SCD as user <default>
Connection Successful
Handshake Header received
Push the data for SCD database
Push the data for SCD database
Exporting  tbl_stationery  .....
Exporting  tbl_banners  .....
Exporting  tbl_watchers  .....
Exporting  tbl_handles  .....
Exporting  tbl_filters  .....
Exporting  tbl_glom_header  .....
Exporting  tbl_glom_detail  .....
Exporting  tbl_mappers  .....
Exporting  tbl_mapper_calendar  .....
Exporting  tbl_rules  .....
Exporting  tbl_queue  .....
Exporting  tbl_queue_destination  .....
Exporting  tbl_device_history  .....
Exporting  tbl_queue_history  .....
Exporting  tbl_users_history  .....
```

```
┌── Command: notepad c:\destiny\stdlist\1998.11.11\uedserv ──────┐
│                                                                 │
│  Exporting  tbl_users    .....                                  │
│  Exporting  tbl_security_roles   .....                          │
│  Exporting  tbl_user_security_roles  .....                      │
│  Exporting  tbl_groups   .....                                  │
│  Exporting  tbl_group_security_roles  .....                     │
│  Exporting  tbl_dist_list   .....                               │
│  Exporting  tbl_dist_list_details  .....                        │
│  Exporting  tbl_nodes   .....                                   │
│  Exporting  tbl_node_communications  .....                      │
│  Exporting  tbl_destinations   .....                            │
│  Exporting  tbl_domains   .....                                 │
│  Exporting  tbl_calendars   .....                               │
│                                                                 │
└─────────────────────────────────────────────────────────────────┘
```

The next step is to start the Spoolman on the Enterprise Server. To do this you must select **Start**, **Programs**, **Destiny**, **Conductor** as shown in Figure 91. This brings up the utility to maintain the Destiny network. What we are going to do is to start the Spoolman on the Enterprise Server. Select the domain that the Enterprise Server was created in. Do this by clicking on **Enterprise Configuration**, **Domains**, and the domain name where the domain name is ITSO in our installation.

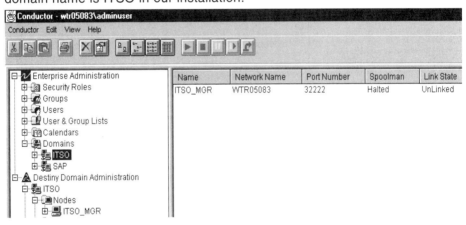

Figure 91. Destiny Conductor

To start spoolman, click on the right hand side of the panel on **ITSO_MGR**.

This action highlights the line. Select **Start, Stop** from the **Conductor** menu. This changes the status of Spoolman from halted to running:

```
ITSO_MGR WTR05083 32222 Running UnLinked
```

We have now successfully done an update of the domain's configuration and put it into operation. Open up a DOS window by clicking on **Start**, **Program**, **Command Prompt** from the task bar on the Windows NT workstation. This will bring up a DOS window. Enter `cd \destiny\demo\incoming` on the command prompt and then type `copy con test_demoweb.txt`. Now type anything that you want and when done press Ctrl+Z to let the operating system know that you are done and a file should be created. If you monitor this directory, c:\destiny\demo\incoming you will see that the file disappears from this directory and a new file is created in c:\destiny\demo\web\docs. The new file is typically something like DemoWeb-?.extension. So in the demo run, test_demoweb.txt was moved into this area as DemoWeb-12.txt and the index.htm file is updated. The following window shows the output on a Web browser.

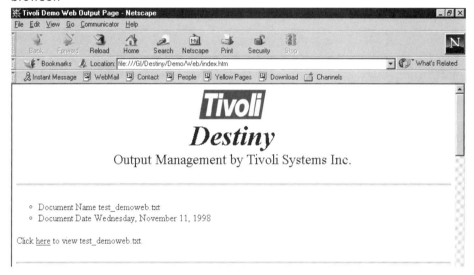

Figure 92. DemoWeb Output

If you click on **Click here to view test_demoweb.txt** in Figure 92 you will get the original text. To get information on what happened during this process you can expand Destiny Domain Administration and walk the Destiny tree through to Domain Name, Nodes, Domain Name Node, Queues, DemoWeb where domain name is ITSO and domain name node is ITSO_Mgr in our example. This portion of Destiny Conductor gives you full status reports on what has happened in the environment. If you do not see your particular result, do a **View**, **Refresh** from the menu to get the latest information from your Domain Manager Server. Figure 93 on page 127 shows all the files that have been processed via wtr05083. If you do not see anything here after hours of waiting refer to the trace files under c:\destiny\stdlist on the Enterprise Server and the client from where you have issued the commands.

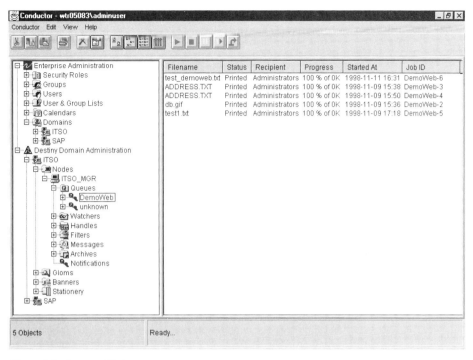

Figure 93. Queues Status

Chapter 4. Using the SAP R/3 Management Environment

In this chapter wo doscribe in detail how to use the management environment for SAP R/3 that we have set up in Chapter 3, "Setting Up the SAP R/3 Management Environment" on page 29. We explain how to use the different management products and also give background information on how the management products communicate with the R/3 system and use information provided by CCMS.

4.1 Tivoli Manager for R/3

In this section we explore the different management functions provided by Tivoli Manager for R/3, including:

- Using Tivoli tasks and jobs to manage the R/3 system

- Deploying the SAPGUI using Tivoli Software Distribution

- Monitoring R/3 using TEC

- Monitoring R/3 using Tivoli Distributed Monitoring

4.1.1 SAP R/3 System Management Tasks and Jobs

In this section we explain how to control the R/3 using Tivoli tasks and jobs, for example, how to take actions on your R/3 system such as start/stop the system, application server, database, client or monitors and also how to show performance information on an application server.

The Tivoli Manager for R/3 provides several predefined jobs to handle your R/3 system.

To control your R/3 System using Tivoli tasks and jobs, start by double-clicking **AMS Module for R/3** on the Tivoli Desktop. Then, select a <System Label> policy region (in our case RDU policy region). There, you will see an icon named <System Label> System Tasks. Double-click it and you will get to the Task Library: RDU System Tasks window as shown in Figure 94 on page 130.

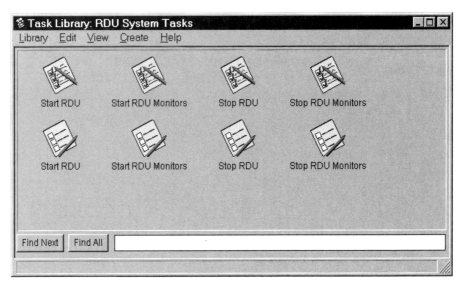

Figure 94. Task Library: RDU System Tasks Window

In this window you can see that we have four predefined jobs (the first four icons) and four predefined tasks (the last four icons) to handle the R/3 system tasks, such as starting/stopping the R/3 system and the server monitors.

> **Note**
>
> Remember that a job runs a task on a predefined list of endpoints, in this case, the RDU Server list profile manager.
>
> A task requires that you specify endpoints when running it.

Additionally, you can view the shell scripts that correspond to these tasks and jobs. They are located in the $BINDIR/../generic_unix/TME/SAP/<System Label>/sh directory.

To control your R/3 System application servers using Tivoli tasks and jobs, start by double-clicking **AMS Module for R/3** on the Tivoli Desktop. Then select a <System Label> policy region and after that <System Label> Servers. There, you will see an icon named <System Label> Server Tasks. Double-click it and you will get to the Task Library: RDU Server Tasks window as shown in Figure 95 on page 131.

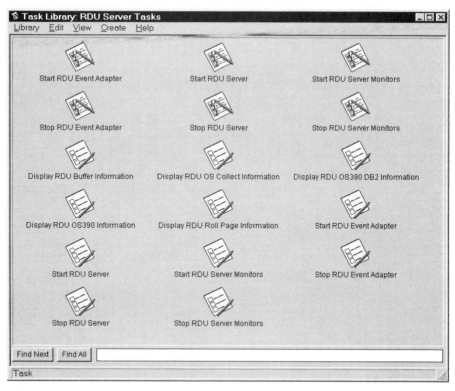

Figure 95. Task Library: RDU Server Tasks

In this window you can see jobs to start/stop the RDU server, start/stop event adapter (event adapters provide the ability to report R/3 alerts to the TEC event server and, consequently, to TEC consoles) and start/stop RDU server monitors. In this window you can also see tasks to get performance information about the RDU application server such as buffer information, roll page and OS collect. To run a task, just double-click on its icon (for example Display RDU OS Collect Information) and you will get a window as shown in Figure 96 on page 132. Note that we have chosen itsosap1_RDU_00 (SapInstance) as the Task Endpoint, as this task must be run on SapInstance endpoints.

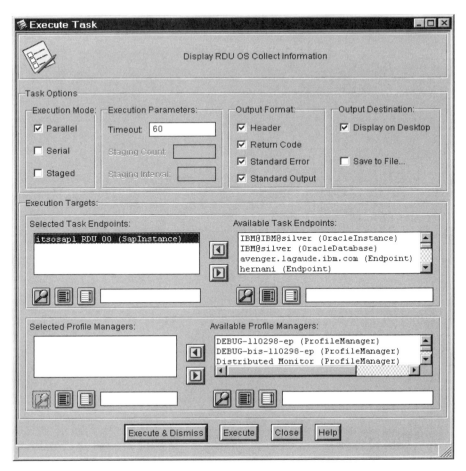

Figure 96. Display OS Collect Information Options

After this, click on **Execute & Dismiss** and you will get the output for this task, as shown in Figure 97 on page 133.

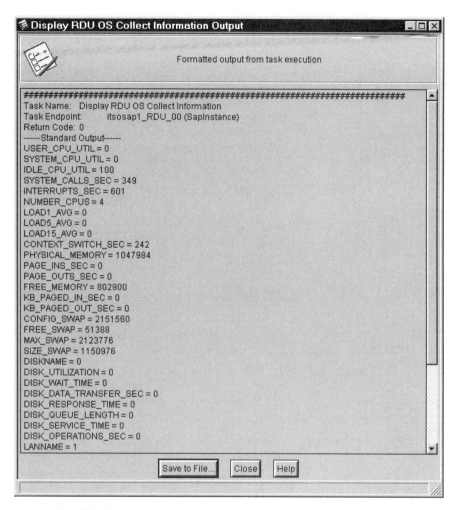

Figure 97. OS Collection Information Output

To control your R/3 system databases using Tivoli tasks and jobs, start by double-clicking **AMS Module for R/3** from the Tivoli Desktop, then select a <System Label> policy region and after that <System Label> Databases. There, you will see an icon named <System Label> Database Tasks. Double-click on it and you will get the Task Library: RDU DatabaseTasks window as shown in Figure 98 on page 134.

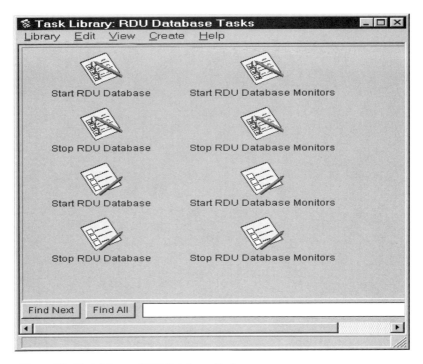

Figure 98. Task Library: RDU Database Tasks

In this window you can see jobs to start/stop the RDU database. There are two important things to be noticed:

1. If the database is on a UNIX database server, when you stop it you will also stop all SID-related application servers on that server.

2. If the database is on Windows NT, this will require customer exit routines, as described in 3.6.4.7, "Configuring the Environment" on page 59.

There are also jobs to start/stop RDU Database Monitors. Note that these monitors run on remote systems, that is they run on SapInstance endpoints contained in the RDU database list and do not affect any monitors that are running on the TMR server.

4.1.2 SAPGUI Distribution

The file package created during the reference installation and the R/3 native installation of the R/3 SAPGUI clients as described in 3.6.6, "Configuration of the R/3 Clients" on page 65, must be distributed to the target machines. Target machines must be defined as subscribers of the appropriate profile managers, according to the type of the installation (reference installation or

R/3 native installation) and the platform of the clients (UNIX, Windows NT or Windows 95).

For clients defined as Managed Nodes or PC Managed Nodes, you just have to subscribe them to the profile managers, and then distribute the profile to these new subscribers. We assume that the reader is familiar with Tivoli Software Distribution. For detailed information about Tivoli Software Distribution refer to the books *New Features in Tivoli Software Distribution 3.6*, IBM Form SG24-2045 and *The TME 10 Deployment Cookbook: Courier and Friends*, IBM Form SG24-4976.

For clients defined as TMAs (Tivoli Management Agents), a customization is required. Indeed, the client install and configuration job's execution creates by default a standard profile manager. Only Managed Nodes and PC Managed Nodes can be subscribed to such a profile manager, but TMAs cannot be subscribed to it, as they are dataless endpoints.

A TMA can *only* be subscribed to a dataless profile manager, and not to a standard profile manager.

Dataless Profile Manager

To get more details about standard and dataless profile managers, and about the subscription in both cases, refer to the Tivoli Framework 3.6 documentation.

4.1.2.1 Customization for TMA Subscription

The first step is to create a new profile manager, with the dataless endpoint mode option. You must give it a different name from the one of the standard profile manager, as Tivoli does not support two objects with the same name.

Then, from the default standard profile manager, clone the profile to the new dataless profile manager. To do that, go into the standard profile manager and select the profile. Then, in the profile manager window, select **Edit** from the menu bar and the **Profiles->Clone...** from the pull-down menu. In the window that appears you will be asked to change the name of the cloned profile, because of the Tivoli rule described above. Select also the dataless profile manager you have created, as the target for the cloned profile, and click the **Clone & Close** button. See Figure 99 on page 136.

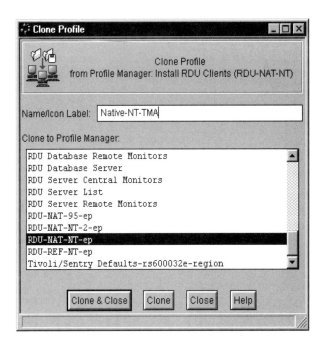

Figure 99. Cloning Profile into Dataless Profile Manager

Now, you can subscribe your TMA to the dataless profile manager. Note that a dataless profile manager can have TMAs, Managed Nodes or PC Managed Nodes as subscribers, but not a subscription list. So you may not delete the standard profile manager, as you may need to subscribe a subscription list.

In our example, shown in Figure 100 on page 137, we have created a dataless profile manager named RDU-NAT-NT-ep, that contains the cloned profile NativeNT. A Windows NT TMA is subscribed to this dataless profile manager.

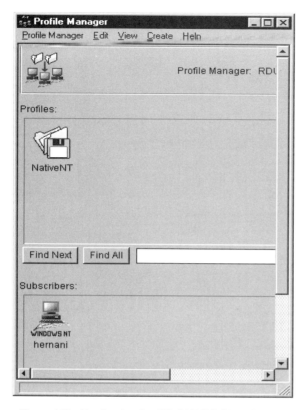

Figure 100. Configuring the R/3 SAPGUI Client File Package: Distribution to a TMA

Now, the file package can be distributed to the TMA. To do so, select the file package from the Profiles section, and the TMA from the Subscribers section. Then, from the menu bar select **Profile_Manager** and **Distribute...** from the pull-down menu. A window will appear to confirm the distribution; click on the **Distribute & Close** button.

4.1.2.2 Result of the SAPGUI Code Distribution

For both methods, a reference installation or an R/3 native installation, once the distribution is completed, the R/3 SAPGUI code is installed on the client machine and the SAPGUI icon for the appropriate R/3 system has automatically been created during the installation, as the installation was performed directly from the CD-ROM image. So, as the sapsetup program was automatically run with the right parameters, the Start menu of the PC client has been updated to provide direct access to the R/3 server, indicated during the job's configuration. See an example of the desktop of a Windows NT SAPGUI client, in Figure 101 on page 138.

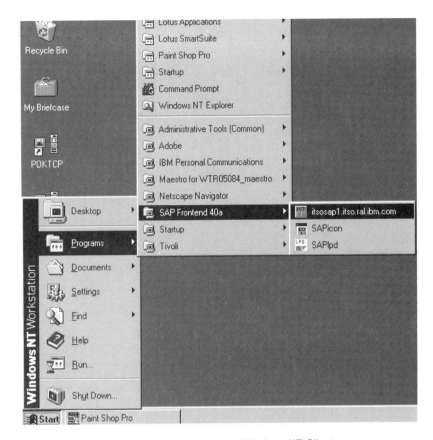

Figure 101. Example of SAPGUI Access on a Windows NT Client

From this menu, you can create other SAPGUI icons for accessing other R/3 servers, by clicking on the **SAPicon** menu.

4.1.3 Monitoring: Behind the Scenes

For monitoring a SAP R/3 system you need a tool to summarize the information in some panels and transactions. The general monitoring tool in the R/3 System is the CCMS (Computer Center Management System). CCMS is integrated in the SAP System and is available on every application server. To get into the CCMS, in the SAPGUI initial window select **Tools** from the menu bar and then **CCMS** from the pull-down menu for SAP 4.X systems. For SAP 3.X systems, in the SAPGUI main window select **Tools** from the menu bar and then **Administration** from the pull-down menu. In the following window select **Computing Center** from the menu bar and the **Management System** from the pull-down menu. As an alternative, you can type in the transaction code SRZL.

One of the transactions in the CCMS is the transaction RZ03 - Alert Details, which gives an overview of the current system status.

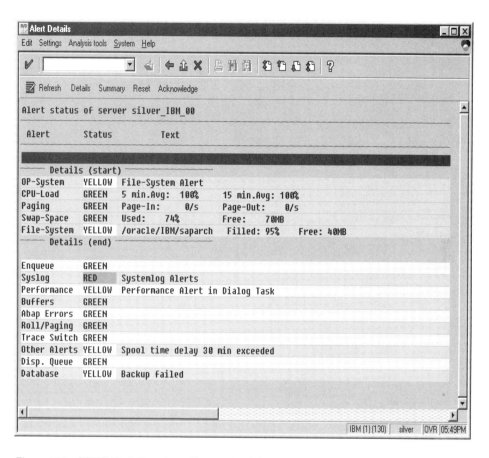

Figure 102. CCMS Alert Overview - Transaction RZ03

The alerts provided by CCMS are also shared with the external world by using an interface, the SAP shared memory segment. Every SAP R/3 application server does have a shared memory segment, also called SAP MIB (Management Information Base), which comprises all alert information from this application server. The MIB is based on SNMP (Simple Network Management Protocol). The information provided in this MIB is monitored by the Tivoli Manager for R/3 with a program, called wr3mib, and a special adapter called TEC event adapter, which translates the MIB alerts to TEC events. More information on the event adapter functioning will be given in 4.1.3.1, "Event Adapter" on page 140.

Another possibility for getting information out of the SAP R/3 system is using Tivoli Distributed Monitoring and the Remote Function Call. Tivoli Distributed Monitoring is the Tivoli core application which provides the functionality for synchronous monitoring. To get information out of SAP R/3, Tivoli Distributed Monitoring operates with the RFC (Remote Function Call) interface and the MIB. The RFC interface is provided by every SAP R/3 system and it is the primary interface for managing R/3 from external management systems. Information is gathered from the SAP system using RFC by the Tivoli program wr3rfc. Getting information from SAP using Tivoli Distributed Monitoring will be discussed in details in 4.1.3.2, "Tivoli Distributed Monitoring" on page 144.

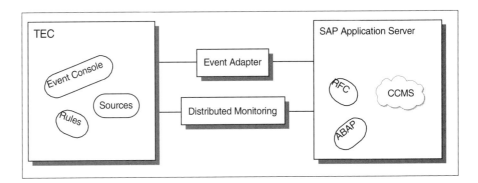

Figure 103. Information Exchange between TEC and R/3 Application Server

4.1.3.1 Event Adapter

For each application server Tivoli Manager for R/3 provides an event adapter that polls periodically the MIB to get the R/3 alerts placed there by CCMS. The tecad_wr3mib program reads the alerts, formats them into TEC events and sends them to the TEC server.

All R/3-related events received by the TEC server can be classified into two categories: specific events and generic events. A specific event is an event that contains all the pertinent information. On the other hand, a generic event only gives a high level indication of the problem. More detailed information must be gathered from the R/3 system through the RFC interface. This process is called a drill-down process in the Tivoli Manager for R/3 terminology.

After reception, the TEC server dispatches the events to its rules engine. The rules specific for R/3 have been previously imported and loaded into TEC server during the event server configuration. One of these rules will be triggered by generic events, based on the event classes (see 4.1.3.3, "TEC

Event Classes and Event Sources" on page 149 and 4.1.3.4, "TEC Rules" on page 152). It will invoke a drill-down and then drop the events. Specific events are directly sent to the TEC consoles.

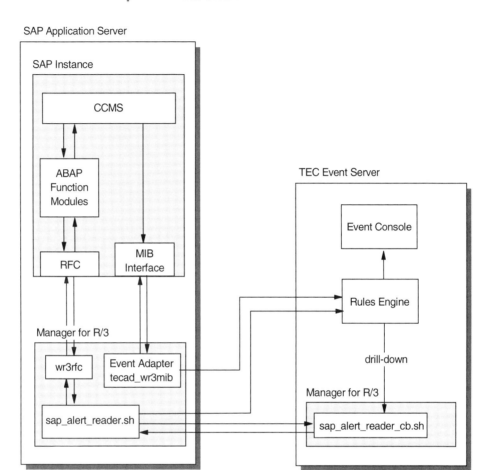

SAP Application Server

Figure 104. Event Adapter: Drill-Down

Drill-Down Process
- When the rule triggers on a generic event, it executes a script named sap_alert_reader_cb.sh located in $BINDIR/TME/TEC/scripts. This script runs on the TEC event server and launches a task with the application server as task endpoint. The corresponding script that is run on the application server is named sap_alert_reader.sh and is located in the $BINDIR/../generic_unix/TME/SAP/2.2C/<SystemLabel>/sh directory of the TMR server.

- When executing, this script calls the wr3rfc program that logs on to the R/3 application server and runs the Z_TV1_ALERT_READER function module imported into the SAP system during the Tivoli Manager for R/3 configuration. The wr3rfc program returns information that is filtered out based on the event class of the generic event that initiates the drill-down (in order to extract the corresponding detailed information). Then the information is formatted into one (in most cases) or several TEC events and sent to the TEC server. The rule engine will forward these specific events to the event consoles.

- If an error occurs during the execution of the sap_alert_reader.sh script, an event of class AMS_WR3MIB_PROCESS_ALERT is sent to the TEC saying "sap_alert_reader.sh failed <error message>". The script also creates automatically a log file residing in the /tmp directory (UNIX) or %DBDIR%\tmp directory (Windows NT) of the application server. The log file is named <SystemLabel>_sap_alert_reader.log.

- If an error occurs during the execution of the sap_alert_reader_cb.sh script, an event of class AMS_WR3MIB_PROCESS_ALERT is sent to the TEC saying "sap_alert_reader_cb.sh failed <error message>". The script also creates automatically a log file contained in the /tmp directory of the TEC server. The log file is named sap_alert_reader_cb.log.

Example

The CUA buffer quality has decreased below the defined level. CCMS will generate an alert on the MIB, notifying that "some" buffer is having a problem. The event adapter reads this alert and formats it into a TEC event of SAP_ALERT_Buf event class (see 4.1.3.3, "TEC Event Classes and Event Sources" on page 149). Then it sends it to the TEC server. The convert_mib_to_internal_alert rule of the TEC triggers on this generic event and launches a drill-down process (see 4.1.3.4, "TEC Rules" on page 152). This rule also drops the event. The drill-down will get the more detailed information executing the Alert Reader task. This uses wr3rfc to read the internal alert table of the SAP system and then it determines which buffer is having a problem, sending that message to the TEC server through an event of SAP_ALERT_BUFF_CUA class. The TEC server will forward it to the event consoles.

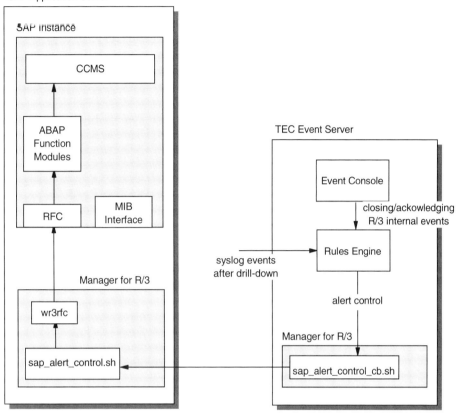

SAP Application Server

SAP instance

CCMS

ABAP
Function
Modules

RFC

MIB
Interface

Manager for R/3

wr3rfc

sap_alert_control.sh

TEC Event Server

Event Console

closing/ackowledging
R/3 internal events

syslog events
after drill-down

Rules Engine

alert control

Manager for R/3

sap_alert_control_cb.sh

Figure 105. Alert Control Process

Alert Control Process

This process can be launched by four rules coming with the Tivoli Manager
for R/3 (see 4.1.3.4, "TEC Rules" on page 152). For example, when an
operator closes (on the TEC console) an event corresponding to an internal
alert, a change rule will trigger in order to reset the corrupting alert in CCMS,
inside the R/3 system. The process is similar to the drill-down:

- When one of these rule triggers, it executes a script named
  sap_alert_control_cb.sh located in $BINDIR/TME/TEC/scripts. This script
  runs on the TEC event server and launches a task with the application
  server as task endpoint. The corresponding script that is run on the
  application server is named sap_control_reader.sh and is located in the
  $BINDIR/../generic_unix/TME/SAP/2.2C/<SystemLabel>/sh directory of
  the TMR server.

- When executing, this script calls the wr3rfc program that logs on to the R/3 application server and runs the Z_TV1_ALERT_CONTROL function module imported in the SAP system during the Tivoli Manager for R/3 configuration. The function module will reset or accolade the alert in CCMS.

- If an error occurs during the execution of the sap_alert_control.sh script, an event of class AMS_WR3MIB_PROCESS_ALERT is sent to the TEC saying `sap_alert_control.sh failed <error message>`. The script also creates automatically a log file residing in the /tmp (UNIX) or %DBDIR%\tmp directory (Windows NT) of the application server. The log file is named <SystemLabel>_sap_alert_control.log.

- If an error occurs during the execution of the sap_alert_control_cb.sh script, an event of class AMS_WR3MIB_PROCESS_ALERT is sent to the TEC saying `sap_alert_control_cb.sh failed <error message>`. The script also creates automatically a log file contained in the /tmp directory of the TEC server. The log file is named sap_alert_control_cb.log.

4.1.3.2 Tivoli Distributed Monitoring

Besides getting alerts out of the SAP R/3 System using the event adapter, the Tivoli Manager for R/3 provides a second way to collect information from SAP: Tivoli Distributed Monitoring.

The interaction between Tivoli Distributed Monitoring and SAP R/3 works in the following way:

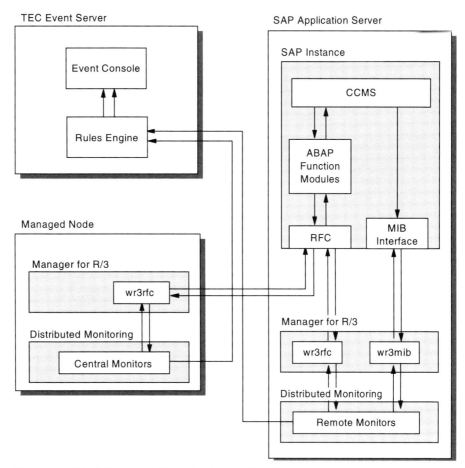

TEC Event Server

Event Console

Rules Engine

SAP Application Server

SAP Instance

CCMS

ABAP
Function
Modules

RFC

MIB
Interface

Managed Node

Manager for R/3

wr3rfc

Distributed Monitoring

Central Monitors

Manager for R/3

wr3rfc

wr3mib

Distributed Monitoring

Remote Monitors

Figure 106. Tivoli Distributed Monitoring in an SAP R/3 System

As you can see in the above figure, there are two kinds of monitors available, the central monitors and the remote monitors.

The remote monitors, running on the SAP application servers, use two interfaces to access the SAP system, the RFC (wr3rfc) and the MIB (wr3mib). The central monitors can run on any other managed node in the TMR, where the Tivoli Manager for R/3 is installed. Typically these monitors run on the TMR Server. They only use the RFC interface as only this interface can be accessed remotely. The MIB interface can not be accessed remotely.

The remote monitors and the central monitors are created from two distinct monitoring collections: <SystemLabel> Server Remote Monitors and

<SystemLabel> Server Central Monitors. If you look at both monitoring collections, you will find that they have some monitor sources in common:

- Page Area
- Roll Area
- Buffer information
- OS Collect Application Server

Besides these common sources:

- <SystemLabel> Server Remote Monitors collection includes:
  - Performance Monitor
  - System availability
- <SystemLabel> Server Central Monitors collection includes:
  - OS database collection
  - OS/390 OS collection
  - OS/390 DB2 collection

The remote monitors use both wr3mib and wr3rfc programs to access respectively the MIB and the RFC interfaces of the SAP system. The performance information and the system availability monitors get their information from the MIB interface and thus use wr3mib. As this program cannot be executed remotely, we only find these two kinds of monitors in the Server Remote Monitor collection.

The central monitors only have the availability to access the SAP systems using the RFC interface. You can execute the wr3rfc from a central point like the TMR server. The Manager for R/3 does not always have direct access to the R/3 database server and it never has direct access to OS/390, which is why the corresponding monitors can only be created from the <SystemLabel> Server Central Monitors collection.

The objoctive of the Server Central Monitors collection is to run the monitors on a machine other than the application servers in order to avoid the consecutive workload on the R/3 machines. But, as the load generated by the monitors running on an application server is generally negligible compared to the load generated by the SAP application itself, we recommend that you use as often as possible the Server Remote Monitors collection. Moreover, the events coming from central monitors will not correlate with those coming from remote monitors. However, for the database monitoring and the OS/390 monitoring, you *must* use the Server Central Monitors collection, as this is the only one that provides this kind of monitor.

Each time a central or remote monitor is running, the gathered SAP R/3 information is compared to the pre-defined threshold. If the current threshold is exceeded, a pre-defined action is executed. Typically an event will be generated and sent to the TEC event server. Each monitoring source contained in the monitoring collections has an associated event class. These event classes are used when a "forward an event to the TEC" action was specified as the action.

The wr3rfc utility is the tool provided by the Tivoli Manager for R/3, which communicates with SAP R/3 through the RFC interface.

As described in Chapter 3, "Setting Up the SAP R/3 Management Environment" on page 29, there must be an RFC user defined and a transport job executed, before the communication can happen. This defined user is a CPIC (Common Program Interface Communication) user, which means that this user can only access the SAP R/3 system through the RFC. To prohibit unauthorized access to the SAP R/3 system with this user, he/she has no authorization to log on using a SAPGUI. The profile of this user only allow him to run the ABAP programs/function modules with minimal a set of authorizations. The transport job imports some function modules that will be executed to get information from the CCMS.

The wr3rfc program can be triggered from Tivoli Distributed Monitoring or by the drill-down. The necessary parameters (for example, user ID, password, client) for the wr3rfc execution are stored in the TMR database after the configuration step "Configure <SystemLabel> Remote Function Call". These parameters can also be entered in the wr3rfc_cfg file in the directory $BINDIR/../generic_unix/TME/SAP/<SystemLabel>/rfc on the machine on which wr3rfc runs. Note that on all platforms the file must be renamed to

.wr3rfc_cfg. This file is only used for troubleshooting the RFC access. The last argument to wr3rfc is always the rfc_interface file, which contains the function module to execute and the export/import parameters needed by this function module.

Note

The import and export parameters stanzas of the rfc_interface file correspond respectively to the export and import parameters of the function module in the SAP system.

When triggering wr3rfc with an rfc_interface file as argument, the specified function module will execute inside the SAP R/3 with the specified import parameters. The function module will end up by assigning the export parameters to wr3rfc. The collected information is now available outside the SAP R/3 system. Depending on which functionality the wr3rfc triggered, the data will be directly sent to the TEC server (for a drill-down) or will be compared to thresholds by the Tivoli Distributed Monitoring engine. In this case and if a threshold is crossed, the pre-defined consecutive action will be taken.

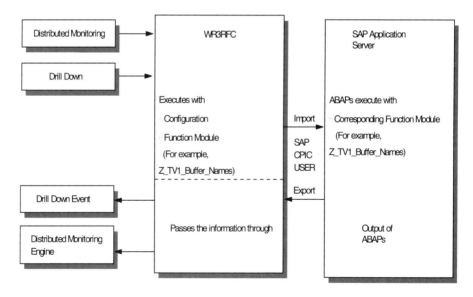

Figure 107. Schema of WR3RFC

The following function modules are provided by the Tivoli Manager for R/3:

- Z_TV1_ALERT_CONTROL

- Z_TV1_ALERT_READER

- Z_TV1_BUFFER_INFO

- Z_TV1_BUFFER_NAMES

- Z_TV1_OS_COLLECT

- Z_TV1_OS390_COLLECT

- Z_TV1_OS390_DB2

- Z_TV1_ROLL_PAGES_SIZES

The corresponding rfc_interface files have the same name and are located in the $BINDIR/../generic_unix/TME/SAP/<SystemLabel>/rfc directory of the Managed Node where the Tivoli Manager for R/3 is installed. Except for the first two, these function modules are all used by the Tivoli Distributed Monitoring monitors.

4.1.3.3 TEC Event Classes and Event Sources
During the configuration of the TEC event server for the Manager for R/3, new event classes defined in two baroc files are imported in the new or extended rule base:

- sap_tecad.baroc that defines event classes used by the event adapter for R/3.

- sap_server_monitor_35.baroc or sap_server_monitor.baroc that defines the event classes used by the Tivoli Distributed Monitoring monitors for R/3. The name of this file depends on the version of Tivoli Distributed Monitoring that is used, sap_server_monitor.baroc is used for versions prior to 3.5.

These baroc files reside in the $BINDIR/TME/TEC/<RuleBaseDir>/TEC_CLASSES directory of the TEC server. Figure 108 on page 150 shows you the hierarchy of these event classes.

A complete list of the event classes of the super classes SAP_Internal_Alert, SAP_MIB_Unique_Alert, SAP_MIB_Generic_Alert and SAP_Server_Monitors can be found in Appendix B, "Event Classes for Tivoli Manager for R/3" on page 267.

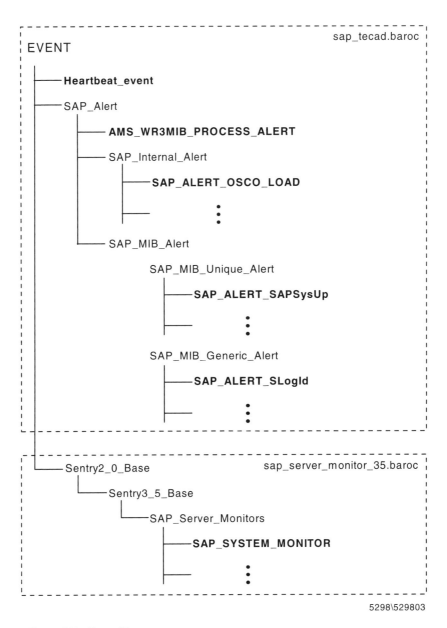

```
                                                    sap_tecad.baroc
 EVENT

 ── Heartbeat_event

 ── SAP_Alert

             ── AMS_WR3MIB_PROCESS_ALERT

             ── SAP_Internal_Alert

                        ── SAP_ALERT_OSCO_LOAD

                                      •
                                      •
                                      •

             ── SAP_MIB_Alert

                  SAP_MIB_Unique_Alert

                        ── SAP_ALERT_SAPSysUp

                                      •
                                      •
                                      •

                  SAP_MIB_Generic_Alert

                        ── SAP_ALERT_SLogId

                                      •
                                      •
                                      •


                                              sap_server_monitor_35.baroc
 ── Sentry2_0_Base

        ── Sentry3_5_Base

             ── SAP_Server_Monitors

                        ── SAP_SYSTEM_MONITOR

                                      •
                                      •
                                      •
```

5298\529803

Figure 108. Event Classes

All event classes under the SAP_MIB_Alert super class correspond to the
CCMS alerts placed by R/3 on its MIB interface. These alerts are read by the
wr3mib program and converted to TEC events of the appropriate class. Some
of them are only high-level indications of a problem and will require a

drill-down process to get more information. These generic events have an event class defined under the SAP_MIB_Generic_Alert. The other events coming from the MIB and not requiring a drill down have an event class defined under SAP_MIB_Unique_Alert.

Drill-down processes get detailed information through the RFC interface of the R/3 system (using the wr3rfc program). Resulting information is formatted into TEC events of classes defined under SAP_Internal_Alert.

The event adapter periodically generates heartbeats that are formatted into events of classes Heartbeat_event.

Events of class AMS_WR3MIB_PROCESS_ALERT are generated when the alert control and alert reader tasks encounter an error.

Note

There is no description for the event classes SAP_ALERT_GenP5 to GENP14 because they map to R/3 Alert Classes that SAP has reserved for future use but that are not used at the moment.

All the events described above (directly sent by the adapter, resulting from drill-down and resulting from reader or control routine error) are sent to the TEC server with WR3MIB as event source.

Tivoli Distributed Monitoring has its own TEC adapter. All alerts detected through the R/3 Remote or Central monitors are forwarded by Tivoli Distributed Monitoring engine to the TEC server with the corresponding event class defined under SAP_SYSTEM_MONITOR.

The Batch, Dialog, Spool and Update Performance monitors mapping respectively to the BATCH_SERVICE_MONITOR, DIALOG_SERVICE_MONITOR, SPOOL_SERVICE_MONITOR and UPDATE_SERVICE_MONITOR event classes use wr3mib to get the information from the SAP system. The SAP System Availability monitor (SAP_SYSTEM_MONITOR class) also uses wr3mib.

Events of the AMS_R3MONITOR_ALERT class are generated when a Tivoli Manager for R/3 DM monitor encounters an error.

All other R/3 monitors use wr3rfc.

All the events described above (generated through Tivoli Distributed Monitoring) are sent to the TEC server with SENTRY as Event Source.

4.1.3.4 TEC Rules

During the configuration of the TEC event server for the Tivoli Manager for R/3, new rules defined in three rule set files are imported in the new or extended rule base:

1. sap_tecad.rls for rules acting on events arising from the event adapter (events source = WR3MIB).

2. sap_monitor.rls for rules acting on events generated from Tivoli Distributed Monitoring (monitors for R/3, event source = SENTRY)

3. sap_default.rls for rules acting on events that need to be correlated across these two different sources.

The sap_tecad.rls rule file provides the following functions:

1. Coordinate Manager for R/3 heartbeat events. This requires detecting when TEC starts, resyncing the heartbeat timer, processing expected heartbeats, processing missing heartbeats. There are five rules that support heartbeat processing:

   - tec_start
   - heartbeat_received
   - heartbeat_ok
   - heartbeat_second_miss
   - heartbeat_first_miss

2. Check for and remove duplicate events. There is one rule that supports duplicate event removal:

   - dup_sap_event

3. Handling harmless events. Harmless events of a few select classes are displayed for 60 seconds, then closed; internal harmless events are closed immediately. There are three rules that support harmless processing:

   - harmless_set_timer
   - drop_new_internal_harmless
   - harmless_still_open

4. Performing drill-down processing. Drill-down is performed when high-level generic events are received from the MIB. Drill-down goes back into R/3 to get more detailed event information. In doing so, the original event is dropped and only the drill-down event is presented on the TEC console (exception: no drill-down for harmless syslog events). There is one rule that supports drill-down processing:

- convert_mib_to_internal_alert

5. Coordinate events with the R/3 application server coming up/going down. This entails closing all outstanding events for that application server and, when the application server is coming up, going out to get all existing alerts in that application server. There are three rules that support R/3 status coordination:

   - handle_sapsysdown
   - sapsysup_close_sapsysdown
   - sapsysup_read_all_internal_alerts

6. Coordinating TEC event acknowledgment/closure with R/3 alert acknowledgment/closure. This ensures that event/alert states are coordinated across the two environments. There are two rules that support event coordination, using alert control processing:

   - ack_sap_alert
   - close_sap_alert

7. Discarding buffer alerts if they occur within 35 minutes of an R/3 operational mode switch. Generally, if an operational mode switch occurs, the R/3 buffers are expected to remove old data and insert new data. Poor buffer performance is expected during these times. There is one rule that supports mode changes, using alert control processing:

   - reset_certain_events_on_statechange

8. Automatically close syslog events as soon as they occur. This is because R/3 only allows one R/3 syslog message to occupy the syslog alert status at a time. By closing the syslog alerts immediately, the probability of getting the next syslog alert is increased. There is one rule that supports closing syslog events, using alert control processing:

   - reset_syslog_alert

9. Forwarding events to alternate TEC servers. There are two rules that support event forwarding:

   - forward_heartbeat_received
   - forward_sap_events

The sap_monitor.rls rule file provides the following functions:

1. Associate DM event with appropriate R/3 system. Based on information in the event, the sub_source slot is assigned to the value of the R/3 system label as defined to Tivoli. There is one rule that supports system label assignment:

- set_r3sapname_slot

2. Check for and remove duplicate events. There is one rule that supports duplicate event removal:

   - dup_sap_monitor_event

3. Handling harmless events. Harmless events of a few select classes are displayed for 60 seconds, then closed. There are two rules that support harmless processing:

   - harmless_set_timer
   - sentry_harmless_still_open

4. Coordinate events with the DM engine or DM host machine coming up/going down. This entails closing all DM outstanding events for the application server(s) on that managed node. There are four rules that support this status coordination:

   - sentry_daemon_or_application_up
   - sentry_daemon_or_application_down
   - sentry_host_up
   - sentry_host_down

5. Coordinate events with the R/3 application server coming up/going down. This entails closing all DM outstanding events for that application server. There are two rules that support R/3 status coordination:

   - sap_system_up
   - sap_system_down

6. Discard DM events if they come in while the corresponding application server is down. There is no need to process these events since there is a larger underlying problem. There is one rule that supports DM event discard:

   - sap_system_down_no_more_entries

7. Discard DM events if they occur within 35 minutes of an R/3 application server coming up. Generally, when an application server is starting, it is loading/refreshing its buffers so poor performance is expected during these times. There is one rule that supports mode changes:

   - drop_sentry_events_on_sentry_sysup

8. Handle operator acknowledgment/closure of DM events. When an operator acknowledges or closes a DM event, the event is forwarded and all duplicates are closed. There are two rules that support operator acknowledgment/closure:

- ack_sap_sentry_alert

- close_sap_sentry_alert

9. Forward events to alternate TEC servers. There is one rule that supports event forwarding:

- forward_all_events

The sap_default.rls rule file provides the following functions:

1. Coordinate DM events with R/3 system up/down status as detected by the MIB; coordinate MIB events with R/3 system up/down status as detected by DM. This generally entails closing all outstanding events for the application server when the R/3 application server changes from down to up and from up to down. There are four rules that support R/3 state coordination:

- drop_sentry_events_if_sapsysdown

- sapsysup_close_sentry_events

- sapsysdown_close_sentry_events

- sapsysdown_close_tecad_events

2. Discard DM events if they occur within 35 minutes of an R/3 application server coming up. Generally, when an application server is starting, it is loading/refreshing its buffers so poor performance is expected during these times. There is one rule that supports mode changes:

- drop_sentry_event_on_statechange

4.1.4 Default Monitoring

The purpose of this section is to show and explain the default monitoring capability provided by the Tivoli Manager for R/3, which is based on the Tivoli Distributed Monitoring concept. Information contained in this section will give the SAP administrator a view of the capabilities and an understanding of the monitoring of the R/3 system by the Tivoli Manager for R/3.

The configuration of the Tivoli Manager for R/3, to enable the monitoring functions on one R/3 system results in an indicator collection, two new monitoring collections, two profile managers and two subscription lists, for each <System Label> policy region. Remember that the <System Label> is an alias for one R/3 system. This set of profile managers and subscription lists is created for each sub-policy region in the <System Label> policy region: <System Label> Clients, <System Label> Servers and <System Label> Database, in order to monitor separately the three components of an R/3 system. The two monitoring collections provide a set of specific new monitors, that allow the management of an R/3 system. Monitoring collections are explained in detail in 4.1.4.2, "Monitoring Collections" on page 159.

Each profile manager contains a Tivoli Distributed Monitoring profile, in which are added some predefined monitors, in order to provide by default a basic monitoring capability, immediately after the initial configuration of the Tivoli Manager for R/3. These monitors are created, by default, among the list of monitors provided by the two new monitoring collections. Profile managers and Tivoli Distributed Monitoring profiles are described in 4.1.4.1, "Default Profile Managers, Subscription Lists, Profiles" on page 156, and the full list of the available monitors is given in 4.1.4.5, "Monitoring Sources Available from Monitoring Collections" on page 173.

4.1.4.1 Default Profile Managers, Subscription Lists, Profiles

For the <System Label> policy region, each profile manager (created by default by the Tivoli Manager for R/3, in the <System Label> Client, <System Label> Database and <System Label> Server sub-policy regions) contains a Tivoli Distributed Monitoring profile. There are two different profile managers per sub-policy region, depending on the monitoring method you want to use: remote monitoring or central monitoring. The names of these profile managers are <System Label> Server Central Monitor and <System Label> Server Remote Monitor.

Tivoli Distributed Monitoring profiles in these profile managers follow the same rule: one Sentry profile contains monitors from the Server Remote monitoring collection, and is created in the remote profile manager; the second Tivoli Distributed Monitoring profile contains monitors from the Server Central monitoring collection, and is created in the central profile manager. The Tivoli Distributed Monitoring profiles have the same name as the profile manager they belong to: <System Label> Server Central Monitor and <System Label> Server Remote Monitor.

To distribute these Tivoli Distributed Monitoring profiles, the Tivoli Manager for R/3 also creates, by default, two subscription lists that contain the right subscribers for each type of profile. Subscribers are the SapInstances. These subscription lists are updated automatically as new R/3 database or application servers are defined to Tivoli, for the R/3 system. However, for the Central profile manager, the default subscriber is the TMR server. The reason is that, as the TMR server has the Tivoli Manager for R/3 installed, it can run the wr3rfc program to execute the monitors remotely, and then work as a proxy in the Central monitoring process. More information about that and the monitoring collections is provided in 4.1.4.2, "Monitoring Collections" on page 159.

The hierarchy provided by the Tivoli Manager for R/3 is illustrated in Figure 109 on page 158. Shown there are all the components created in one *System Label*: RDU, in our sample. Only the hierarchy in the RDU Server policy region is described, as it is duplicated for the two other policy regions, RDU Database and RDU Client.

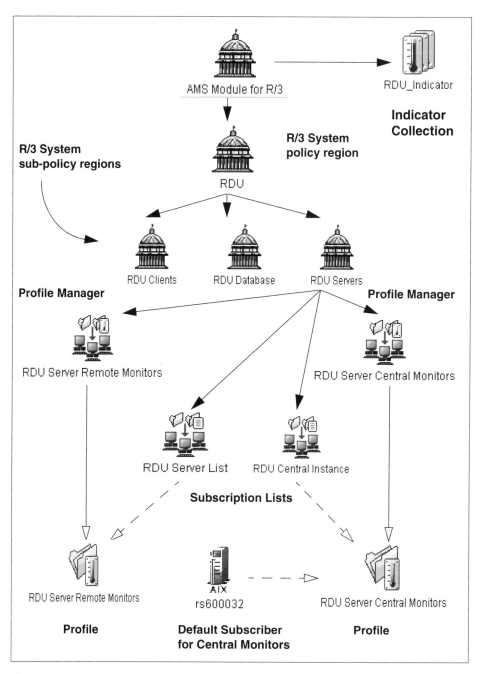

Figure 109. Default Profile Managers, Subscription Lists and Profiles

This picture shows the hierarchy for the RDU R/3 system. First, the configuration of the monitoring capability has created an Indicator Collection icon, in the AMS Module for R/3 policy region (level 1). A new icon is created each time you configure the module for another R/3 system. In this Indicator Collection are stored the alerts sent by the monitors. Let's now examine the policy region RDU (level 2). Three sub-policy regions are created, for the three components of the RDU R/3 system. The remainder of this example is based on the sub-policy region RDU Server (level 3). The two other policy regions present the almost same structure.

The sub-policy region RDU Server is made up of two profile managers, RDU Server Remote Monitors and RDU Server Central Monitors, and two subscription lists, RDU Server List and RDU Central Instance.

The profile manager RDU Server Remote Monitors contains a Tivoli Distributed Monitoring profile named RDU Server Remote Monitor, and has by default the subscription list RDU Server List as its subscriber.

The profile manager RDU Server Central Monitors contains a Sentry profile named RDU Server Central Monitor, and has by default the TMR server as subscriber.

4.1.4.2 Monitoring Collections

Thanks to these two monitoring collections, you get a wide set of internal and external R/3 monitors, not only for the monitoring of the R/3 application itself, but also for the operating system it runs on and the database. Monitors are contained in the Server Remote Monitors monitoring collection and in the Server Central Monitors monitoring collection. These two monitoring collections are available for each R/3 system you will manage in your TMR. The monitoring collections are run against R/3 application servers only.

For R/3 database servers, you have to use monitors provided by the monitoring collections in the Tivoli database management products, for example the Tivoli Manager for Oracle, in our case.

The following figure shows the two monitoring collections added by the configuration of Tivoli Manager for R/3 for the RDU system.

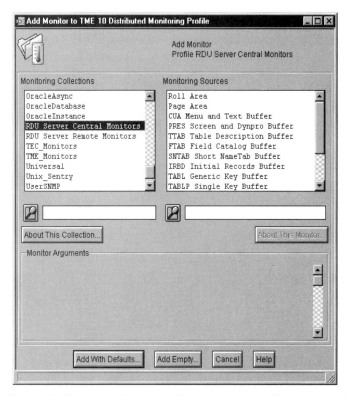

Figure 110. Monitoring Collections Provided by the Tivoli Manager for R/3

The monitors from each of the two monitoring collections differ in where they are supposed to be distributed and run. They do not differ in what they are monitoring, as both monitoring collections have the same set of monitors, except for SAP system availability, performance and OS/390 monitors.

Monitors belonging to the Server Remote Monitors collection must be run on a specific machine, and will monitor that machine directly. Such monitors are distributed and run on an SapInstance. This means that the Tivoli Distributed Monitoring profile containing these monitors must have a SapInstance as subscriber, and not a Managed Node, for example.

On the other hand, monitors from the Server Central Monitors collection can be compared to proxies. This means they are distributed to a machine and monitor other machines remotely, using the wr3rfc program. According to that characteristic, Server Central monitors have to be distributed to the TMR server, for example, or whichever Managed Node has the Tivoli Manager for

R/3 installed. Then, these monitors will run on behalf of a SapInstance. This SapInstance is specified as a parameter when you create the monitor.

Also, another difference between the two monitoring collections is the monitoring of the SAP system availability, the performance of an R/3 server and the monitoring of OS/390.

Indeed, only the Server Central monitoring collection provides monitors for the operating system running the database server, the DB2 database on OS/390 and OS/390 itself. On the other hand, the SAP system availability and performance monitors are provided only by the Server Remote monitoring collection. In 4.1.4.5, "Monitoring Sources Available from Monitoring Collections" on page 173, all the monitoring sources are described, with their functions and the monitoring collection they belong to. You can also refer to 4.1.3.2, "Tivoli Distributed Monitoring" on page 144 for a detailed explanation about these two monitoring collections.

4.1.4.3 Predefined Default Monitors

After you finish installing and configuring Tivoli Manager for R/3, you will see some predefined default monitors ready to use and to start monitoring your SAP system. There are predefined default monitors for server, database and client in both central and remote collections.

To access predefined default monitors for servers, start by double-clicking **AMS Module for R/3** from the Tivoli Desktop, then a System Label policy region and then System Label Servers. You will see two icons, one for System Label Server Central Monitors and other for System Label Server Remote Monitors. By clicking on the first icon, and then again on the profile icon, you will see the predefined default monitors for <System Label> Server Central Monitors as seen in Figure 111 on page 162.

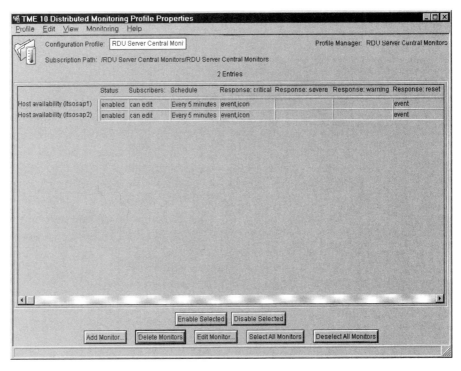

Figure 111. RDU Predefined Server Central Monitors

Then, by double-clicking on the second icon and then again on the profile icon, you will see the predefined default monitors for <System Label> Server Remote Monitors as seen in Figure 112 on page 163.

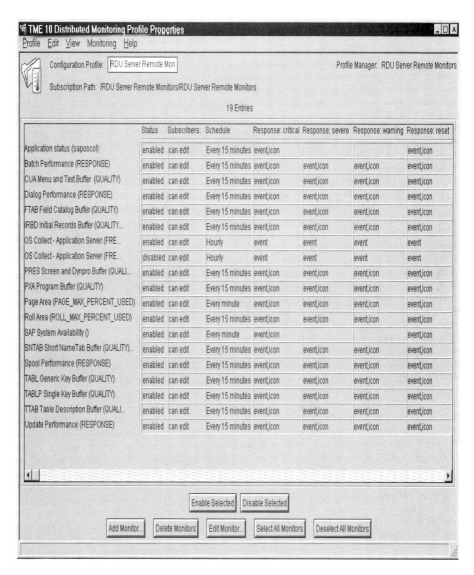

Figure 112. RDU Predefined Server Remote Monitors

To access predefined Default Monitors for Database, start by double-clicking
AMS Module for R/3 from the Tivoli Desktop, then select a <System Label>
policy region and then a <System Label> Database. You will see two icons,
one for <System Label> Database Central Monitors and another one for
<System Label> Database Remote Monitors. By clicking on the first icon, and
then again on the profile icon, you will have the predefined default monitors

for <System Label> Database Central Monitors as seen in Figure 113 on page 164.

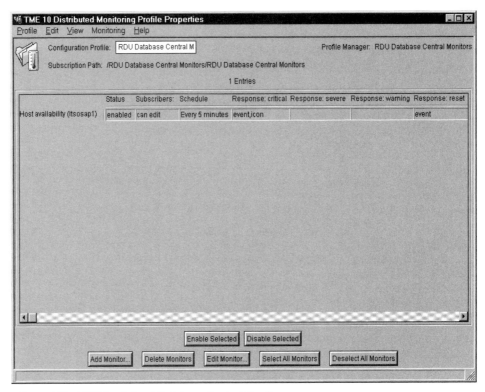

Figure 113. RDU Predefined Database Central Monitors

Note

Notice that there are no predefined default monitors for database remote monitors. In this case, you should use the monitoring collections of the Tivoli Manager for Oracle (in our environment). For more information, please refer to 4.1.4.2, "Monitoring Collections" on page 159.

To access predefined Default Monitors for Clients, start by double-clicking **AMS Module for R/3** from the Tivoli Desktop, then select a <System Label> policy region and then <System Label> Clients. You will see two icons, one for <System Label> Client Central Monitors and other for <System Label> Client Remote Monitors.

> **Note**
>
> Notico that there are no predefined default monitors for Client Central Monitors. For more information, please refer to 4.1.4.2, "Monitoring Collections" on page 159.

By double-clicking on the second icon, and then again on the profile icon, you will get the predefined default monitors for *System Label* Client Remote Monitors as seen in Figure 114 on page 165.

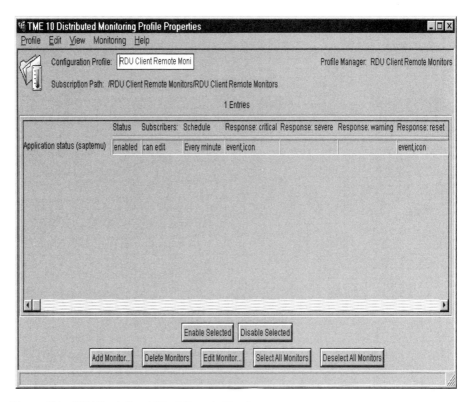

Figure 114. RDU Predefined Client Remote Monitors

4.1.4.4 Distribution and Functioning

Once you have enabled the default monitors you want to see in your TEC console, you have two steps to follow: first, distribute the profile to the subscribers you have defined. Then start the event adapter on the SAP Instance you want to monitor.

To distribute the profile select it in your profile manager and select the subscribers you want to distribute to. Then select **Profile Manager** from the menu bar and **Distribute...** from the pull-down menu. See Figure 115 on page 166 for details.

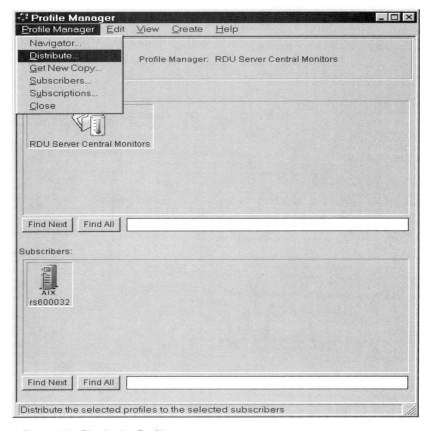

Figure 115. Distributing Profile

To start the event adapter on the SAP Instance you want to monitor, select an application server icon, click the right mouse button and select **START_EVENT_ADAPTER** from the pull-down menu. See Figure 116 on page 167 for details.

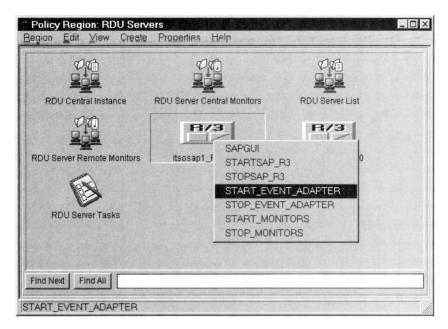

Figure 116. Starting Event Adapter

After performing these steps, you now have your default monitors running against your SAP system and you can see the default alerts on the TEC Console, as shown in Figure 117 on page 168.

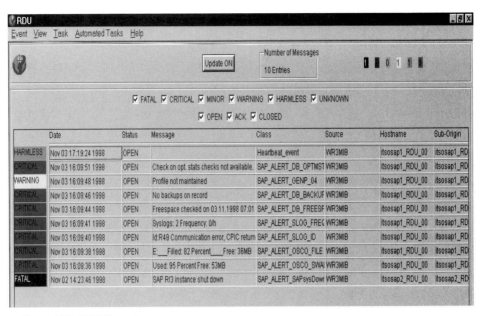

Figure 117. TEC Console

If you want to modify a given monitor, from the Tivoli Desktop double-click on **AMS Module for R/3**, then double-click on the RDU policy region, then **RDU Servers** and finally on **RDU Server Central Monitors**. Within this profile manager you can access the profile provided by default, that is, RDU Server Central monitor and then get to the two provided default monitors. By selecting one of them and clicking the **Edit Monitor...** button you will get what can be seen in Figure 118 on page 169.

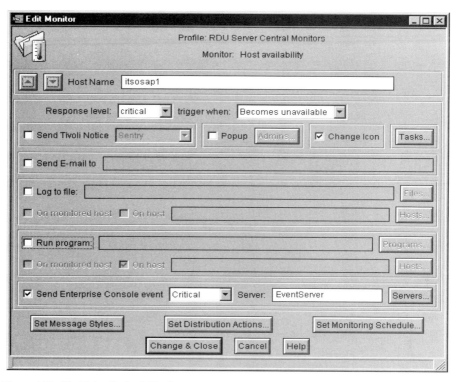

Figure 118. Modifying Default Monitors

In this window you can modify a set of predefined fields for this monitor in order to customize the way you want to be notified when it occurs and also the way you want to react when it occurs. This second option can be done by clicking **Run program** and then selecting which program you want to run, either on the monitored host or on the TME Managed Node of your choice. For more information on all fields you can modify and what they will do, simply click the **Help** button.

If you want to create a new monitor, you can start from the window shown on Figure 119 on page 170 and select the **Add Monitor...** button.

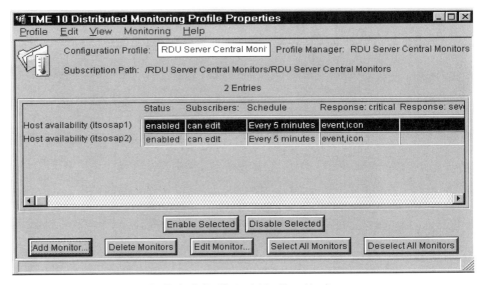

Figure 119. Edit Properties for Default Profile to Add a New Monitor

When this is done, you will see the Add Monitor to TME 10 Distributed Monitoring Profile window, where you can select on the left the Monitoring Collections available and on the right the Monitoring Sources for each Monitoring Collection. When you select a Monitoring Source, you will also have a field where you can select the attribute to this Monitor Source and also the application servers available to run this monitor. For example, let us select **RDU Server Central Monitors** as our Monitoring Collection and **Roll Area** as our Monitoring Source. The Roll Area Attribute is Roll Currently Used and the Application Server is itsosap1_RDU_00. In Figure 120 on page 171 you can see the selections we have made in this example.

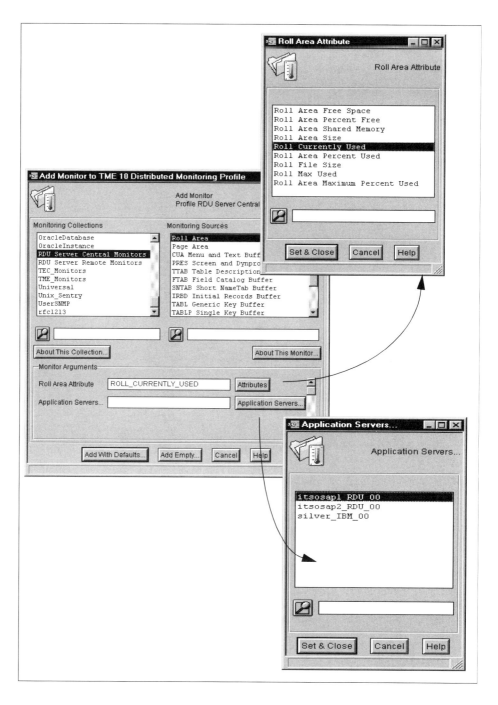

Figure 120. Add a Monitor Window Navigation

After making the selections you want, simply click the **Add Empty...** button and you will have all available options to your new monitor to customize as you want. See Figure 121 on page 172 for details.

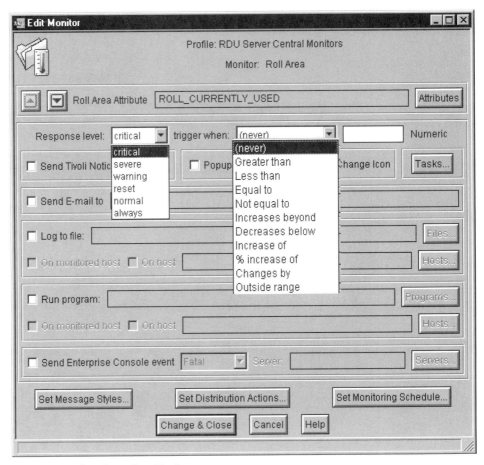

Figure 121. Creating a New Monitor

After selecting the options you want for your new monitor, click the **Change & Close** button to create it. After this, you have to select the Indicator Collection for your new Monitor. In this example, we simply choose the default RDU Indicator, but you can create another one if you want. The result of our selections can be seen on Figure 122 on page 173.

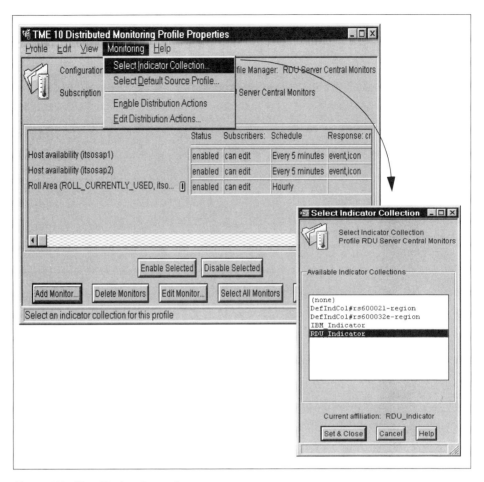

Figure 122. New Monitor Created

As the last step, select **Profile** from the menu bar and then **Save** from the pull-down menu to finish creating your new monitor.

4.1.4.5 Monitoring Sources Available from Monitoring Collections

The purpose of this section is to show what the Tivoli Manager for R/3 can monitor on a SAP R/3 system, using Tivoli Distributed Monitoring monitors, coming from the two monitoring collections, provided by the module. Tivoli Manager for R/3 provides 20 monitoring sources that monitor the R/3 application itself, the operating system the R/3 application runs on and the database. For the R/3 application, the module offers the capability to monitor the memory allocations, such as the different R/3 buffers, the space allocations, such as the pages, the response time performance and the availability of a SAP system. For the operating system, monitoring sources are available to monitor the operating system of either the R/3 application server, or the R/3 database server. The monitoring of the operating system also includes a monitoring source for the OS/390 operating system. Then, for the database itself, Tivoli Manager for R/3 proposes a monitor source to monitor the DB2 database running on OS/390.

The following table lists these monitoring sources, associated with their monitoring collection. Note that for each monitoring source a list of attributes is available to configure the monitor. These lists are presented in Appendix A, "Monitor Sources and their Attributes" on page 261, and you can also refer to the SAP R/3 documentation for details and explanations about these attributes.

Monitor Sources	Server Remote Collection	Server Central Collection
Roll Area	◆	◆
Page Area	◆	◆
Buffer (*)	◆	◆
Performance (*)	◆	
SAP System Availability	◆	
OS Collect - Application Server	◆	◆
OS Collect - Database Server		◆
OS/390		◆
OS/390 DB2		◆

(*) The Buffer and Performance label represent groups of monitoring sources. For the Buffer label, here is the list of the monitor sources: CUA Menu and Text buffer, PRES Screen and Dynpro buffer, TTAB Table Description buffer, FTAB Field Catalog buffer, SNTAB Short NameTab buffer, IRBD Initial Records buffer, TABL Generic Key buffer, TABLP Single Key buffer, PXA Program buffer.

For the label Performance, here is the list of the monitor sources: Dialog performance, Update performance, Batch performance and Spool performance.

4.1.5 SYSLOG Configuration

The SAP system log is the logging facility in the SAP R/3 system. All errors, warnings and other information about what is going on in the SAP system is logged here. To get into the SYSLOG enter the transaction code SM21. Here you can specify which information should be displayed (problems only, problems and warnings or all information), either local, remote or central system log, or which errors, timeframes and users.

The interface to provide the syslog messages outside the SAP R/3 system is the MIB interface. If a syslog message is generated and if this kind of message (syslog IDs) was previously defined as alertable in the SYSLOG, an alert will be placed on the MIB interface saying that a syslog message has been generated. The event adapter of the Tivoli Manager for R/3 will read this alert and a drill-down will be generated to get the real message content through the RFC interface. When this event arrives in the TEC, an alert control process will be performed to reset the syslog alert in the R/3 system itself.

Monitoring the SAP system log with a system management tool like the Tivoli Manager for R/3 is always a challenge, because you have several kinds of SAP R/3 systems. Production, test and development systems have different importance and the alerts gathered locally in the SYSLOG have different severities for the customer, monitoring them from outside. For instance, in a production system all ABAP errors should be alerted to the Tivoli Manager for R/3, but in the development system these errors can be ignored.

Therefore, it is necessary to configure the SYSLOG in each SAP system defining which syslog IDs must be alerted from the SYSLOG to the outside world and thus provided to the systems management tool.

In each SAP R/3 system you configure the SAP system log with the transaction RZ06. Select the application server and click on the change button. Select **Syslog**. The following window will appear.

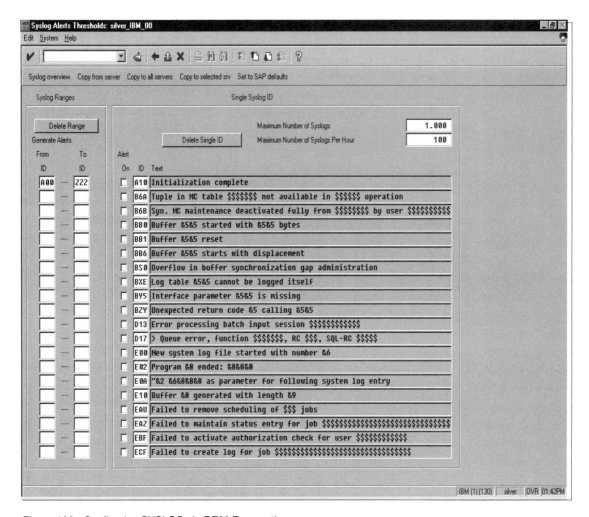

Figure 123. Configuring SYSLOG via RZ06 Transaction

On the left side you specify the alert syslog ranges, which should be alerted to the MIB interface. The range for SAP R/3 is A00 to ZZZ. Alert exceptions can be chosen in the fields on the right side by entering the Alert ID. At the top of the screen, you see the field Maximum Number of Syslogs Per Hour, which describes the alert frequency.

The information in the system log is stored in several tables. The configuration table is called TALIM. This table reflects all entries made in the transaction RZ06. Check it by displaying the table contents by using transaction SE12.

The other tables available in the SAP system log are shown in the following figure.

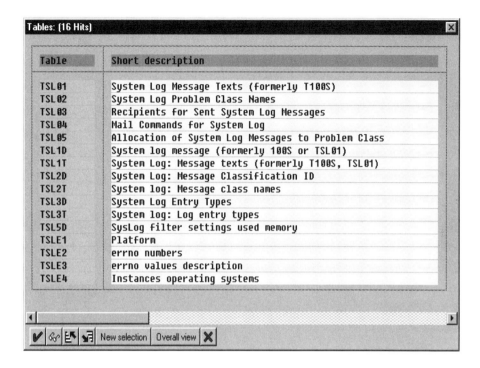

Figure 124. SYSLOG Tables

> **Note**
>
> It is possible that you will not get all the syslog messages in the TEC console. This can happen when more than one syslog alert occurs in less than a few seconds. Before being able to get the new message in the console, the previous one must be gathered through the drill-down and then it must be closed in the SAP system through the alert control process. A new alert won't occur on the MIB interface if the previous syslog alert is not reset.
>
> It may be three to five seconds before next R/3 SYSLOG entry can be read.

4.2 Tivoli Workload Scheduler (Maestro)

In this section we work with Tivoli Workload Scheduler (Maestro) that we have previously installed as described in 3.8, "Installing and Configuring Tivoli Maestro" on page 79.

Here we give detailed information about how Maestro works and show how to use it in combination with SAP R/3.

4.2.1 Tivoli Maestro Basics

The role of Tivoli Maestro is to provide us with the ability to automate batch job scheduling in a multiplatform environment. The batch job is basically operating system support commands or scripts; however, Tivoli in addition, offers an extended method to control application batch jobs, such as SAP R/3 and BaaN IV.

In this section, we describe the basic function and usage of Tivoli Maestro so you will understand how Tivoli Maestro works in an SAP R/3 environment and to evaluate the true benefit which Tivoli Maestro can offer you. A full functional description of Tivoli Maestro is beyond the scope of this book. Those who install Tivoli Maestro in their environment should consult the appropriate Tivoli Maestro manuals.

4.2.2 Tivoli Maestro System Configuration

We use Tivoli Maestro Version 6.0, which introduced the concept of the Maestro Domain.

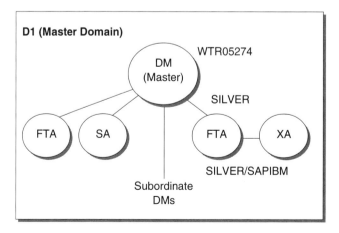

Figure 125. Tivoli Maestro Domain

There is a Master/Domain Manager, which is basically the centralized operational point and contains the centralized master files used to document the scheduling objects. It creates the production control file at the start of each day, and performs all logging and reporting. In our case, the Master Domain Manager is wtr05274, which is a Managed Node of the rs600032e policy region. The domain members are Master and Agents. There are agents, named Fault-Tolerant-Agent (FTA), Standard Agent (SA) and eXtended Agent (XA), respectively.

- FTA is an agent CPU (please refer to 4.2.4, "Tivoli Maestro Job Scheduling Object Definition" on page 181) which is capable of resolving local dependencies and launching its jobs in the absence of a domain manager. In our environment silver is the FTA.

- SA is an agent CPU that launches jobs only under the direction of its domain manager.

- XA is an agent CPU that launches jobs only under the direction of its host. Extended agent can be used to interface Tivoli Maestro with non-Maestro systems and applications, in our case, with SAP R/3.

  The host mentioned in the XA agents part can be any Maestro CPU, except for another extended agent. In our case the FTA on silver was chosen.

The Maestro domain can be configured to connect with another domain or to have a backup domain controller; however, these items are beyond the scope of this book.

4.2.3 Tivoli Maestro Internals

After you create your job scheduling network in Tivoli Maestro, you have a Symphony file which has job scheduling information as a result. In the production cycle, the contents of the Symphony files must be delivered to the FTAs. Tivoli Maestro offers the Jnextday script file to perform this work, which usually runs once a day. Both in the Master Domain Manager and in the FTA system, Maestro processes, Batchman, Jobman, and Jobmon will run to execute and monitor the job launched from Maestro. The XA jobs are controlled by Master or FTA.

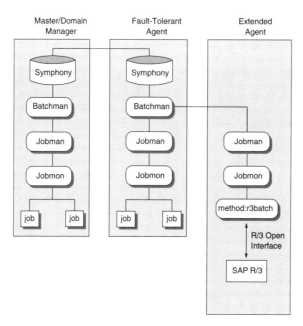

Figure 126. Maestro Job Execution

The Batchman process resolves all job dependencies to ensure the correct order of execution, and then issues a job launch message to the Jobman process, which runs Jobmon. Jobmon sets the environment variables and executes the standard configuration script, *maestrohome*/jobmanrc.cmd (in Windows NT, which is our case).

Stdlist output is created by Jobman which contains header, trailer, echoed command, stdout and stderr from the program. However, care should be taken because in the case of an SAP R/3 extended agent, we cannot get the output from an SAP R/3 job from the Stdlist.

Launching SAP R/3 jobs is the responsibility of the extended agent. This mechanism will be shown later in 4.2.6, "Tivoli Maestro SAP R/3 Extended Agent" on page 188. Launching jobs for XA is done through the method provided by each of the XA products. The method is located in the *maestrohome*/methods directory of its host CPU machine. In our case, it is in the usr/lib/maestro/methods/r3batch directory of silver. This method is located in the *maestrohome*/methods directory on wtr05274, which is the Maestro Master machine.

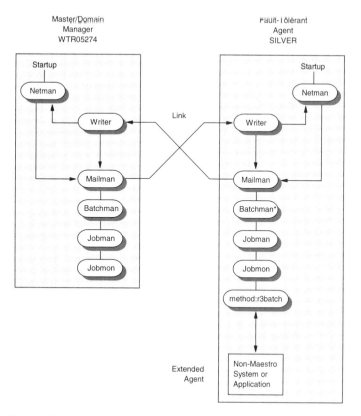

Figure 127. Tivoli Maestro Network Processes

At the end of this section, we show the network process of Tivoli Maestro (Figure 127 on page 181). Netman is started as a service in a Windows NT environment and should be started as a daemon in a UNIX environment. It is up to the Tivoli Maestro system administrator to start Netman in advance. You must log in as the Maestro user to start Maestro and run the `conman start` command. Netman handles all tasks for Maestro network communications.

4.2.4 Tivoli Maestro Job Scheduling Object Definition

In this section we explain all the objects you have to define in the Maestro environment.

1. CPU

   The Tivoli Maestro CPU denotes the processing objects, individual computers, on which Tivoli Maestro schedules jobs. For each Tivoli Maestro CPU the number of jobs for simultaneous launching can be defined. CPUs must be defined as Tivoli Maestro objects before you begin scheduling.

Remember that the name of a Tivoli Maestro CPU is defined in its installation process. Care should be taken when establishing the naming convention of the CPU. You cannot have duplicate CPU names in your Maestro network.

2. CPU Class

In a large system configuration environment, you may optionally define a set of CPUs according to a logical unit of CPU class. CPU classes permit schedules to be replicated over multiple systems. A Tivoli Maestro CPU class maps the schedule onto every CPU in the CPU class.

3. Calendar

Tivoli Maestro optionally allows you to define your corporate calendar or manufacturing calendar. For example, you can define a calendar named paydays containing a list of dates and a calendar containing a list of your company's holidays. You are requested to prepare your calendar in advance to define your Tivoli Maestro schedule when you need calendar-based scheduling. You don't have to create multiple definitions for the identical job to be launched.

4. Resource

Tivoli Maestro optionally allows you to define your custom resources for your job's requirement. The custom resources can be physical or logical ones on your system. For example, suppose your job needs a tape processing unit. You can define the tape unit as a Tivoli Maestro custom resource. While the job runs that uses the tape unit, other jobs which require the tape unit are prevented from launching. You are requested to prepare your custom resources in advance to define your Tivoli Maestro schedule when you need a custom resource in your scheduling.

5. Prompt

Tivoli Maestro optionally allows you to set a custom prompt for each job or scheduler. This function enables the operator to confirm job launching manually. The operator action is required from Tivoli Maestro Console Manager. There are two kinds of prompts: global and local. When a global prompt is issued, only one reply is necessary to release all jobs and schedules that use it. Local prompts, on the other hand, are linked to an individual job or schedule.

6. Parameter

Parameters can be optionally used as substitutes for defining Tivoli Maestro jobs and dependencies. The parameters have the advantage of being global in nature, unliko ohcll variables which must be exported.

7. User

   Every Tivoli Maestro program and command checks the user's capabilities against the definition contained in the Maestro security file. The Maestro security permits you to control access to every Maestro object and to specify exactly what types of access will be permitted.

   A Tivoli Maestro user ID must exist on the operating system. The default user ID is maestro.

8. Job (Standard Job in Tivoli Maestro)

   What is a job in Tivoli Maestro? In Tivoli Maestro, it is a script file or a command in standard usage. In an extended agent like that of SAP R/3, it has a different meaning. It is jobs predefined in SAP R/3. You must define your jobs both in SAP R/3 and Tivoli Maestro. Generally, jobs are defined independently of schedules and must be defined in advance to create your schedule. To define a standard job in Tivoli Maestro, you are requested to specify:

   - The CPU which the job runs on.

   - The unique job name on each CPU.

   - The user name under which the jobs run.

   - A script file name or command. The script must reside on the target CPU file system. The files option doesn't allow you to search your script file on the remote CPU and you must type the name of the script in this case. For Windows NT, include the file extension for the script name. The command will be executed directly and unlike a script file, the configuration script (jobmanrc script) is not used.

   - Interactive option for Windows NT interactive desktop applications.

   - Load balancing option for users who have the Tivoli Load Balancer program product.

   - Recovery options for Stop, Continue, Rerun conditions in case of the job abend.

   - Recovery job name and the CPU name on which it runs if the original job abends. Recovery jobs are run only once for each abended instance of the original job.

   - Recovery prompt for job abends. The recovery prompt is a local prompt.

9. Schedule

Tivoli Maestro scheduling is an outline of batch processing consisting of a list of jobs. Each schedule is dated so that it can be selected automatically by Maestro for execution. In defining your schedule, Tivoli Maestro allows you to specify various dependency conditions which must be satisfied before the job or schedule will be launched. A single job or schedule is permitted up to 40 dependencies. To define a schedule, you are requested to specify:

- Unique schedule name within CPU.

- On/Except panel to specify when the schedule will, or not will execute. You can specify everyday, weekdays, workdays (holiday calendar must be exits for this option), request (no automatic selection), and Monday-Sunday, respectively. Or, you can choose calendar.

- Options panel to specify:

  - The At field defines the time of day the schedule is launched. The time is based on Maestro CPU local time which is specified in the schedule definition.

  - The Until Time field defines the time of day after which a schedule will not be launched, regardless of other dependencies. When using At and Until time you must make certain that Until time is later than At time.

  - The schedule priority and job limit.

  - Carry forward option. For this option, refer to 4.2.5, "Job Scheduling Production Cycle" on page 186).

Job Priority

Tivoli Maestro defines the priority from 0-101 for both jobs and schedules. HIGH and GO priority means priority number 100 and 101, respectively. You can choose the priority number from 0-99. HIGH and GO jobs are launched as soon as their dependencies are satisfied. If you specify HI or GO in a schedule all the jobs in the schedule are given HIGH or GO priority. The default priority number is zero if you leave it blank.

- Follows Sched/Job panel to specify the schedules and jobs that must be completed successfully before the schedule can be launched. You must have the jobs and schedules defined in advance to define this panel. Figure 128 on page 185 shows an example definition of Follow job for the schedule named ITSOMSTR#RDEP1(ITSOMSTR is the CPU name assigned to this schedule and RDEP1 is the schedule name). After entering production stage, you can find the schedule has a dependency of SAPJOB1.SAP1 in the Tivoli Maestro Console Manager Display as shown in Figure 129 on page 185.

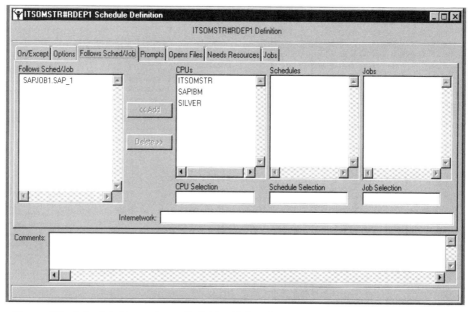

Figure 128. Schedule Dependency Definition/Follow SchedJob Panel

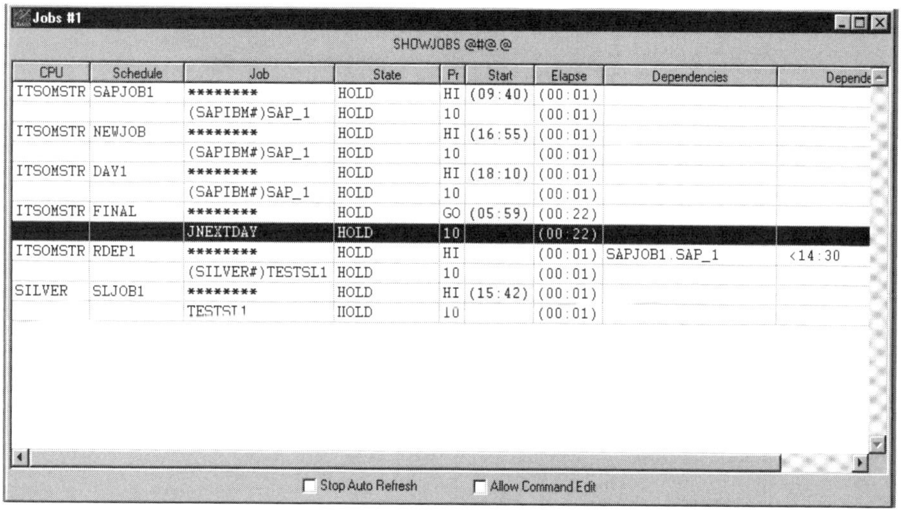

Figure 129. Maestro Console Manager View of Jobs

- Prompt panel to specify a prompt for a job, which must be issued or answered affirmatively before the job can be launched. The prompt must be defined in advance.

- Open Files panel to specify the necessary files to be ascertained before a job can be launched. File dependency provides a convenient way to prevent jobs from failing due to unavailable files. However, care should be taken because this facility doesn't guarantee locking the files for this job. You can choose the test qualifier.

- Needs Resource panel to specify the need for a custom resource for the schedule to be launched. The resource must be defined in advance.

4.2.5 Job Scheduling Production Cycle

Tivoli Maestro processing begins at the time defined by the Global Option start time which is set by default to 6:00 a.m. The Tivoli Maestro user's guide describes the Global option file in detail. You can create your schedule by issuing the job Jnextday provided by Tivoli Maestro daily. Tivoli provides the schedule named Sfinal which was executed in the installation procedure also. Normally, once a day, Tivoli Maestro constructs a schedule of the day from its schedule definition file (acts as a template file) named mastsked and located in the *maestrohome*/mozart directory. The production schedule file, named *maestrohome*/mozart /prodsked, contains the schedules selected for execution on a particular date. The file is built and loaded and its contents are merged into the Production Control file named Symphony file during the Jnextday job processing.

Eventually, the Symphony file will contain the scheduling information needed by the production control process Batchman. During the production phase, it is continually updated to indicate the current status of production processing-work completed, in progress, and work to be done. You can change the content of the Symphony file dynamically from the Tivoli Maestro Console Manager GUI Interface to reflect the change occurring in the daily system management activity. For example, in the production runtime, you can add a dependency.

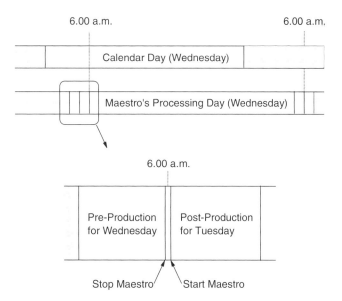

Figure 130. Production Cycle - A Day in Tivoli Maestro

In the Jnextday processing (transition from the past day to new day scheduling), the following procedures are processed:

1. Scheduler processing to select the appropriate schedules to execute:
   - Input: mastsked file
   - Output: prodsked file
2. Complier processing to create new production file:
   - Input: prodsked file
   - Output: Symnew file
3. Stop Maestro.
4. Stageman processing to
   - Carry forward uncompleted schedules from the previous day. An option for enabling a schedule is to check the Carry Forward option in the Options panel of the Schedule Definition window. The SFinal schedule has this option by default. There are several options related to Carry Forward; for detailed information, please see the Maestro user's guide.
   - Log the Production Control file from the previous day.
   - Install the new Production Control file.
5. Start Maestro.

The detailed Stageman processing model is shown In Figure 131 on page 188. During this processing, a copy of a production file - called a Sinfonia file - is also created for fault-tolerant agent CPUs.

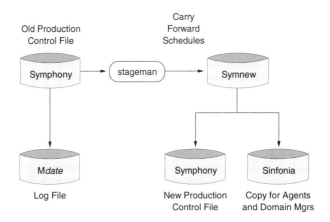

Figure 131. Stageman Processing during Jnexday Job

4.2.6 Tivoli Maestro SAP R/3 Extended Agent

Tivoli Maestro SAP R/3 Extended Agent serves as an interface to an external, non-Maestro system, for example, SAP R/3. It is defined as a Maestro CPU with an access method. In our case, the access method is r3batch.

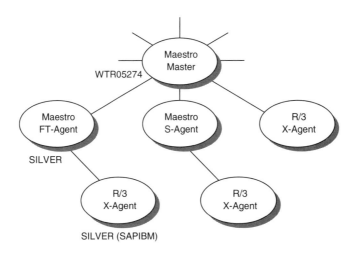

Figure 132. SAP R/3 Extended Agent

SAP R/3 Extended Agent can be configured under Master, SA or FTA. Here, Master is wtr05274. The R/3 X-Agent is under FTA and called silver as shown in Figure 132 on page 188. For the valid configuration of SAP R/3 XA, you must have SAP R/3 XA running on the SAP R/3 application server. The options are to have your SAP R/3 machine as:

- Maestro Master
- Maestro SA
- Maestro FTA

as shown in Figure 132 on page 188. Here, we make silver, which is the SAP R/3 control instance, as the Maestro FTA.

4.2.6.1 r3batch Method - Interaction with SAP R/3

The r3batch access method of Tivoli Maestro SAP R/3 Extended Agent is responsible for the interaction between Tivoli Maestro and SAP R/3. The r3batch method must be installed on the machine where SAP R/3 is running; here it is silver.

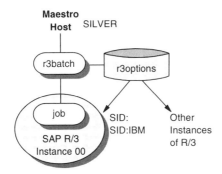

Figure 133. R3batch Access Method

The XA method is defined in the *maestrohome*/method directory. When a request from Maestro to SAP R/3 occurs, r3batch invokes an RFC (Remote Function Call) which was imported during the installation process. The r3batch method consults with the r3options file in which these items are defined:

- XA Maestro CPU name
- Hostname of R/3
- Hostname of R/3 gateway if you have one
- R/3 SID

- R/3 instance number

- R3 client number

- SAP R/3 user. This user must have appropriate roles.

- Password. The password is stored in encrypted format.

- Minimum interval in seconds for R/3 Jobs status updates. The default is 30.

- Maximum interval in seconds for R/3 Jobs status updates. The default is 300.

To update the information in the r3options file, you can use `r3setup -maintain`.

```
/usr/lib/maestro/methods > cat r3batch.opts
LJuser=maestro
IFuser=maestro
JobDef=r3batch
/usr/lib/maestro/methods > cat r3options
SAPIBM silver  IBM 00 130 maestro #At3-bRIp-6Y3F-4m 30 300 0
```

Figure 134. R3options File for Tivoli Maestro r3batch Methods Definition

4.2.6.2 Managing SAP R/3 Jobs Using Tivoli Maestro

You must follow five steps to manage your SAP R/3 jobs with Tivoli Maestro:

1. Define jobs in SAP R/3. You must not specify a start time here. You only define the SAP R/3 job steps.

2. Define jobs in Tivoli Maestro. You must use the SAP R/3 Extended Agent CPU name for the Maestro CPU. In this step you have to select the name of the SAP R/3 job defined in step 1. You can retrieve a SAP R/3 job list by pushing the **Retrieve** button in the Tivoli Maestro Job Definition window. You can specify in the window:

   - R/3 jobname is filled after your selection of an R/3 job by pushing **Retrieve** button.

   - R/3 user name is filled after your selection of an R/3 job by pushing **Retrieve** button.

   - R/3 job ID is filled after your selection of an R/3 job by pushing **Retrieve** button.

   - R/3 job class is filled after your selection of an R/3 job by pushing **Retrieve** button.

- Logon is the user name to run the job under in Tivoli Maestro. You need to fill this field manually.
- Advanced options:
  - -v[n] variants, where [n] specifies the step in the R/3 job.
  - You can type `-debug -trace` to get debugging information in case you experience problems. The `-debug` option creates an additional list in stdlist and the `-trace` option creates the dev_rfc file in the m*aestrohome* directory.
- No BDC wait makes Tivoli Maestro not wait for the completion of BDC sessions that were started by the R/3 job.

3. Scheduling Process is the same as the normal processing of Tivoli Maestro described in Chapter 4.2.4, "Tivoli Maestro Job Scheduling Object Definition" on page 181.

4. Run production cycle. This can be attained by scheduling the SFinal schedule or running the Jnextday command. This is the same as normal Tivoli Maestro processing.

- Tivoli Maestro creates a copy of an R/3 job defined in step 1 at run time.
- The authorization user fields are not changed for R/3 jobs by Tivoli Maestro. Permissions are neither gained or lost relative to running the same jobs without Tivoli Maestro.
- You can make use of Tivoli Maestro's unique functionality of managing batch input jobs in R/3. Refer to Tivoli Maestro SAP R/3 Extended Agent manuals for more details.

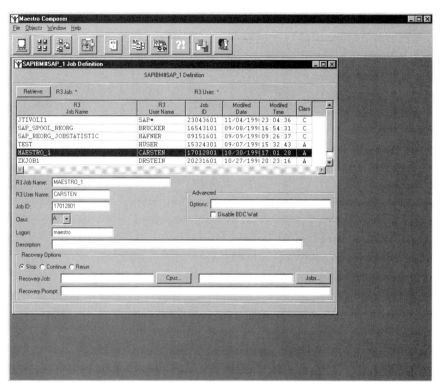

Figure 135. SAP R/3 Job Definition in Tivoli Maestro

5. Monitor the status of SAP R/3 jobs from Tivoli Maestro Console Manager. This is the same as normal Tivoli Maestro processing.

   You can specify to rerun R/3 jobs from Tivoli Maestro Console Manager from the beginning or from any step within the jobs. This function is not attained by SAP R/3 original job scheduling function.

The following table compares the Maestro job state and the R/3 job state.

Table 6. Maestro and R/3 Job States

Maestro Job State	R/3 Job State
intro	n/a
wait	ready
exec	active
succ	finished
abend	cancelled

4.2.7 Batch Job Network Design Under Tivoli Maestro

In this section, we show an example of the batch job network design under Tivoli Maestro.We need to compose the Maestro objects for the jobs to work correctly. There is not a general rule you must obey in making your job network; however, you can improve your management workload and quality if you design properly.

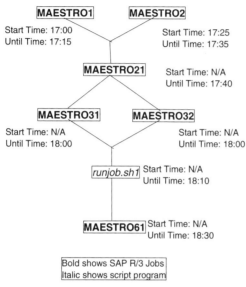

Figure 136. Job Network Example

Figure 136 on page 193 shows the sample job network we are planning to configure for our Tivoli Maestro environment. We have 6 SAP R/3 jobs which are to be run on a single SAP instance called IBM. These jobs are MAESTRO1, MAESTRO2, MAESTRO21, MAESTRO31, MAESTRO32, and MAESTRO61 respectively (Figure 137 on page 194). You can find the job dependencies in the previous figure.

Here, we set a different start time and until time specification between MAESTRO1 and MAESTRO2 to show how to synchronize Tivoli Maestro job dependency.

We have another script job, runjob.sh1, which is to be run on the SAP R/3 host, silver, after the successful completion of the two SAP R/3 jobs MAESTRO31 and MAESTRO32. Also, we have a job MAESTRO61 which follows script job runjob.sh1. Thus, this example shows, in the first stage, how to manage an SAP R/3 internal jobs network, and in the latter part how to manage the interdependency between the operating system script and the SAP R/3 job.

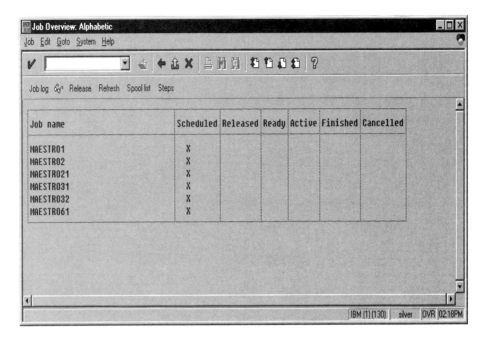

Figure 137. SAP Jobs Defined in SAP GUI

First, you must define the SAP R/3 jobs through the SAPGUI. You should not specify the start time for SAP R/3 jobs in the SAPGUI.

Then, you must create a Maestro job for each of the SAP R/3 jobs. The Maestro CPU for these jobs must be SAPIBM as shown in Figure 138 on page 195. So far, this is rather straightforward.

CPU	Job	Creator	Last Runtime
SAPIBM	MAE1	maestro	11/17/98
SAPIBM	MAE2	maestro	11/17/98
SAPIBM	MAE21	maestro	11/17/98
SAPIBM	MAE31	maestro	11/17/98
SAPIBM	MAE32	maestro	11/17/98
SAPIBM	MAE61	maestro	11/17/98
SILVER	TESTSL1	maestro	11/17/98

LIST JOB = S@#@

Figure 138. Maestro Jobs List

The question is how we can combine multiple jobs into a single schedule? As the schedule can have multiple jobs, it will make it easy when you combine multiple jobs in a logical unit of schedule. For example, the logical unit of a schedule can be multiple table backup activities performed as individual jobs.

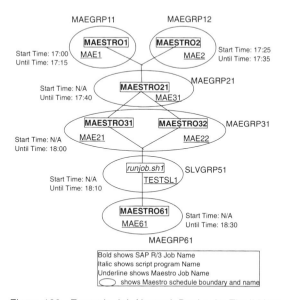

Figure 139. Example Job Network Design by Tivoli Maestro

Figure 139 on page 195 shows the result of the design in our example. The jobs which have an independent start time or until time specification must be put in an individual schedule even if they have a common follow-on job specification from the next job. MAESTRO1 and MAESTRO2 are to be specified as the follow-on jobs for MAESTRO21.

If this is the only dependency for MAESTRO21, we can put MAESTRO1 and MAESTRO2 in the same schedule; however, in this case they have different start and until time specifications, and thus, each must have its own schedule.

On the other hand, MAESTRO31 and MAESTRO32 can share the until time specification, and can be in the same schedule, here named MAEGRP31. You can put both external jobs (external from SAP R/3) and SAP R/3 jobs in the same schedule when they don't have dependencies between them.

It depends on your management policy. If you think that the logical unit of scheduling for these jobs fits for a single management object, it will suit you to have them in a single schedule. If you want to separately manage external jobs from jobs in SAP R/3, you should divide jobs into two groups.

As you divide sets of jobs in higher resolution, the level of management detail will increase; however, this may result in increasing complexity.

Figure 140 on page 196 shows the schedule list we created. In this case, all of the jobs are to be run in the same machine, silver, so we defined the Maestro CPU for these schedules as SAPIBM.

CPU	Schedule	Creator	Last Updated	
ITSOMSTR	FINAL	maestro	11/05/98	
SAPIBM	MAEGRP11	maestro	11/17/98	
SAPIBM	MAEGRP12	maestro	11/17/98	
SAPIBM	MAEGRP21	maestro	11/17/98	
SAPIBM	MAEGRP31	maestro	11/17/98	
SAPIBM	MAEGRP61	maestro	11/17/98	
SILVER	SLVGRP51	maestro	11/17/98	

List of Schedules
LIST SCHED = @#@

Figure 140. Maestro Schedule List

After completion of Jnextday processing, we see the Maestro Console Manger as shown in Figure 141 on page 197. The SHOWSCHEDULES window offers a view of all dependencies we defined in Maestro Composer.

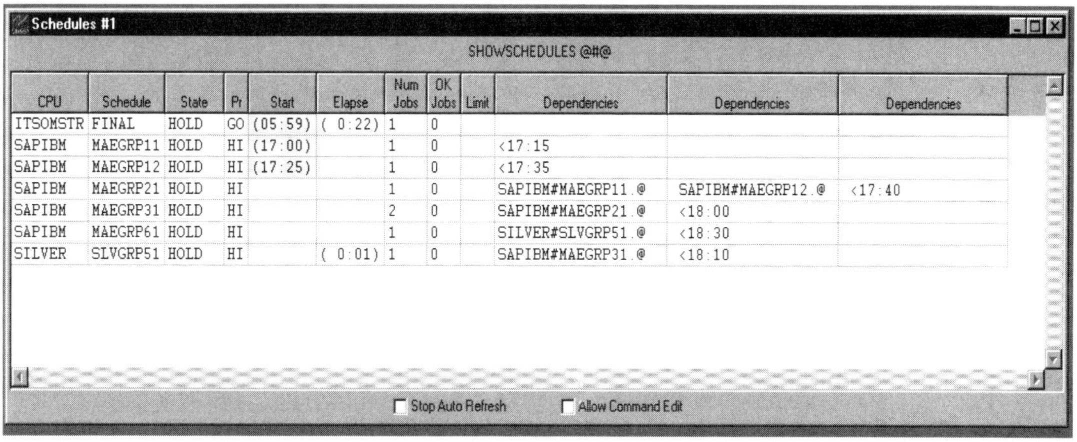

Figure 141. Maestro Console Manager SHOWSCHEDULES Window

Just after the scheduling, you can grasp the whole jobs list in the SHOWJOBS display in the Maestro Console Manager as shown in Figure 142 on page 198. All of the jobs are shown with their dependencies and in the state of HOLD at this time.

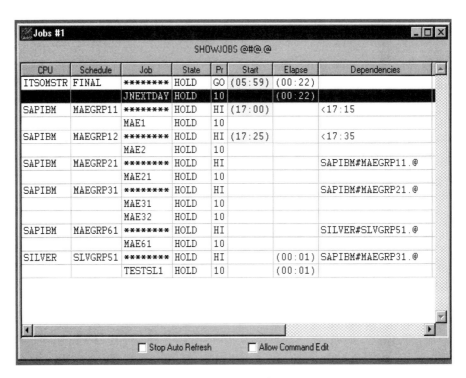

CPU	Schedule	Job	State	Pr	Start	Elapse	Dependencies
ITSOMSTR	FINAL	********	HOLD	GO	(05:59)	(00:22)	
		JNEXTDAY	HOLD	10		(00:22)	
SAPIBM	MAEGRP11	********	HOLD	HI	(17:00)		<17:15
		MAE1	HOLD	10			
SAPIBM	MAEGRP12	********	HOLD	HI	(17:25)		<17:35
		MAE2	HOLD	10			
SAPIBM	MAEGRP21	********	HOLD	HI			SAPIBM#MAEGRP11.@
		MAE21	HOLD	10			
SAPIBM	MAEGRP31	********	HOLD	HI			SAPIBM#MAEGRP21.@
		MAE31	HOLD	10			
		MAE32	HOLD	10			
SAPIBM	MAEGRP61	********	HOLD	HI			SILVER#SLVGRP51.@
		MAE61	HOLD	10			
SILVER	SLVGRP51	********	HOLD	HI		(00:01)	SAPIBM#MAEGRP31.@
		TESTSL1	HOLD	10		(00:01)	

☐ Stop Auto Refresh   ☐ Allow Command Edit

Figure 142. Maestro Console Manager SHOWJOBS Window

As time progresses, you receive feedback of the job processing as shown in Figure 143 on page 199.

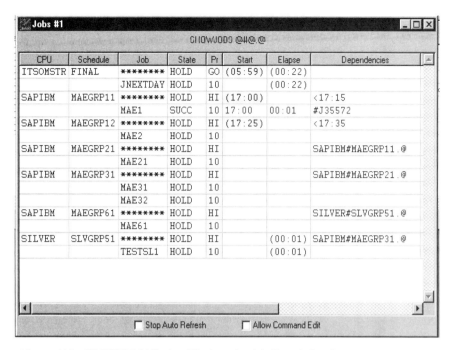

Figure 143. SHOWJOBS Window Displays the Job Completion Status

Finally, you can ascertain the result of the whole jobs network in the SHOWJOBS window of the Maestro Console Manager as shown in Figure 144 on page 199.

Jobs #1 — SHOWJOBS @#@.@

CPU	Schedule	Job	State	Pr	Start	Elapse	Dependencies	Dependencies	Dependencies
ITSOMSTR	FINAL	********	HOLD	GO	(05:59)	(00:22)			
		JNEXTDAY	HOLD	10		(00:22)			
SAPIBM	MAEGRP11	********	HOLD	HI	(17:00)		<17:15		
		MAE1	SUCC	10	17:00	00:01	#J35572		
SAPIBM	MAEGRP12	********	HOLD	HI	(17:25)		<17:35		
		MAE2	SUCC	10	17:26	00:01	#J7186		
SAPIBM	MAEGRP21	********	HOLD	HI			SAPIBM#MAEGRP11.@	SAPIBM#MAEGRP12.@	<17:40
		MAE21	SUCC	10	17:27	00:01	#J31614		
SAPIBM	MAEGRP31	********	HOLD	HI			SAPIBM#MAEGRP21.@	<18:00	
		MAE31	SUCC	10	17:28	00:01	#J34842		
		MAE32	SUCC	10	17:28	00:02	#J24094		
SAPIBM	MAEGRP61	********	HOLD	HI			SILVER#SLVGRP51.@	<18:30	
		MAE61	SUCC	10	17:31	00:01	#J31866		
SILVER	SLVGRP51	********	HOLD	HI		(00:01)	SAPIBM#MAEGRP31.@	<18:10	
		TESTSL1	SUCC	10	17:30	00:01	#J27454		

Figure 144. Final Result of Example Job Scheduling

From Figure 144 on page 199, we can see both the planned run time and actual run time. You can also find the elapsed time of each job.

This is the way Tivoli Maestro manages both SAP R/3 internal jobs and external jobs.

Finally, let us see how the jobs were carried out in SAP R/3 using the R/3 SM37 transaction. You can find that the original jobs are kept in Scheduled status and a new copy of the jobs was made and ended in Finished status.

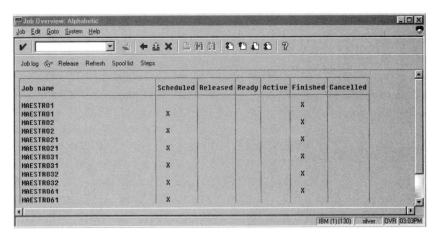

Figure 145. R/3 SM37 Transaction

4.2.8 Tivoli Maestro SAP R/3 Extended Agent Summary

In this section we have shown how to use Maestro in combination with R/3 and how Maestro can complement the native R/3 job scheduling.

Maestro can enhance R/3 job scheduling in the following ways:

- You can eliminate the need in R/3 to repeatedly define jobs, even if the content of the job does not change. With Tivoli Maestro you define the job in R/3 once and then re-use it.

- You can manage jobs that have dependencies with other R/3 instances or even other resources or jobs originating from other sources. You can create dependencies that allow you to structure your workflow and model your business process.

- You can define recovery jobs in case your R/3 job fails. This helps in network automation and helps you to take quick action to recover from a failed job.

4.3 Tivoli Output Manager (Destiny)

In this section we describe how to use Tivoli Output Manager (Destiny) that we have previously installed and configured as described in 3.9, "Installing and Configuring Tivoli Output Management (Destiny)" on page 113.

4.3.1 Destiny Enterprise Server

Enterprise Server is responsible for all the updates to the environment and maintains UED, SCD and NEWS. The structure of UED, SCD and NEWS is shown in Appendix D, "Destiny Database Structure" on page 277. It is useful to know the structure to determine what data is flowing from UED to SCD to NEWS so that major changes can be done at night. To browse the databases a utility is included with Destiny called SQLView, residing under C:\Destiny\Util where C: is the installation drive and is very useful to determine discrepancies and problems in the databases.

The utility that is used to modify the output network is Destiny Composer. This utility resides under C:\Destiny\Client where C: is the installation drive. To use Composer click on **Start**, **Program**, **Destiny**, **Composer**. The first time you run it from the desktop you must provide the following information: Network Node and Default Domain in the Configuration for Composer window, Figure 146 on page 201. The network node is the machine hosting the UED database or the Enterprise Server. There is only one node in the Destiny network with the UED database. After clicking **OK**, enter the username (adminuser) and password (none) in the Username/Password window.

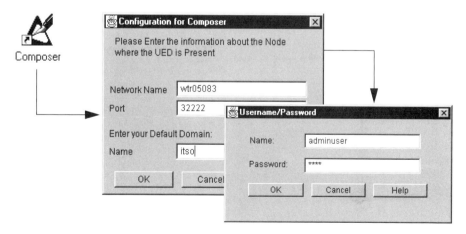

Figure 146. Composer Logon Windows

All the information you provided is stored in composer.ini. The program composer.exe will read this file and log you on to the same node every time. If you want to change the logon node information you have to delete the ini file and specify the new information to the Configuration for Composer window.

Composer has two sections: Enterprise Configuration and Destiny Domain Configuration. The Enterprise Configuration section is where you add physical objects, for example, users, groups, destinations, rights and schedules. All these objects control the way that users use destinations. Destinations are definitions for printers, other users, pagers, Web servers, e-mail gateways, faxes, etc. Once a user is validated to use the destination the intelligence is left to the process objects in the Destiny Domain Configuration section. In this section you define the dependencies and interactions between the hierarchy of objects that controls destinations, such as stationary, banners, watchers, filters, etc. In Figure 147 on page 202 you can see the objects found under the discussed sections: Enterprise Configuration and Destiny Domain Configuration.

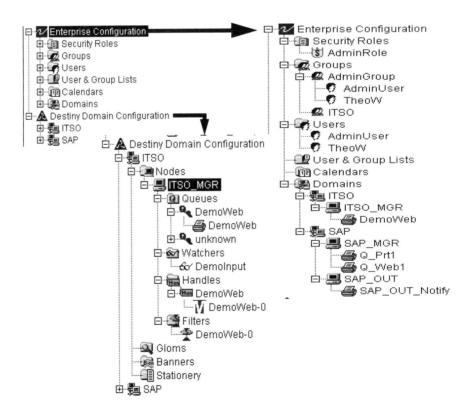

Figure 147. Composer Objects

The menu icons of Composer are shown in Figure 148 on page 203. You can either use these icons or Composer's Composer/Edit menus. Some of these icons only work when you are in the right environment so if you don't get any update the icon is not meant for the operation that you want to execute.

Icon	Description	Icon	Description
	Creates an object of the selected type		Displays large icons of the objects
	Cuts an object to the clipboard		Displays small icons of the objects
	Copies an object to the clipboard		Displays spool files with all the attributes
	Pastes the clipboard to current cursor location		Displays spool files by name
	Prints the Composer screen		Moves a filter up in the list of filters
	Deletes the selected item		Moves a filter down in the list of filters
	Displays the properties for the selected item		Starts the Report Wizart to define automatic routing schemes

Figure 148. Composer Icons

4.3.1.1 Domain Updates with Enterprise Server

Once you are finished with your environment definitions it is time to activate them by clicking on **Composer, Push, All** for the specific domain. This will start the database updates for the selected domain. The enterprise configuration parameters go to the Output Server and the domain configuration parameters go to the Domain Manager Server and Output Server. All the communication happens via TCP/IP but is encrypted before transfer.

The tables which are synchronized via Enterprise Configuration pushes are:

- tbl_calendars
- tbl_destinations
- tbl_dist_list
- tbl_dist_list_details
- tbl_domains
- tbl_groups
- tbl_group_security_roles
- tbl_nodes
- tbl_node_communications

- tbl_security_roles
- tbl_users
- tbl_user_security_roles

The tables which are synchronized via Destiny Domain Configuration pushes are:

- tbl_banners
- tbl_device_history
- tbl_filters
- tbl_glom_detail
- tbl_glom_header
- tbl_handles
- tbl_mappers
- tbl_mapper_calendar
- tbl_queue
- tbl_queue_destination
- tbl_queue_history
- tbl_rules
- tbl_stationery
- tbl_users_history
- tbl_watchers

4.3.2 Domain Manager Server

The Domain Manager server is responsible for internal domain functions and cross domain functions. The Domain Manager server also provides logon capabilities for Destiny Direct to minimize the traffic over slow links.

The Destiny database that all the configurations are kept in is called SCD. This database resides under C:\Destiny\DB where C: is the installation drive. Not much interaction is seen from the surface between Composer and Conductor but when jobs are spooled the Domain Manager Server comes into play. It controls the flow and interaction between the Output Server and the security rights of the specific queues and destinations. Once the job is transferred to the queue the Domain Manager does no longer plays a role and the Output Server spools without any interaction from the Domain Manager Server. There are situations like pausing, replaying and modifications where the Domain Manager Server regain control and reprocess the specific job back into the queue for the specific output device.

4.3.3 Output Server

Output Server handles the spooling of jobs to the output devices. It monitors the jobs and determines appropriate actions if needed. Output Servers communicate with the Domain Manager Server for the specific domain and receive updates from the Domain Manager Server for the domain under which the Output Server operates and the Enterprise Server. The Output Server has the ability to handle Destiny Direct clients running under Microsoft Windows NT and Microsoft Windows 95. This makes the output network very hierarchical and structured, based on the enterprise policies.

Once the files are in the queue of the Output Server, no more interaction with the Destiny Domain is needed to finish the spooling of the job to the output device. In scenarios where the physical output device fails interaction back to the Domain Manager will be needed, but is very infrequent.

4.3.4 Typical Domain Structure

It is not very difficult to see the ideal enterprise structure for Destiny. The following components must be placed: Enterprise Server, Domain Manager Server and Output Server. Because there can only be one Enterprise Server, it is obvious to put this component in the middle of the network. The question is now where to locate the Domain Manager Server and when to split the Domain Manager and Output Manager. Let's say you want to manage by department and then by location, for example: payroll devices should be grouped together over several locations with wide area links between these devices. It would then be advisable to put the Domain Manager for payroll in the center of all the locations and place one Output Server per location. If the management environment is location and then department: a Domain Manger would be put onsite with the Output Server on the same machine as the Domain Manager Server.

4.3.5 SAP R/3 Interface

At this time there is no native interface for SAP R/3; however, one is planned for the future. So, when speaking about the interface to SAP R/3, it could just as well be referred to as the interface to Lotus Notes or Microsoft BackOffice.

There are two ways of putting data into the Destiny output network: Destiny Direct client and printer spooler catchers. Destiny Direct client runs only on Microsoft Windows NT and Microsoft Windows 95. The example that we discuss here is how to use spooler catchers.

These are the steps that we use:

- Change the print spooler on the Windows NT machine.
- Set up a watcher for the client.
- Direct the watcher to an output device.

We took an existing printer definition on the R/3 machine and modified the print processor by clicking on **Start, Settings, Printers**. Once you highlight the destination printer click on **Properties**.

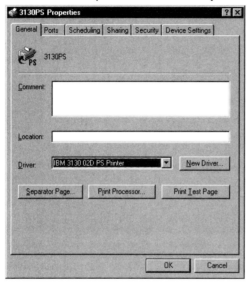

Figure 149. Changing Print Processors

Click now on **Print Processor** as shown in Figure 149 on page 206 to bring up the available print processors installed on the particular Windows client. If you have Destiny Direct Client installed on your machine you will see SplNtPP on the list. Select this option as well as **NT EMF 1.003** as shown in Figure 150 on page 207. It is really up to the memory in the printer and hard disk space on the local machine if you want to enable Always spool RAW datatype as shown in Figure 150 on page 207.

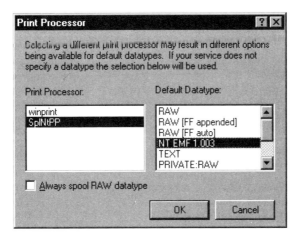

Figure 150. Choosing Print Processors

The above steps divert the NT spool system into the Destiny network. Be careful when you create a destination in SAP R/3 because your data will be encapsulated in the type of data format you specify and would be very difficult to switch between Destiny endpoints. The best destination to select for SAP R/3 is a line printer where there are no control characters added to your data stream.

The next objective is to set up the Destiny network to watch for input from this client and define output paths and schedules. To do this you must launch Composer. Any new definition to the Destiny output network must go through these steps:

- Select **Enterprise Configuration, Domains, Specific Domain Name, Specific Domain Node, New**.

  This step creates a new destination on the selected node. Destinations can be anything from faxes, Web servers, e-mail gateways to disk space for archive purposes. A destination can also be marked as a confidential destination and would then fall into a different category. You also assign the destination fixed formats here like paper size and 600 dpi for instance so that all the user defaults could be overwritten. Destinations belong to a certain domain and a certain Output Server. The rights needed to access this device are handled by the Domain Manager Server and are also updated by Composer through the users and group section.

- Select **Destiny Domain Configuration, Specific Domain Name, Nodes, Specific Domain Node, Queues, New**.

Here you create a new queue to the destination that you have specified. This is the last entity that Destiny controls before it starts the data stream to the physical output device. Once the job is in the queue it does not need the Destiny domain structure anymore just the Output Server.

Be sure to select a destination and also the way the queue is going to operate (fifo or linear). See Figure 151 on page 208 for details.

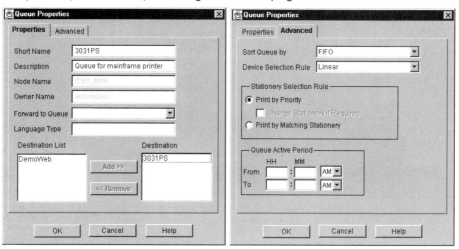

Figure 151. Queue Properties

The other properties like queue activation are also handy features to define when a certain destination is confidential.

- Select **Destiny Domain Configuration, Specific Domain Name, Nodes, Specific Domain Node, Watchers, New**.

Watchers are the objects in Destiny which scoop the data and put it through the process definitions. Watchers work together with Handles to enable filters and rules on certain queues. There are not really any parameters for Watchers except when destinations require certain executables to run when data is received into a certain queue. This executable name field is definable in the Watchers window.

- Select **Destiny Domain Configuration, Specific Domain Name, Nodes, Specific Domain Node, Handles, New**.

After data has passed through the Handles section it has a unique handle and can be processed via the filters and finally the queue. When data is not assigned a handle the data is discarded by the Destiny Output Server. Handles are a way of telling the system that a certain match was performed on the data stream and the data is valid. Once a handle is created a mapper must be created to tell Destiny when the data stream is supposed to be processed and to which destination. Mappers allow complex scenarios for when data is supposed to flow to certain output devices and when not. This can be very useful for peak time processing and non-peak time processing of huge output devices. Be sure to fill in the Calendar and Send To fields in the specific mappers. In the Mapper field you can also choose to archive the data stream for security reasons. See Figure 152 on page 209.

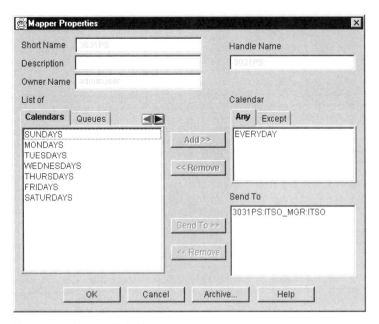

Figure 152. Mapper Definitions

- Select **Destiny Domain Configuration, Specific Domain Name, Nodes, Specific Domain Node, Filters, New**.

  It is not mandatory to define filters for a destination. Filters need to know on which handle and destination to act.

Once you have taken all the previous steps you must push the configuration to the Domain Manager Server and the Output Server. Issue a **Conductor, Push, All** and your new Destiny objects will be active.

Any SAP R/3 printing is now diverted into the Destiny network as shown in Figure 153 on page 210.

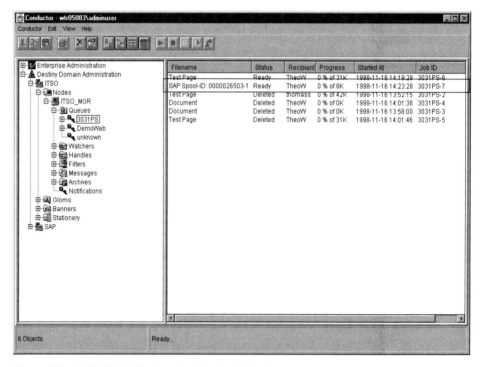

Figure 153. SAP R/3 Printing into the Destiny Network

The other possibility for SAP R/3 printing is to define the normal system printer destination in SAP R/3 and where you must type the printer name you enter `destiny1` as the name of the Windows printer. Obviously, there is not a destiny1 printer at this stage but you are going to use the Destiny Direct client to create a printer with these settings.

Open any application where you can print from, like Wordpad: **Start, Program, Accessories, WordPad**. Issue a print command and change your printer to the Destiny printer which was installed via the Destiny Direct Client. As soon as you choose **OK** from the print window it will bring up the Destiny authentication window. Log on as a privileged user as shown in Figure 154 on page 211.

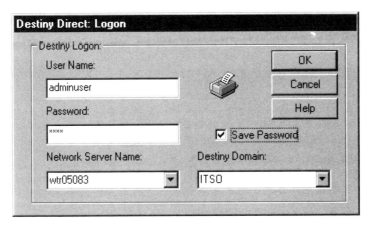

Figure 154. Direct Client Logon Screen

After you click on **OK** you will see the Print Destinations window of Destiny. Here, you can select the output device(s) in the left pane of the window.

Notice that you can select more than one device and it will print to all the destinations at the same time. This is useful when you want to print, for example, end-of-the month reports, which require large amounts of processing. By defining a SAP R/3 system in this way it will process the report only once in SAP R/3 and think that it sends it only once to a printer called destiny1. What happens in Destiny is that the Watchers will pick up the data and send it to all the queues in parallel with the least amount of overhead on all the systems.

Once you have your device(s) selected click on **Save As Printer** and give it the name destiny1. Now it acts like a physical device in Windows NT but is really a software destination channel in Destiny. See Figure 155 on page 212.

These are the only ways to define printer locations in business application where the applications does not ask a user for a specific device, but output the data stream into predefined values.

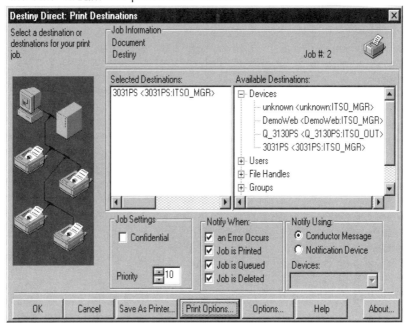

Figure 155. Saving Selections as Destiny Printers

Chapter 5. Management Scenarios

In this chapter we give design guidelines that will help a technical consultant to create an integrated systems management solution for SAP R/3 environments. This chapter is valuable for consultants that have to position and propose an integrated management solution for SAP R/3 as well as for personnel who have to design an SAP R/3 management solution for large deployments.

The examples we discuss are typical for customer environments and will give you guidelines on how to approach the situation and resolve the problem.

The following scenarios will be discussed:

- "Creating a Custom SAP Monitor" on page 213
- "Critical Monitoring" on page 228
- "Monitoring SAP R/3 Using a Standard Numeric Script Monitor" on page 243
- "Interconnected TMRs" on page 250

> **Note**
>
> The scenarios in this chapter are included to show you some typical real life scenarios, however, it is beyond the scope of this book to provide a comprehensive solution for any kind of real life situation. Hence, the scenarios can get you started when planning a solution deployment or customer engagement but will need to be adjusted and enhanced for any specific environment.

5.1 Creating a Custom SAP Monitor

In this section we show you how to create a custom monitor for R/3 using ABAP and the Tivoli Distributed Monitoring MCSL language. This is useful when you want to create monitors that are not covered by Tivoli Manager for R/3.

Tivoli is extremely open, including the Tivoli SAP R/3 offering. If there is a monitor or task that is needed, it can be written quite easily in ABAP and called from Tivoli, allowing the roles and policies of Tivoli to be leveraged.

5.1.1 Overview

The Tivoli Manager for R/3 provides a number of Tivoli Distributed Monitoring monitors that get information from the SAP application servers through their RFC interface. As explained in "Using the SAP R/3 Management Environment" on page 129, these monitors use the wr3rfc program to execute a function module on the application server. After execution, the resulting information is returned to wr3rfc. These ABAPs provided by Tivoli had been previously imported into the R/3 system during the configuration of Tivoli Manager for R/3. The wr3rfc program provides remote execution of *any* function modules that support the RFC interface. So, it can be used in custom tasks or monitors to get information from the R/3 system through the execution of ABAPs not provided by Tivoli (ABAPs provided by SAP or custom ABAPs).

In this scenario, we show you an example where we create our own custom monitor that will use the wr3rfc program to execute a function module provided by SAP: SAPTUNE_NUM_OF_WP. This function module returns the number of dialog, batch, spool, update and enqueue work processes configured for the application server on which it is executed. We will use this function module just for example purposes, since monitoring the number of processes defined is not really interesting. We just want to show you a way to create your own monitors that use your own ABAPs.

5.1.2 Technical Details

In the following sections we show the technical details of our custom monitor, such as the R/3 definitions, the ABAP code and the custom monitoring script.

5.1.2.1 Creating the rfc_interface File

We first have to create an rfc_interface file that will be specified as an argument to the wr3rfc command. In such a file, we specify which function module must be executed in the R/3 system and the corresponding import/export parameters or tables. For a complete description, refer to Appendix A of the *Tivoli Manager for R/3 User's Guide*.

> **Note**
>
> The import and export parameters stanzas of the rfc_interface file correspond to the export and import parameters of the function module in the SAP system.

You can display the characteristics of the function module by performing the SE37 transaction in a SAPGUI. Then enter SAPTUNE_NUM_OF_WP in the function module field and click the **Display** button. Figure 156 on page 215 shows you the administration folder of the function module characteristics.

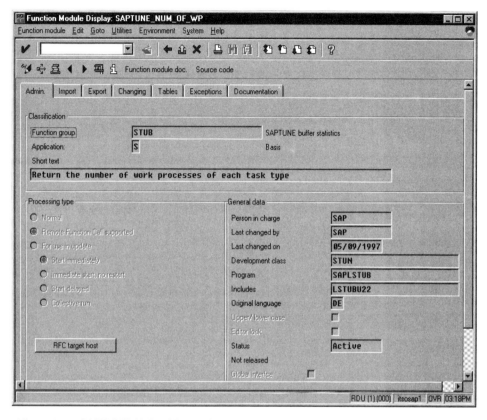

Figure 156. SAPTUNE_NUM_OF_WP Characteristics

We can also test the function module using the SE37 transaction. Enter its name, click the **Snlg. test** button and in the resulting window, click the **Execute** icon. The result is shown in Figure 157 on page 216. We see there that the function module has five export parameters (DIA, ENQ, BTC, SPO and VB) which correspond to an integer value. It permits us to write the rfc_interface file as shown in the Figure 158 on page 217. We have named this file SAP_WP.

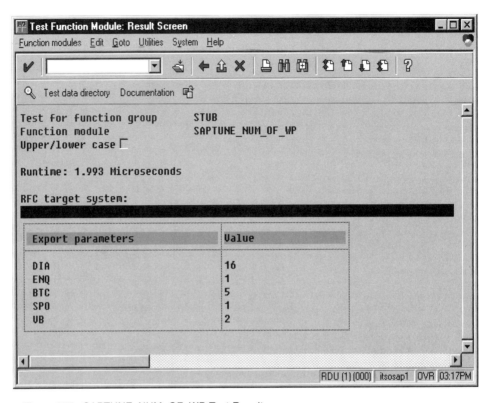

Figure 157. SAPTUNE_NUM_OF_WP Test Result

```
COMMAND OPTIONS:
MODULE = CAPTURE_NUM_OF_WP

IMPORT PARAMETER:
NAME = DIA
TYPE = TYPINT
FORMAT = VERBOSE

IMPORT PARAMETER:
NAME = ENQ
TYPE = TYPINT
FORMAT = VERBOSE

IMPORT PARAMETER:
NAME = BTC
TYPE = TYPINT
FORMAT = VERBOSE

IMPORT PARAMETER:
NAME = SPO
TYPE = TYPINT
FORMAT = VERBOSE

IMPORT PARAMETER:
NAME = VB
TYPE = TYPINT
FORMAT = VERBOSE
```

Figure 158. SAP_WP rfc_interface File

5.1.2.2 Testing the rfc_interface File

We copy the file to the /tmp directory of our TMR server and then execute the following command:

```
export PATH=$PATH:$BINDIR/TME/SAP/2.2C
wr3rfc -d IBM -h silver -s 00 SAP_WP
```

This returns the following lines which indicate that it works properly:

```
Warning: open failed for config file .wr3rfc_cfg errno=2,
processing continues
DIA = 3
ENQ = 1
BTC = 2
SPO = 1
VB = 1
```

5.1.2.3 Creating the Custom Monitor

Creating a custom monitor consists of two steps: writing the script that will get the needed information, and integrating this script in Tivoli Distributed Monitoring so that the information can be compared to predefined thresholds and allow actions to be taken. For this second step, we will use MCSL in order to create our own monitoring collection that will contain our custom monitor.

We first have to write a shell script that gets the number of work processes for a specific type of work process: DIA, ENQ, BTC, SPO or VB. This type is passed to the script as its first argument. The script has a second argument: the Tivoli object ID of the application server. This second argument is temporary and it is only used when executing the script manually for debugging purposes.

When the script is integrated in Tivoli Distributed Monitoring and after the monitor is run, this OID will reside in the ENDPOINT_OID variable of the Tivoli Distributed Monitoring engine environment. These OIDs can be retrieved from the Tivoli database by typing:

```
wlookup -ar SapInstance
```

The script will also get the INTERP variable from the Tivoli Distributed Monitoring engine environment when integrated. For manual execution, the Tivoli environment must be set in order to use this variable. The script assumes that the SAP_WP interface file resides in the $BINDIR/../generic_unix/TME/SAP/2.2c/rfc directory of the application server on which it will run. As it is a short and simple script, we wrote a single script that can run on UNIX or Windows NT and not two platform-specific scripts.

```
#The process type is the first argument
TYPE=$1
#The endpoint object id is the second argument
ENDPOINT_OID=$2
#Defining the temporary directory in function of the OS
if [ "$INTERP" = "w32-ix86" ] ; then
  TMP=`wtemp`
else
  TMP=/tmp
fi
#Redirecting the errors to a log file
exec 2> ${TMP}/ITSO_WP_monitor.log
set -x
#Setting up the environment to dispose of $BINDIR
if [ "$INTERP" = "w32-ix86" ] ; then
  . $SystemRoot/system32/drivers/etc/Tivoli/setup_env.sh
else
  . /etc/Tivoli/setup_env.sh
fi
#Locating the wr3rfc program and the rfc_interface file
WR3RFC=$BINDIR/TME/SAP/2.2C/wr3rfc
RFCDIR=$BINDIR/../generic_unix/TME/SAP/2.2C/rfc
cd $RFCDIR
#Getting the hostname on which the monitor is running
HOST=`idlattr -t -g $ENDPOINT_OID HostName string`
HOST=`eval echo $HOST`
#Getting the instance number of the application server
SAPSYSTEM=`idlattr -t -g $ENDPOINT_OID InstanceID string`
SAPSYSTEM=`eval echo $SAPSYSTEM`
#Getting the SID of the R/3 system
SAPSYSTEMNAME=`idlattr -t -g $ENDPOINT_OID SystemID string`
SAPSYSTEMNAME=`eval echo $SAPSYSTEMNAME`
#Getting the info from wr3rfc
OUTPUT=`$WR3RFC -h "$HOST" -d "$SAPSYSTEMNAME" -s "$SAPSYSTEM" SAP_WP`
#Parsing the output for the process type
WPLINE=`echo "$OUTPUT" | grep "^$TYPE ="`
WPNUM=`echo $WPLINE | awk -F= '{print $2}'`
#Returning the value as result
echo $WPNUM
exit 0
```

Figure 159. Custom Script

We copy the script and the SAP_WP file on our application servers (UNIX and Windows NT), set up the Tivoli environment and then execute it to be sure everything works (for Windows NT you must launch a bash shell before executing the script). On our UNIX system we have to change the authorizations of the SAP_WP file (`chmod 755 SAP_WP`). When executed, the script automatically generates a log file located in the /tmp (UNIX) or %DBDIR%\tmp (Windows NT) directory. The log file is named ITSO_WP_monitor.log.

We use MCSL to wrap our script and make it available to Tivoli Distributed Monitoring. This is done by using the mcsl command, which is part of Tivoli Distributed Monitoring. MCSL enables us to create our own monitoring collection with our own monitoring source.

The work-processes type will be specified as an attribute when adding a new monitor from this source through the Tivoli GUI. All these definitions have to be written in an MCSL source file.

The csl files provided by the Tivoli Manager for R/3, containing the definitions of the related monitors have been very helpful for writing our own csl file. These files are located in the $BINDIR/../generic_unix/TME/SAP/2.2C/csl directory of any managed node where the product is installed. You can find our csl file in Appendix C, "Custom Monitor MCSL Source File" on page 273. Just note that we have specified there the event class that should be used in case an alert is forwarded to a TEC event server. We have specified a new event class specific for our monitor instead of using an existing one in order to avoid any side effect with the TEC rules that could act on existing event classes.

We won't go into the details on how we wrote this file but we refer you to the redbook *Creating Custom Monitors for Tivoli Distributed Monitoring*, IBM Form SG24-5211.

We have copied the file to the /tmp directory of our TMR server and then compiled it using MCSL:

```
mcsl -Pcat -x ./testITSO.col ./testITSO.csl
```

Now we can install the collection using:

```
mcsl -R -i ./testITSO.col
```

To see the new collection and its monitors in the Tivoli Distributed Monitoring user interface, we have to recycle the object dispatchers on all the connected nodes using:

```
odadmin reexec all
```

We use the sap_server_monitor_35.baroc file in order to define our own event class. This file resides in the $BINDIR/TME/TEC/<RuleBaseDir>/TEC_CLASSES directory of the TEC server. We copy it to the /tmp directory of the event server and add the following statement at the end of the file:

```
TEC_CLASS :
  NUM_WP_MONITOR ISA SAP_Servers_Monitors;
END
```

Then, we delete the non-modified sap_server_monitor_35.baroc file from the active rule base, re-import the modified file, compile the rule base, re-load it and stop/re-start the event server using the following commands:

```
wdelrbclass sap_server_monitor_35.baroc "ITSO RuleBase"
wimprbclass /tmp/sap_server_monitor_35.baroc "ITSO RuleBase"
wcomprules "ITSO RuleBase"
wstopesvr
wloadrb "ITSO RuleBase"
wstartesvr
```

5.1.2.4 Creating a TEC Rule to Reformat the Event Message

Now our custom monitor is really like any Tivoli Distributed Monitoring monitor. We can choose thresholds and actions to be taken when these thresholds are exceeded. Typically, we will forward an event to the TEC server.

The problem with the event adapter of Tivoli Distributed Monitoring is that it formats the message field in a way so that the useful and interesting part of the message is not displayed on the event console. Each time you receive such a message from Tivoli Distributed Monitoring you have to edit it in order to understand the alert. Figure 160 on page 222 shows you an example when monitoring the filesystem /tmp with Tivoli Distributed Monitoring.

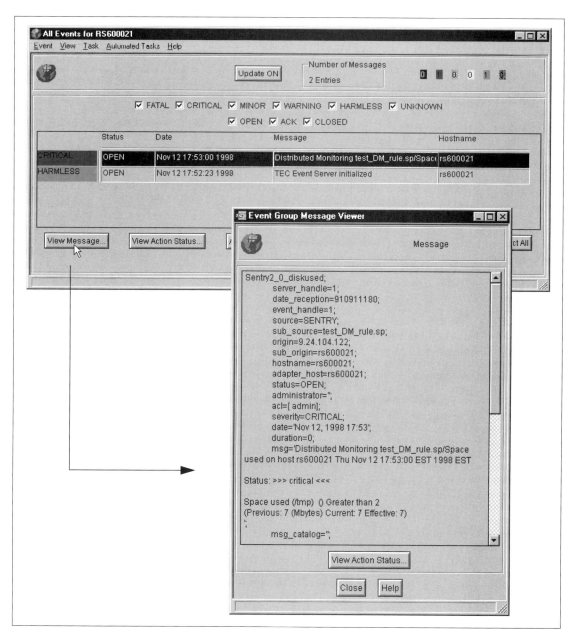

Figure 160. Distributed Monitoring Events

To solve this problem for our custom monitor, we create a TEC rule that re-formats the message slot of Tivoli Distributed Monitoring events in a way that allows the message to start with the pertinent information. This rule acts on all event classes derived from the Sentry2_0_Base superclass.

Sometimes you encounter event classes that depend on this superclass but that do not need to be re-formatted. A good example is the AMS_R3MONITOR_ALERT class coming with the Tivoli Manager for R/3, which is used for events indicating that the monitor has encountered a problem. To handle such cases we write a second rule that will mark such event classes, so that they will not trigger on the first rule.

We wrote our two new rules in a single rule set dm_msg_format.rls. You can see the content of the file in Figure 161 on page 224. The rule dm_msg_reformat_exclude triggers on the AMS_R3MONITOR_ALERT events and fills the sub_origin slot with the string 'no_dm_reformat'. The rule dm_msg_reformat triggers on all event classes defined below the Sentry2_0_Base superclass with the sub_origin slot different from no_dm_reformat. It reformats the message slot to start with the fifth line of the message. The new format consists of the fifth line, two carriage returns, the first line, space, the third line, space, the sixth and following lines. All the information is thus conserved, only the order is changed. For further information about the programming of TEC rules, see the *Tivoli Enterprise Console Rule Builder's Guide*.

To activate the rules, we copy the file to the /tmp directory of the TEC server and execute the following commands:

```
wimprbrules /tmp/dm_msg_format.rls "ITSO RuleBase"
wcomprules "ITSO RuleBase"
wloadrb -u "ITSO RuleBase"
```

```
rule:
dm_msg_reformat_exclude:
(
 description: 'Mark the sub-origin slot for DM events that must not be reformatted',
 event: _event of_class within ['AMS_R3MONITOR_ALERT']
  where [
        sub_origin: _sub_origin
        ],
reception_action:
(
_mark = 'no_dm_reformat',
bo_set_slotval(_event,sub_origin,_mark)
)
).

rule:
dm_msg_reformat:
(
 description: 'Reformat the msg slot for DM events non previously excluded',
 event: _event of_class within ['Sentry2_0_Base']
where [
        sub_origin: outside ['no_dm_reformat'],
        msg: _msg
        ],
reception_action:
(
atomlength(_msg,_L1),
atompart(_msg, '
', _start1, _L),
_l1 is _L1 - _start1 - 1,
_start2 is _start1 + 2,
atompart(_msg, _right1, _start2, _l1),
_end1 is _start1 - 1,
atompart(_msg, _left1, 1, _end1),
atomlength(_right1,_L2),
atompart(_right1, '
', _start3, _Z),
_l2 is _L2 - _start3 - 1,
_start4 is _start3 + 2,
atompart(_right1, _right2, _start4, _l2),
_end2 is _start3 - 1,
atompart(_right1, _left2, 1, _end2),
atomlength(_right2, _L3),
atompart(_right2, '
', _start5, _Y),
_l3 is _L3 - _start5,
_start6 is _start5 + 1,
atompart(_right2, _right3, _start6, _l3),
_end3 is _start5 - 1,
atompart(_right2, _left3, 1, _end3),
atomconcat([_left3,'

',_left1,' ',_left2,' ',_right3],_newmsg),
bo_set_slotval(_event,msg,_newmsg)
)
).
```

Figure 161. Dm_msg_format.rls Rule Set

Figure 162 on page 225 shows the same event as in Figure 160 on page 222 for the filesystem /tmp, but with the Message field reformatted. Editing the alert is no longer required.

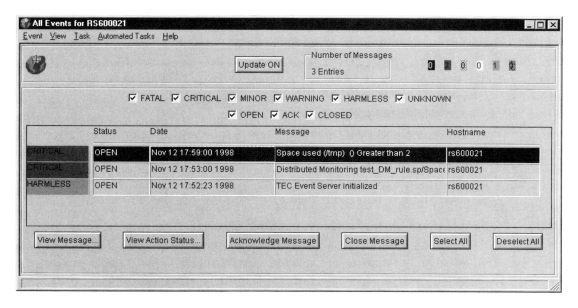

Figure 162. Reformatted Distributed Monitoring Events

5.1.3 Results

The new event class and the new rules are loaded into the TEC server. The new collection is imported into the TMR server. We now have everything needed to add our monitors in a Tivoli Distributed Monitoring profile and distribute it to a SAP instance.

We added a custom monitor for the dialog work processes to the already existing IBM Server Remote Monitors profile, as shown in the Figure 163 on page 226. This Tivoli Distributed Monitoring profile already has the right user ID for the execution of monitors using wr3rfc.

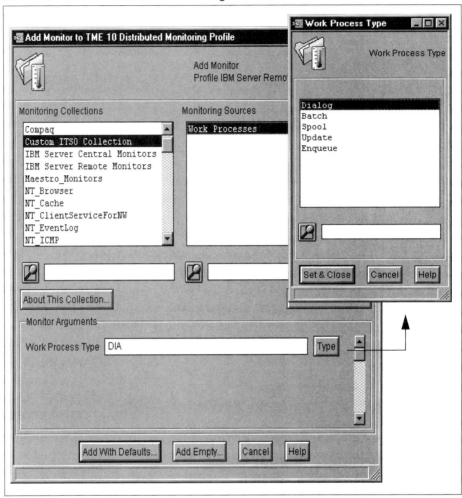

Figure 163. Adding a SAP Custom Monitor

We then specify that the monitor must trigger when the number of dialog work processes is different from five. The action to be taken is to forward an event of WARNING severity to the TEC server. We also change the scheduling characteristics.

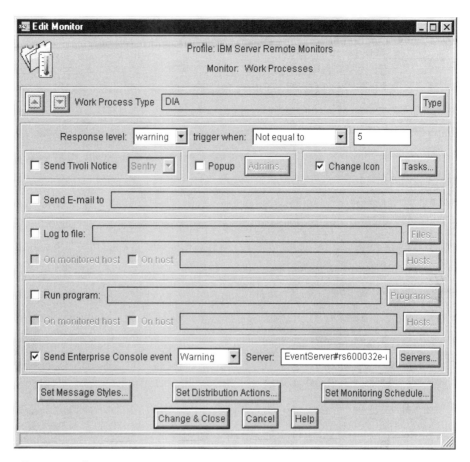

Figure 164. Customizing our New Monitor

Afterwards, we re-distribute the profile to the SAP instance silver_IBM_00. As we know that the number of dialog processes configured for this instance is three, we expect an alert at the TEC console. Figure 165 on page 228 shows you this alert. We see that the pertinent information is well displayed in the Message field.

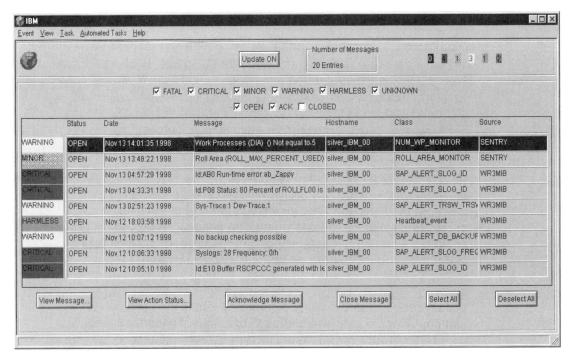

Figure 165. Event from our Custom Monitor in the TEC Console

5.2 Critical Monitoring

In this section we discuss which of the monitors provided in Tivoli Manager for R/3 are most useful for a typical environment and what other Tivoli products can be used to provide comprehensive monitoring of the entire environment.

5.2.1 Overview

A typical environment consists of critical systems that have to be monitored 24 hours a day. The monitoring is performed through Tivoli at the network, operating system, database, middleware and application levels. All alerts detected through this monitoring are centralized in a unique console constantly watched by operators. When an event arrives in the console, the operator calls the right person to fix the problem (the network administrator, the system engineer, the application administrator, etc.). In such an environment, each event that arrives at the console should reveal a serious problem that requires direct intervention. For example, a critical file system that is nearly full falls in that category, but a decrease in buffer quality does not necessarily.

In this scenario, we will give some ideas on how to integrate the monitoring of SAP in such an environment. We will try to define what should be used in the monitoring capabilities offered by Tivoli in order to get only meaningful alerts.

5.2.2 Technical Details

Monitoring SAP does not only include the monitoring of the application layer itself. It is also important to monitor the underlying layers, such as the database, the operating system and the network. Tivoli offers products for the management/monitoring of each of these layers:

- Application SAP: Tivoli Manager for R/3
- Database: Tivoli Manager for Oracle, Informix, DB2, Sybase or MS SQL
- Operating system: Tivoli Distributed Monitoring
- Network: Tivoli NetView

We use these products for their monitoring capability, which allows them to send alerts to the Tivoli Enterprise Console (TEC), which will then manage the events.

The monitoring capability of the Tivoli Manager for R/3 relies mainly on the monitoring capability of CCMS in the way that Tivoli Manager for R/3 gets information from CCMS through its MIB or RFC interface. CCMS performs monitoring at the four layers already mentioned, because its aim is to centralize the management/monitoring of a particular R/3 system in a single tool.

In getting information from CCMS, the Tivoli Manager for R/3 also permits some monitoring at the four layers. For the network, operating system and database layer, it can be redundant with the monitoring capability offered by the other products designed for each of the layers. For example, the Manager for R/3 provides a monitor for the average load (5 min); the same monitor is provided by Tivoli Distributed Monitoring.

The advantage of using the different products is that you can use the complete monitoring capability for each layer. Moreover, it is always better to get the information directly at the layer level and not through an upper layer level. For example if a function module of CCMS encounters a problem when getting information on the free tablespace of the Oracle database, you will miss this alert through the Tivoli Manager for R/3 but not if you were monitoring the database through the Tivoli Manager for Oracle. Moreover

CCMS does not always provide current information since the collector program runs certain checks only at specified hourly intervals.

In a small environment, using only Tivoli Manager for R/3 can provide you with sufficient monitoring for all layers without the work and cost of setting up Tivoli NetView and the Tivoli Manager for the database (Tivoli Distributed Monitoring is still required for the functioning of Tivoli Manager for R/3).

In this scenario, we assume that we are in a large environment, where the use of the different Tivoli products is a real plus. When duplicate monitoring capability occurs, we use the most appropriate product to get the information.

5.2.2.1 Network Layer

The client/server architecture of R/3 is composed of the database server, the application servers and the presentation clients. The external communication between these components is based on TCP/IP. In all client/server systems, the network is one of the critical elements.

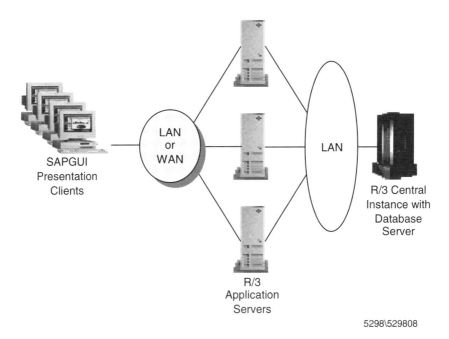

5298\529808

Figure 166. Typical R/3 Topology

Tivoli NetView allows you to closely manage/monitor all elements of the network, such as routers, bridges, hubs, switches, etc. NetView is based on SNMP, on top of TCP/IP. The monitoring capability consists of SNMP traps sent by the critical components of the network to the NetView server. It also consists of getting information from the SNMP MIB of these components through a polling process initiated by the NetView server. Tivoli NetView has its own console, centralizing all traps and pertinent information, but you can configure it in order to forward selected traps and messages to the Tivoli Enterprise Console.

This is what we advise in this scenario: forwarding the most critical information to TEC, our focal point for the monitoring that allows us to correlate all events coming from different sources. This most critical information must reveal problems for the communication between the three components of the R/3 systems (database, application and presentation) and will depend on the topology of the network.

For example, we advise monitoring the availability of the servers running the databases and the SAP instances (availability means here that we can ping the IP address of the interfaces), the availability of the routers and bridges that play a significant role in the topology and the network collisions.

5.2.2.2 Operating System Layer
Database servers and application servers typically run on operating systems such as UNIX, AS/400 and Windows NT. Tivoli Distributed Monitoring provides many monitors for operating systems. Here is the list of critical items that we identified to monitor on SAP servers. In this scenario, we assume that the SAP servers have UNIX as the operating system and Oracle as the database.

1. File systems that must not fill up:
   - /oracle/<SID>/saparch
   - /sapmnt/<SID>
   - /usr/sap/<SID>
   - /usr/sap/trans

2. Processes that must run:
   - saposcol
   - Minimum number of work processes
   - SQL*NET V1 or V2 listener (orasrv or tnslsnr)

3. The swap space

4. The average load (15 minutes)

5. The error report (permanent hardware errors)

6. The status of the print queues to which the SAP print jobs are sent

Except for the error report, we advise monitoring these items using Tivoli Distributed Monitoring monitors, specifying Send Enterprise Console Event as the action to be taken when a threshold is exceeded.

Monitoring the error report has to be done through the Tivoli logfile adapter. The adapter will format the new errors coming in from the error report into TEC events and send them to the TEC server. You can configure the adapter to filter the events you want to send, for example, the permanent hardware errors. We won't go into details about how to setup this monitoring but we refer you to the *Tivoli Enterprise Console Adapters Guide*.

5.2.2.3 Database Layer

R/3 supports different relational database systems such as Oracle, Informix, DB2, Adabas or MS SQL Server. Our scenario focuses on Oracle databases. We identified the following important items to be monitored at the database level:

1. The RDBMS status (ability to connect to the instance)

2. The free space in the tablespaces

3. Missing indices

4. The free space required for the next extent of a segment

5. The number of extents which can still be allocated before reaching the maximum extents limit

6. The free space fragmentation index for all tablespaces

Except for missing indices, this monitoring can be easily set up by using the Tivoli Manager for Oracle that provides a wide range of Tivoli Distributed Monitoring monitors especially for databases.

Missing indices must be monitored using the Tivoli Manager for R/3. This monitor triggers when the physical database schema does not correspond to the logical data model stored in R/3.

5.2.2.4 Application Layer

For this layer, we identified the following list:

1. The SAP status

2. The enqueue table filling up

3. Errors generated in ABAP update processes

4. Errors generated in ABAP background processes

5. Errors generated in ABAP dialog processes

6. SQL errors generated in ABAP programs

7. The system log (SYSLOG)

Tivoli Manager for R/3 brings us the ability to monitor these items. As explained in the previous chapter the monitoring capability of this product is based on event adapters reading the MIB interfaces and Tivoli Distributed Monitoring monitors.

We have full control of the Tivoli Distributed Monitoring monitors as we can choose which one we want to use. For the event adapter, it is rather different. Indeed, when you enable the event adapter, it reads everything that is placed by CCMS on the MIB interface and sends the information to the TEC server without providing a filtering capability with the current version.

It results in many messages arriving at the TEC console, critical or not. In our scenario, we want to have full control of what we monitor and we advise the following bypass in order to achieve this full control. We filter the events on the TEC server by deleting the uninteresting event classes from the rule base. When events of these classes arrive in the reception engine, it will not validate them and they will be dropped. This is not an optimal solution as the filtering is not performed locally on the application server itself.

We also want to have full control of the syslog messages that can appear in the console. Therefore, we have to configure the system log in R/3 in order to specify which kinds of messages (syslog IDs) are alertable, and thus can be seen through Tivoli.

5.2.3 Results

In this section we give concrete recommendations on which monitors to use for specific environments and how to set up profile managers and profiles.

5.2.3.1 Tivoli Distributed Monitoring Monitors

Several monitors that have to be created depend on the R/3 system you want to monitor (SID, number of work processes defined, etc.). Therefore, we group our monitors per R/3 system in a profile manager that we name Critical Monitoring <SID>_PM. In an environment where R/3 systems are monitored through Tivoli you find several kinds of endpoints to which the monitors must be distributed.

Monitors provided by the Tivoli Manager for R/3 are distributed to SAP Instances. Monitors provided by the Tivoli Manager for Oracle are distributed to Oracle databases or to Oracle instances. Standard Tivoli Distributed Monitors are usually distributed to Managed Nodes. But you must also consider that some of your standard Tivoli Distributed Monitoring monitors must be distributed to Managed Nodes that are application servers and others to Managed Nodes that are databases servers. To cover all these cases we create five profile managers that contain the different endpoints and that will be used as subscribers of our sentry profiles.

- SAP_INST-<SID>_PM contains all SAP instances in the <SID> R/3 system.

- ORA_DB-<SID>_PM contains all Oracle databases in the <SID> R/3 system.

- ORA_INST-<SID>_PM contains all Oracle instances in the <SID> R/3 system.

- APP_MN-<SID>_PM contains all Managed Nodes that are application servers in the <SID> R/3 system.

- DB_MN-<SID>_PM contains all Managed Nodes that are database servers in the <SID> R/3 system.

We create the corresponding Tivoli Distributed Monitoring profiles to structure our monitors following the different layers previously described and that have to be distributed to the profile managers mentioned above.

- SAP-SAP_INST-<SID>_SP for the SAP monitors that have to be distributed to the SAP instances.

- DB-ORA_DB-<SID>_SP for the database monitors that have to be distributed to Oracle databases.

- DB-ORA_INST-<SID>_SP for the database monitors that have to be distributed to Oracle instances.

- OS-APP_MN-<SID>_SP for the operating system monitors that have to be distributed to application server Managed Nodes.

- OS-DB_MN-<SID>_SP for the operating system monitors that have to be distributed to database server Managed Nodes.

From the above, you can hopefully see the significant role of a naming convention. Figure 167 on page 235 shows you all these objects for the R/3 system IBM.

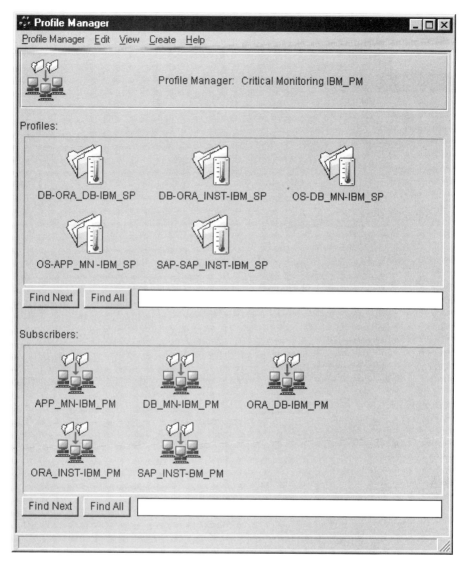

Figure 167. Profile Managers and Tivoli Distributed Monitoring Profiles Created

For each of the Tivoli Distributed Monitoring profiles, here is the complete description of the monitors we created, for the monitoring of our IBM R/3 system.

OS-APP_MN-IBM_SP Tivoli Distributed Profile

Monitoring the minimum number of work processes:

Table 7. Work Processes

Collection	Universal
Source	Application instances
Attribute	dw.sapIBM_DVEBMGS00
Schedule Frequency	15 minutes

Severity	Trigger When	Action
Critical	Decreases below 9	TEC event with CRITICAL severity
Warning	Increases beyond 8	TEC event with HARMLESS severity

Monitoring the swap space:

Table 8. Swap Space

Collection	Unix_Sentry
Source	Available swap space
Attribute	
Schedule Frequency	15 minutes

Severity	Trigger When	Action
Critical	Decreases below 5 Mbytes	TEC event with CRITICAL severity
Severe	Decreases below 10 Mbytes	TEC event with WARNING severity
Warning	Increases beyond 9 Mbytes	TEC event with HARMLESS severity

Monitoring the saposcol process:

Table 9. Saposcol

Collection	Unix_Sentry
Source	Daemon status
Attribute	saposcol
Schedule Frequency	15 minutes

Severity	Trigger When	Action
Critical	Becomes unavailable	TEC event with CRITICAL severity

Severity	Trigger When	Action
Warning	Becomes available	TEC event with HARMLESS severity

Monitoring the load average:

Table 10. Load Average

Collection	Unix_Sentry
Source	Load average (fifteen minutes)
Attribute	
Schedule Frequency	15 minutes

Severity	Trigger When	Action
Critical	Increases beyond 5 ready jobs	TEC event with CRITICAL severity
Warning	Decreases below 6 ready jobs	TEC event with HARMLESS severity

Monitoring the /sapmnt/<SID> filesystem:

Table 11. /sapmnt/<SID> Filesystem

Collection	Universal
Source	Percent space in use
Attribute	/sapmnt/IBM
Schedule Frequency	15 minutes

Severity	Trigger When	Action
Critical	Increases beyond 95%	TEC event with CRITICAL severity
Severe	Increases beyond 90%	TEC event with WARNING severity
Warning	Decreases below 91%	TEC event with HARMLESS severity

Monitoring the /usr/sap/trans filesystem:

Table 12. /usr/sap/trans Filesystem

Collection	Universal
Source	Percent space in use
Attribute	/usr/sap/trans
Schedule Frequency	15 minutes

Severity	Trigger When	Action
Critical	Increases beyond 95%	TEC event with CRITICAL severity
Severe	Increases beyond 90%	TEC event with WARNING severity
Warning	Decreases below 91%	TEC event with HARMLESS severity

Monitoring the /usr/sap/<SID> filesystem:

Table 13. /usr/sap/<SID> Filesystem

Collection	Universal
Source	Percent space in use
Attribute	/usr/sap/IBM
Schedule Frequency	15 minutes

Severity	Trigger When	Action
Critical	Increases beyond 95%	TEC event with CRITICAL severity
Severe	Increases beyond 90%	TEC event with WARNING severity
Warning	Decreases below 91%	TEC event with HARMLESS severity

Monitoring the status of a print queue:

Table 14. Print Queue

Collection	Unix_Sentry
Source	Status of print queue
Attribute	sapq
Schedule Frequency	15 minutes

Severity	Trigger When	Action
Critical	Becomes unavailable	TEC event with CRITICAL severity
Warning	Becomes available	TEC event with HARMLESS severity

OS-DB_MN-IBM_SP Tivoli Distributed Monitoring Profile

Monitoring the SQL*NET listener:

Table 15. Orasrv

Collection	Unix_Sentry
Source	Daemon status
Attribute	orasrv
Schedule Frequency	15 minutes

Severity	Trigger When	Action
Critical	Becomes unavailable	TEC event with CRITICAL severity
Warning	Becomes available	TEC event with HARMLESS severity

Monitoring the saparch filesystem:

Table 16. /oracle/<SID>/saparch Filesystem

Collection	Universal
Source	Percent space in use
Attribute	/oracle/IBM/saparch
Schedule Frequency	15 minutes

Severity	Trigger When	Action
Critical	Increases beyond 95%	TEC event with CRITICAL severity
Severe	Increases beyond 90%	TEC event with WARNING severity
Warning	Decreases below 91%	TEC event with HARMLESS severity

DB-ORA_DB-IBM_SP Tivoli Distributed Monitoring Profile

Monitoring the free space required for the next extent of a segment:

Table 17. Free Space Deficit

Collection	OracleDatabase
Source	Free Space Deficit
Attribute	No, No
Schedule Frequency	30 minutes

Severity	Trigger When	Action
Critical	Decreases below 2 equity	TEC event with CRITICAL severity
Severe	Decreases below 5 equity	TEC event with WARNING severity
Warning	Increases beyond 4 equity	TEC event with HARMLESS severity

Monitoring the free space fragmentation index for all tablespaces:

Table 18. Free Space Fragmentation

Collection	OracleDatabase
Source	Free Space Fragmentation
Attribute	No
Schedule Frequency	1 day

Severity	Trigger When	Action
Critical	Decreases below 10 FSFI	TEC event with CRITICAL severity
Severe	Decreases below 20 FSFI	TEC event with WARNING severity
Warning	Increases beyond 19 FSFI	TEC event with HARMLESS severity

Monitoring the free space in the tablespaces:

Table 19. Free Tablespace

Collection	OracleDatabase
Source	Free Tablespace
Attribute	No, No
Schedule Frequency	15 minutes

Severity	Trigger When	Action
Critical	Decreases below 5%	TEC event with CRITICAL severity
Severe	Decreases below 10%	TEC event with WARNING severity
Warning	Increases beyond 9%	TEC event with HARMLESS severity

Monitoring the number of extents which can still be allocated before reaching the maximum extents limit:

Table 20. Maximum Extents

Collection	OracleDatabase
Source	Maximum Extents
Attribute	No, No
Schedule Frequency	1 hour

Severity	Trigger When	Action
Critical	Decreases below 1 extent	TEC event with CRITICAL severity
Severe	Decreases below 3 extents	TEC event with WARNING severity
Warning	Increases beyond 2 extents	TEC event with HARMLESS severity

5.2.3.2 DB-ORA_INST-IBM_SP Tivoli Distributed Monitoring Profile

Monitoring the ability to connect to the instance:

Table 21. RDBMS State

Collection	OracleInstance
Source	RDBMS State
Attribute	
Schedule Frequency	15 minutes

Severity	Trigger When	Action
Critical	Becomes unavailable	TEC event with CRITICAL severity
Warning	Becomes available	TEC event with HARMLESS severity

SAP-SAP_INST-IBM_SP Tivoli Distributed Monitoring Profile

Monitoring the SAP status:

Table 22. SAP System Availability

Collection	IBM Server Remote Monitors
Source	SAP System Availability
Attribute	
Schedule Frequency	2 minutes

Severity	Trigger When	Action
Critical	Becomes unavailable	TEC event with FATAL severity
Warning	Becomes available	TEC event with HARMLESS severity

> **Note**
>
> The user and group ID of a Tivoli Distributed Monitoring profile determines the operating system context under which the monitors contained in the profile are executed. Do not forget to specify these for each profile. You must specify an operating system user that is in the Edit Logins list of a Tivoli administrator that has the right TMR role for executing the monitors.
>
> The Tivoli Distributed Monitoring engine has a timeout value of one minute, so ensure that any monitors you run will complete within this time frame. To see if this is true, run them and watch the SentryStatus notices.

5.2.3.3 TEC Event Server

As previously stated, the TEC event server must be reconfigured to restrict the alerts coming to it from the event adapters running on each application server. In our rule base, we deleted all leaf event classes specified in the tecad.baroc file except for the following:

SAP_ALERT_SAPSysUp (the application server has been started)

SAP_ALERT_SAPSysDown (the application server has been stopped)

SAP_ALERT_SlogId (an alertable syslog message has been generated) and SAP_ALERT_SLOG_ID (drill-down)

SAP_ALERT_SlogFreq (an excessive number of syslog messages have been generated) and SAP_ALERT_SLOG_FREQ (drill-down)

SAP_ALERT_Enqueue (the enqueue table is filling up) and
SAP_ALERT_ENQU_ENQ (drill-down)

- SAP_ALERT_AbapUpd (an occured in an ABAP update process) and
  SAP_ALERT_ABAP_VB (drill-down)

- SAP_ALERT_AbapErr (an error occured in an ABAP dialog or background
  process) and SAP_ALERT_ABAP_ERR (drill-down)

- SAP_ALERT_AbapSql (an SQL error occured in an ABAP) and
  SAP_ALERT_ABAP_SQL (drill-down)

- SAP_ALERT_DbIndcs (a required index is missing in the database) and
  SAP_ALERT_DB_INDICES (drill-down)

- AMS_R3MONITOR_ALERT (a Manager for R/3 monitor has encountered
  an error)

- AMS_WR3MIB_PROCESS_ALERT (alert control or alert reader process
  has encountered an error)

- Heartbeat_event

For the configuration of SysLog alerts, we refer you to 4.1.5, "SYSLOG
Configuration" on page 175. We also advise importing the rule developed in
5.1.2.4, "Creating a TEC Rule to Reformat the Event Message" on page 221.
This rule will reformat any Distributed Monitoring message in order to get the
pertinent information displayed on the console.

5.3 Monitoring SAP R/3 Using a Standard Numeric Script Monitor

In this section we show how to monitor a SAP R/3 system using a Numeric
Script monitor from the Universal monitoring collection in Tivoli Distributed
Monitoring. Unlike the previous example, we don't use MCSL here to create
our custom monitor but instead just use a standard monitor provided by Tivoli
Distributed Monitoring.

5.3.1 Overview

In 5.1, "Creating a Custom SAP Monitor" on page 213 we described how to
create a SAP custom monitor by using the `mcsl` command. The monitor
developed in 5.1, "Creating a Custom SAP Monitor" on page 213
communicates with SAP R/3 instances through the wr3rfc command provided
by Tivoli Manager for R/3. In this section, we take another approach for
adding a monitor by making use of the Universal collection Numeric Script
monitor which is provided by Tivoli Distributed Monitoring.

The way to communicate with the SAP R/3 instance is also via wr3rfc provided by Tivoli Manager for R/3 which is the same as that described in 5.1, "Creating a Custom SAP Monitor" on page 213. Thus, we don't describe how wr3rfc communicates with SAP R/3. Please refer to 5.1, "Creating a Custom SAP Monitor" on page 213 for details.

Here, we create our own remote function module named Z_KUB_RS1, which monitors the response time for querying the table BSEG. There is no specific intention for the monitoring contents or in selecting this table. The aim of this section is to show the process to add your own Numeric Script monitor of the universal monitoring collection which invokes your own remote function module or other remote function module, if any, through wr3rfc. You may be able to create your String Script monitor of the Universal monitoring collection in the same way as described in this section.

5.3.2 Steps Needed to Add the Numeric Script Monitor

You need to follow the steps below:

1. Identify what you need to monitor in your SAP R/3 system. Here, it is to monitor the query response time for a table access. It should return the response time, if possible.

2. Look for appropriate function modules which are provided by SAP or other vendors. If you cannot find one, you need to create an ABAP/4 program which collects data from the SAP R/3 instance. Here, we create a simple ABAP/4 program which queries the table using a select statement.

3. Identify the import/export parameters that the remote function module provides, or define them in the SE37 transaction.

4. Develop your script which invokes the wr3rfc command.

5. Create your rfc_interface file which defines your remote function module name and import/export parameters.

6. Add a Numeric Script monitor of the Universal monitoring collection in Tivoli Distributed Monitoring. You can optionally specify to send an event to TEC. You must define your monitoring threshold in advance.

7. Distribute the monitor to your SAP R/3 machine; here, this is Silver.

8. Perform production monitoring using your monitor.

5.3.3 Details of Customization

In this section we show the scripts we use for our monitoring example.

5.3.3.1 Function Module Z_KUB_RS1

```
FUNCTION Z_KUB_RS1.
*"----------------------------------------------------------------------
*"*"Local interface:
*"      EXPORTING
*"          VALUE(RESPONSE_TIME) LIKE  SY-UZEIT
*"----------------------------------------------------------------------
DATA: START_TIME LIKE SY-UZEIT,
   PROCESS_TIME LIKE SY-UZEIT,
   END_TIME LIKE SY-UZEIT.
TABLES: BSEG.
DATA:     BEGIN OF INT_TAB OCCURS 1000.
       INCLUDE STRUCTURE BSEG.
DATA:     END OF INT_TAB.
GET TIME.
START_TIME = SY-UZEIT.
WRITE / 'Start of Module' .
WRITE / START_TIME.
SELECT * FROM BSEG INTO TABLE INT_TAB.
GET TIME.
END_TIME = SY-UZEIT.
WRITE / END_TIME.
IF END_TIME > START_TIME.
   PROCESS_TIME = END_TIME - START_TIME.
   ELSE.
     WRITE /  'In the else'.
     PROCESS_TIME = '240000'.
     PROCESS_TIME = PROCESS_TIME - START_TIME.
     PROCESS_TIME = PROCESS_TIME + END_TIME.
   ENDIF.
WRITE / PROCESS_TIME.
RESPONSE_TIME = PROCESS_TIME.

ENDFUNCTION.
```

Figure 168. ABAP/4 Program for Checking Table Availability

Figure 168 on page 245 shows the ABAP/4 program list we used. This program just queries the BSEG table and returns the response time calculated from the time obtained by GET TIME ABAP statement. The result is stored in the export parameter RESPONSE_TIME.

In creating the function module, don't forget to specify the **Remote Function Call supported** option in the administration data panel as shown in Figure 169 on page 246.

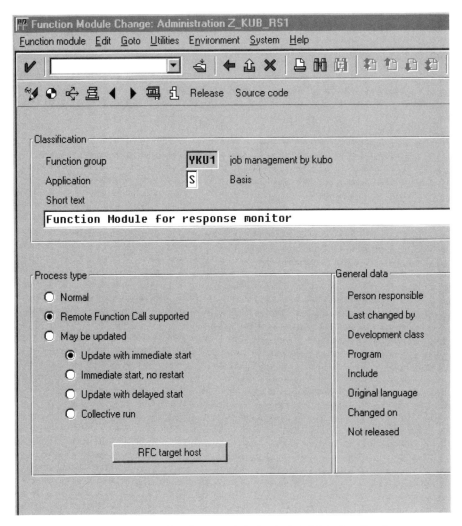

Figure 169. Remote Function Call Supported Option in Administration Panel

We must define the export parameter as shown in Figure 170 on page 247.

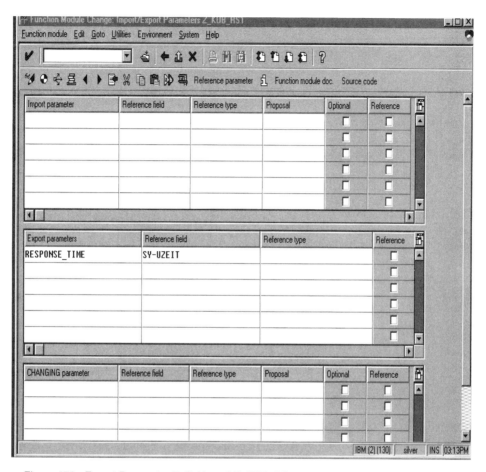

Figure 170. Export Parameter Definition of Z_KUB_RS1

We recommend that you have your remote function module tested on the SAP instance as described in 5.1, "Creating a Custom SAP Monitor" on page 213. Here, we show the result of the test in Figure 171 on page 248. This shows that the export parameter has a value of 000003. The Numeric Script monitor makes use of this value.

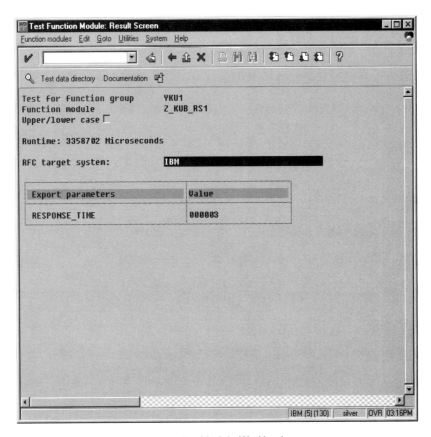

Figure 171. Test of Remote Function Module We Used

5.3.3.2 Numeric Script

The role of Numeric Script monitor is to be launched by the Tivoli Distributed Monitoring engine periodically and return the appropriate numeric value to stdout.

```
#!/bin/ksh
. /etc/Tivoli/setup_env.sh
cd /usr/local/Tivoli/bin/generic_unix/TME/SAP/IBM/rfc
/usr/local/Tivoli/bin/generic_unix/TME/SAP/IBM/rfc/wr3rfc /usr/local/Tivoli/bin/generic_unix/TME/SAP/IBM/rfc/Z_KUB_RS1
exit 0
```

Figure 172. Numeric Script

Figure 172 on page 248 shows our numeric script. This script invokes wr3rfc using the rfc_interface file named Z_KUB_RS1.

5.3.3.3 Create Your Interface File for the wr3rfc Command

Figure 173 on page 249 shows the interface file named Z_KUB_RS1 which we use. We specify the FORMAT option not as VERBOSE but as RESULT because we don't need additional shell coding by using this option. This figure also shows the test result of executing the wr3rfc Z_KUB_RS1 command at the command prompt.

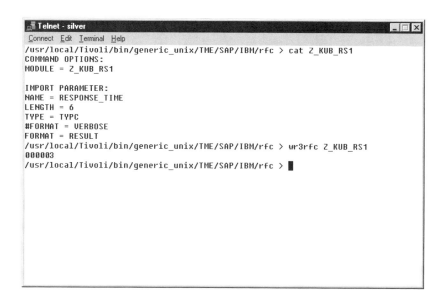

Figure 173. wr3rfc Command Interface File

5.3.3.4 Adding the Numeric Script Monitor to Your Profile

In the Add Monitor window, you have to choose the Numeric Script monitor from the list of the Universal monitoring collection. Then you can specify the numeric value that is taken as a threshold value by the monitor with an appropriate scheduling interval time in the Edit Monitor window as shown in Figure 174 on page 250. After distributing the monitor to the host where the wr3rfc command is run, it invokes the remote function module periodically.

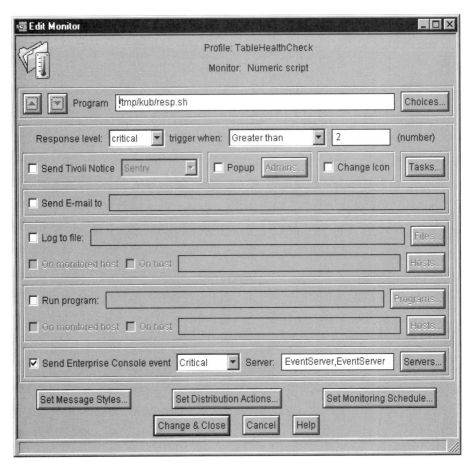

Figure 174. Edit Monitor Window of Tivoli Distributed Monitoring

In this section, we briefly showed how to make use of the Numeric Script monitor in combination with the wr3rfc command. The same approach can be taken to define your String Script monitor.

5.4 Interconnected TMRs

In this section, we discuss how Tivoli Manager for R/3 Version 1.5 behaves in an interconnected TMR design. This design if often employed in large environments, such as in outsourcing environments.

5.4.1 Overview

Another typical environment that you can find in the real world is the managomont of oyotcmo with interconnected TMRs. The aim of such a design is to manage several systems in a common way, from the first level TMR (also referred to as master TMR or focal TMR). The added value of such a solution is not only to have a common and easy way to manage a large number of different systems plugged into the first level TMR, but also to provide a reusable system management architecture for each new system you want to manage.

Managing a system through an interconnected TMR environment means, for example, distributing a Tivoli Distributed Monitoring profile created in the upper TMR, to the Managed Nodes or TMAs of the lower TMRs, or sending alerts from the lower TMR machines directly to the TEC server installed in the first level TMR.

Normally, you create your Tivoli objects, such as monitors, tasks and file packages in the upper TMR and you use them with endpoints defined in the lower TMRs. All the administration is done through the desktop of the upper TMR. For the book, we set up our environment in a way that reflects an interconnected TMR architecture.

The purpose of this scenario, even if Tivoli Manager for R/3 Version 1.5 does not support fully transparent cross-TMR management, is to show the level of support provided by the product for useful and meaningful management actions.

5.4.2 Technical Details

In this section we discuss some of the specific behavior in an interconnected TMR design.

5.4.2.1 Using the Navigator

Using the Navigator in an interconnected TMR environment allows you to directly open policy regions, profile managers, etc. from a remote TMR, without opening a second desktop. Normally, the purpose of an interconnected TMR architecture as described in the overview is to perform all management actions from the upper TMR desktop only. But the Tivoli Manager for R/3 must be installed and configured in the TMR where the SAP Managed Nodes reside, which means in the lower TMRs. The objects, such as monitors and tasks are created only there, which is why the navigator is useful here.

Editing SAP monitors from remote Tivoli Distributed Monitoring profiles and changing their customized settings can be done through the navigator. You can add new monitors or delete some. You can also distribute remote Tivoli Distributed Monitoring profiles to remote SAP instances.

Executing SAP tasks from remote task libraries won't succeed because you cannot assign the required TMR roles for these tasks (<SystemLabel>_admin and <SystemLabel>_super) to your upper TMR administrator. Indeed, these roles are not available even after an update of resources. The solution is to create manually the roles on the upper TMR, using Tivoli commands, as shown below. In our example, the System Label is IBM. You must run these commands on the upper TMR server, logged as an operating system user corresponding to the main Tivoli administrator:

```
AO='wlookup Administrators'
ROLE=IBM_admin
idlcall "AO" add_supported_role \"""ROLE\"""
idlcall "AO" add_supported_tmr_role \""ROLE\""
```

Then, using the Tivoli GUI, you can assign these two new roles to the upper TMR's main Tivoli administrator. You must repeat this for all the R/3 systems you have in the lower TMRs. Then the execution of the SAP tasks, such as stopping an event adapter, stopping SAP, etc. will work through the navigator.

Through the navigator, you can also go to remote file packages you have created in the remote TMRs for the distribution of the SAPGUI. You can edit and update the file packages and distribute them to remote Managed Nodes or TMAs.

5.4.2.2 SAPGUI File Package Creation and Configuration
It is possible to create a SAPGUI file package in the upper TMR that we can distribute to endpoints of the lower TMRs. Therefore, you must install the module on the upper TMR and configure it for a virtual R/3 system. As the System Label must be unique across the interconnected TMRs you cannot use the same one for your lower TMRs. Then you dispose of tasks and jobs that enable you to create file packages for the SAPGUI distribution. You will have to modify the distribution scripts in order to create the right icon for the R/3 server you want to access and not the wrong virtual R/3 system of the upper TMR.

5.4.2.3 Tasks/Jobs Execution and Monitors
SAP tasks and monitoring collections are related to the System Label (corresponding to the SID) of the R/3 system. Each time you configure a new R/3 system, you create new monitoring collections and new tasks. The

System Label must be unique across the interconnected TMRs, so you cannot configure the module for virtual R/3 systems on the upper TMR with the same System Label as those of your lower TMRs. So, creating SAP monitors or executing SAP tasks/jobs locally on the upper TMR (not through the navigator) is really impossible.

5.4.2.4 Send SAP Events to a TEC Server in Another TMR

One of the limitations of the current version of the Tivoli Manager for R/3 is that a TEC server must be located in the Tivoli region where the SAP managed nodes reside. This TEC server has to be configured to receive the wr3mib and wr3rfc events coming from the R/3 machines and act on them (drill-down, alert control, etc.).

Eventually, it can be configured to forward the events to a TEC server residing in an interconnected TMR, the upper TMR for instance. In the architecture described in this scenario, we would like to have only one TEC server residing in the upper region.

The limitation is due to the alert reader process (drill-down), the alert control process and the way Tivoli Distributed Monitoring monitors are coded. Indeed, the alert reader scripts are coded in order to send events to the local TEC server only. In case of problems during the execution of Tivoli Distributed Monitoring monitors or alert reader and control scripts, events are generated and sent to the local TEC server. Another limitation are the roles needed in order to execute the alert reader and control tasks from the upper TMR.

The solution we propose here offers a bypass of these limitations and allows you to have only one TEC server in the upper region. We assume in this scenario that there is only one lower region.

1. Configuring the event server in the upper region

The first step is to configure the event server of the upper region. To do this, you must first install the Tivoli Manager for R/3 on the upper TMR and TEC servers. Then, configure the event server for the Tivoli Manager for R/3, by executing the job Configure Event Server for R/3. To perform this, follow the next steps:

- Open the Tivoli desktop (main administrator) of the upper TMR server and double-click on the **AMS Module for R/3** policy region.

- Double-click on the **AMS Module for R/3 Utilities** task library and then on the job **Configure Event Server for R/3**. You will get a window as shown in Figure 175 on page 254.

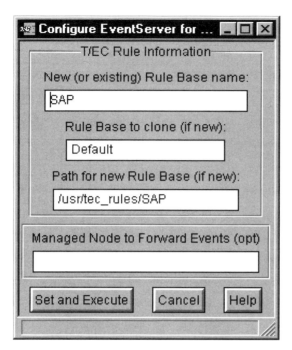

Figure 175. Configure the Upper Event Server

Enter your parameters and click on the **Set and Execute** button.

2. Configuring the Manager for R/3 event adapters in the lower regions

The second step is to configure the event adapters provided by the Tivoli Manager for R/3, to make them send the events to the TEC server of the upper region. You must do this configuration for each R/3 application server you manage in your lower region. To do it, follow the next steps:

- Open the main Tivoli desktop of the lower TMR server and double-click on the **AMS Module for R/3** policy region.

- Double-click on the **AMS Module for R/3 Utilities** task library and then on the job **Configure Event Adapter**. You will get a window as shown in Figure 176 on page 255.

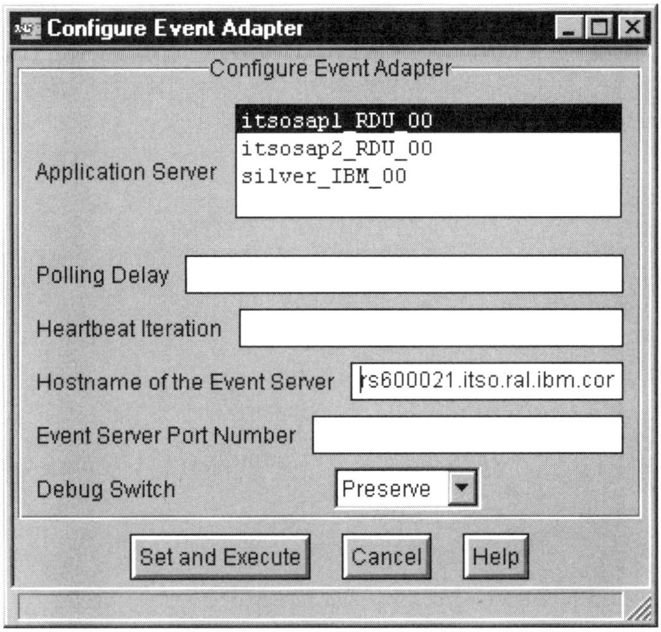

Figure 176. Configure Event Adapter

From the Application Server area, select your R/3 application server, and give the hostname of your upper TMR's TEC server in the Hostname of the Event Server field. In our example, we are giving the hostname of the upper TMR server which also runs the TEC server. Then, press the **Set and Execute** button.

Repeat the operation for all application servers shown in the Application Server area.

Do not forget to stop and re-start all event adapters.

At this point of the procedure, the MIB events are sent to the upper TMR's TEC server, but the alert reader and alert control process cannot be done. Indeed, even if the scripts called by the TEC rules (sap_alert_reader_cb.sh and sap_alert_control_cb.sh) are present in the upper TEC server, after having installed the Tivoli Manager for R/3, the main administrator of the upper TMR does not have the appropriate roles to run these scripts that execute the alert_reader and alert_control tasks.

3. Creating the missing roles in the upper TMR

The roles required to run these scripts and execute these tasks are the <SystemLabel>_admin and <SystemLabel>_super roles. These roles are set to the lower TMR main administrator because the Tivoli Manager for R/3 is installed and configured there.

Even after updating the resources between the two interconnected TMRs, you don't dispose of these roles in the upper TMR. As already described for the navigator, the solution is to create manually the roles in the upper region, using Tivoli commands. Repeat the following for each System Label:

```
AO='wlookup Administrators'
ROLE=<SystemLabel>_admin
idlcall "AO" add_supported_role \"""ROLE\"""
idlcall "AO" add_supported_tmr_role \""ROLE\""
```

Repeat the operation with the ROLE variable set to <SystemLabel>_super.

Then, using the Tivoli GUI, you can give these new roles to the upper TMR's main administrator.

At this point, the sap_alert_reader_cb.sh and sap_alert_control_cb.sh scripts can be run and the alert_reader and alert_control tasks residing in the lower TMR server can be executed. Two scripts correspond to these two tasks: sap_alert_reader.sh and sap_alert_control.sh. When executing the tasks, these scripts are copied on the application server and then run. They are coded to send events to the local TEC server but we would like to send them to the TEC residing in the remote region.

4. Modifying the alert control and reader scripts

We must modify the following scripts:

1. sap_alert_reader_cb.sh and sap_alert_control_cb.sh residing in the upper TEC server in the $BINDIR/TME/TEC/scripts directory

2. sap_alert_reader.sh and sap_alert_control.sh residing on the lower TMR server in the $BINDIR/../generic_unix/TME/SAP/<SystemLabel>/sh directory. They have to be modified for each R/3 system (so in each <SystemLabel> directory.

We must export the object ID of the name registry of the upper TMR in the first two scripts and use it in the other scripts to locate the event server. Update the scripts as follows:

- sap_alert_reader_cb.sh and sap_alert_control.sh

   Add the following lines to the script before using the wruntask command, as shown in Figure 177 on page 257.

```
TNR='wlookup NameRegistry'
```

```
export TNR
```

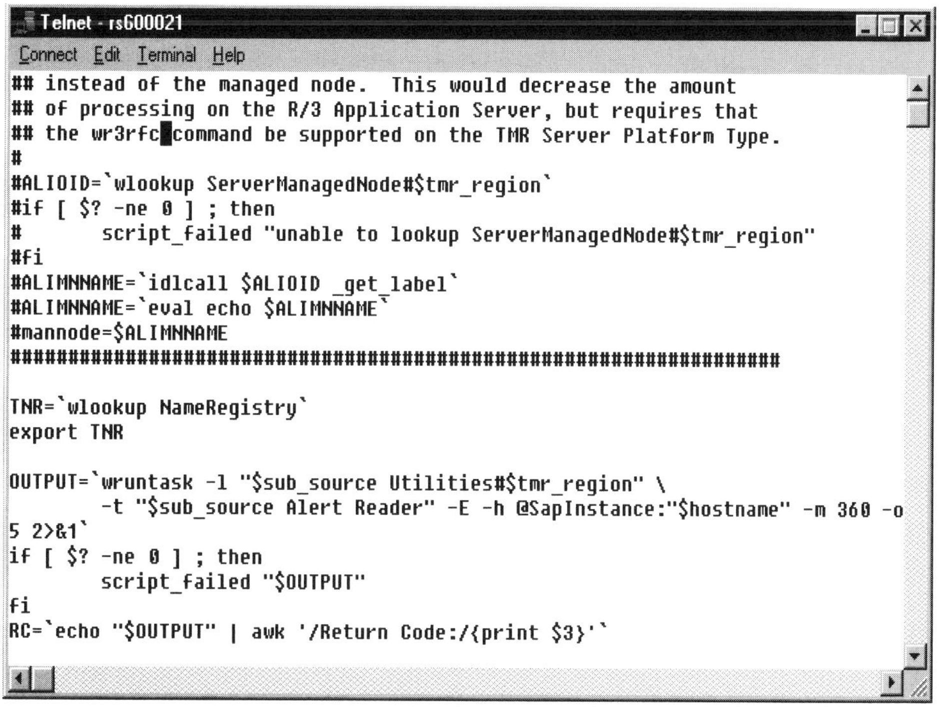

```
Telnet - rs600021

Connect  Edit  Terminal  Help
## instead of the managed node.  This would decrease the amount
## of processing on the R/3 Application Server, but requires that
## the wr3rfc▮command be supported on the TMR Server Platform Type.
#
#ALIOID=`wlookup ServerManagedNode#$tmr_region`
#if [ $? -ne 0 ] ; then
#       script_failed "unable to lookup ServerManagedNode#$tmr_region"
#fi
#ALIMNNAME=`idlcall $ALIOID _get_label`
#ALIMNNAME=`eval echo $ALIMNNAME`
#mannode=$ALIMNNAME
####################################################################

TNR=`wlookup NameRegistry`
export TNR

OUTPUT=`wruntask -l "$sub_source Utilities#$tmr_region" \
        -t "$sub_source Alert Reader" -E -h @SapInstance:"$hostname" -m 360 -o
5 2>&1`
if [ $? -ne 0 ] ; then
        script_failed "$OUTPUT"
fi
RC=`echo "$OUTPUT" | awk '/Return Code:/{print $3}'`
```

Figure 177. sap_alert_reader_cb.sh Script

- sap_alert_reader.sh and sap_alert_control.sh

  Replace the TNR definition with the following lines, as shown in Figure 178 on page 258. Repeat this for each R/3 system.

  ```
  if [ "$TNR" = "" ]; then
  TNR=`wlookup NameRegistry`
  fi
  ```

```
Telnet - rs600032                                                    _ □ X
Connect  Edit  Terminal  Help

#BINDIR=`echo $PATH | awk -F: '{print $1}' | sed 's,/bin$,,'`
EVENTFILE=${TMP}/sap_alert_reader.$$
SAPDIR=$BINDIR/../generic_unix/TME/SAP

if [ "$TNR" = "" ]; then
TNR=`wlookup NameRegistry`
fi

ES=`idlcall $TNR local_lookup '"EventServer" "EventServer"'`
EUS=`idlarg 1 $ES`

# all of the event variables are in the process environment because
# we are being called from a script that called the wruntask with the
# -E option to pass the process environment
if [ -z "$r3alertAgentHostName" ] ; then
        echo "this task may only be executed from the T/EC" >&2
        script_failed "this task may only be executed from the T/EC"
fi

if [ "$r3alertSystemNumber" -lt 10 ] ; then
        r3alertSystemNumber=`expr $r3alertSystemNumber + 0`
        r3alertSystemNumber="0$r3alertSystemNumber"
```

Figure 178. sap_alert_reader.sh Script

To make the changes to the sap_alert_reader.sh and sap_alert_control.sh
scripts effective in the corresponding tasks, you have to edit the tasks and
re-fill the field with the script paths. You have to do this for each R/3 system.

At this point, everything is set up correctly to send the MIB events directly to
the upper TEC server and this server can perform the drill-down process and
the alert control process.

Sending events from the SAP sentry monitors to the upper TEC server can be
done by specifying the right TEC server to send events to in the monitors
properties. But when they encounter a problem, these monitors are coded to
send an event to the local TEC. This non-critical limitation is difficult to
bypass. One solution, if you really want to be able to get these error alerts in
the upper TEC, is to modify the two csl files provided by the module, just after
installation. Indeed, it is only when the R/3 systems are configured that the
monitoring collections are created. So you can modify these files
(sap_central_server.csl and sap_remote_server.csl), which reside in the

$BINDIR/../generic_unix/TME/SAP/2.2C/csl directory on the lower TMR server. For example for each monitor you can hard code the TNR object ID of the upper TMR.

5.4.3 Results

In conclusion, we can say that although the Tivoli Manager for R/3 Version 1.5 does not directly support interconnected TMR designs, it can still be used efficiently in such environments. We have seen that you can still perform some maintenance actions from the first level TMR through the navigator. If you install the module in this region you will be able to create your SAPGUI file packages there. We have also seen that it was possible to send the SAP events to a TEC server residing in the upper region. The biggest limitation is that the sentry monitors cannot be created in the upper TMR.

Appendix A. Monitor Sources and their Attributes

The following table summarizes the monitoring sources in the monitoring collections provided by Tivoli Manager for R/3.

Monitor Sources	Attributes
Roll Area	Roll Area Free Space (Roll Area Free - Roll Currently Used)
	Roll Area Percent Free (Roll Area Free / Roll Area Size)
	Roll Area Shared Memory (KB)
	Roll Area Size (Total size of roll area)
	Roll Currently Used (KB)
	Roll Area Percent (%)
	Roll File Size (On disk, in KB)
	Roll Max Used (KB)
	Roll Max Percent Used (%)
Page Area	Page Area Free Space (Page Area Size - Page Currently Used)
	Page Area Percent Free (Page Area Free / Page Area Size)
	Page Area Shared Memory
	Page Area Size (Total size of page area)
	Page Currently used (KB)
	Page Area Percent Used (%)
	Page File Size (On disk, in KB)
	Page Max Used (KB)
	Page Max Percent Used (Page Max Used / Page Area Size)
SAP System Availability	Host Availability of an SAP System

Monitor Sources	Attributes
Buffer	Allocated Memory (KB)
	Available Memory (KB)
	Free Memory (KB)
	Free Memory Percent (%)
	Used Memory
	Used Memory Percent (Used Memory / Available Memory)
	Number of DB Accesses
	Number of DB Accesses Saved
	Frames Swapped
	Free Directory Entries
	Free Directory Entries (%)
	Max Directory Entries
	Used Directory Entries
	Used Directory Entries Percent (Used Directory Entries / Max Directory Entries)
	Number of Hits
	Hits Ratio (%)
	Late Reset Date
	Late Reset Time
	Total Resets
	Quality (DB access quality -%)
	Number of Requests
	Object Swapped
Performance	Frequency per minute
	Average Response Time in milliseconds
	Average Wait Time in milliseconds

Monitor Sources	Attributes
OS Collect	CPU Utilization, Uoor, Syotem, Idle (%)
	System Calls per second
	Interrupts per second
	Number of CPUs
	Load Average in 1, 5, 15 minutes
	Context Switches per second
	Available Physical Memory (KB)
	Physical Memory Free (KB)
	Pages In/Out per second
	Kilobytes paged In/Out per second
	Configured swap space size (KB)
	Free swap space (KB)
	Maximum swap space (KB)
	Actual swap space size (KB)
	Disk Utilization (%)
	Disk Average Wait time (ms)
	Disk kilobytes transferred per second
	Disk Response time (ms)
	Disk Average Queue length
	Disk Average Service time (ms)
	Disk Operations per second
	LAN packets In/Out per second
	LAN packets in errors per second
	LAN packets out errors per second
	LAN packets Collisions per second

Monitor Sources	Attributes
OS/390	CPU Utilization (%)
	CPU System Utilization (%)
	Paging Rate
	Pages In/Out per second
	Pages Into Private per second
	Pages Out of Private per second
	Pages to Expanded Storage per second
	Pages from Expanded Storage per second
	Blocked pages paged in
	Blocks paged in
	Unused Interval count
	Available frames in expanded storage
	Migration age
	Total Available frames

Monitor Sources	Attributes
OS/390 DB2	Activate page of buffer pool with maximum active (%)
	Hit ratio of buffer pool with minimum hit ratio (%)
	Buffer Pool 0 hit ratio (%)
	Buffer Pool 2 hit ratio (%)
	Buffer Pool 3 hit ratio (%)
	32 KB Buffer Pool hit ratio (%)
	Buffer Pool shortage - any active pool
	Hiper pool concern - any active pool
	Buffer Pool 0 maximum active pages
	Buffer Pool 2 maximum active pages
	Buffer Pool 3 maximum active pages
	32 KB Buffer Pool maximum active pages
	Deadlocks
	Lock Suspensions
	Lock Timeouts
	Failures due to EDM pool full
	EDM Utilization (%)
	Dynamic cache hit ratio (%)
	Number of times MAXKEEPD was exceeded
	Indication of deferred close threshold reached
	Commits
	Rollbacks
	Checkpoints

Appendix B. Event Classes for Tivoli Manager for R/3

The following TEC event classes are introduced by Tivoli Manager for R/3.

Super Class	Event Class
SAP_MIB_Unique_Alert	SAP_ALERT_NULL
	SAP_ALERT_StateChange
	SAP_ALERT_SAPsysUp
	SAP_ALERT_SAPsysDown
SAP_MIB_Generic_Alert	SAP_ALERT_SlogId
	SAP_ALERT_SlogFreq
	SAP_ALERT_Buf
	SAP_ALERT_Enqueue
	SAP_ALERT_Rollpag
	SAP_ALERT_Trace
	SAP_ALERT_DpQueue
	SAP_ALERT_PerfDia
	SAP_ALERT_PerfUpd
	SAP_ALERT_PerfBtc
	SAP_ALERT_PerfSpo
	SAP_ALERT_AbapUpd
	SAP_ALERT_AbapErr
	SAP_ALERT_AbapSql
	SAP_ALERT_DbIndcs
	SAP_ALERT_DbFreSp
	SAP_ALERT_DbArcSt
	SAP_ALERT_DbBckup
	SAP_ALERT_Spo

Super Class	Event Class
	SAP_ALERT_Arch
	SAP_ALERT_GenP3
	SAP_ALERT_GenP4
	SAP_ALERT_GenP5
	SAP_ALERT_GenP6
	SAP_ALERT_GenP7
	SAP_ALERT_GenP8
	SAP_ALERT_GenP9
	SAP_ALERT_GenP10
	SAP_ALERT_GenP11
	SAP_ALERT_GenP12
	SAP_ALERT_GenP13
	SAP_ALERT_GenP14
	SAP_ALERT_GenP15
SAP_Internal_Alert	SAP_ALERT_OSCO_LOAD
	SAP_ALERT_OSCO_PAGE
	SAP_ALERT_OSCO_SWAP
	SAP_ALERT_OSCO_FILE
	SAP_ALERT_ENQU_ENQ
	SAP_ALERT_SLOG_ID
	SAP_ALERT_SLOG_FREQ
	SAP_ALERT_PERF_DIA
	SAP_ALERT_PERF_VB
	SAP_ALERT_PERF_ENQ
	SAP_ALERT_PERF_BTC
	SAP_ALERT_PERF_SPO
	SAP_ALERT_PERF_V2

Super Class	Event Class
	SAP_ALERT_BUFF_PXA
	SAP_ALERT_BUFF_TABL
	SAP_ALERT_BUFF_TABLP
	SAP_ALERT_BUFF_PRES
	SAP_ALERT_BUFF_CUA
	SAP_ALERT_BUFF_DBST
	SAP_ALERT_BUFF_TTAB
	SAP_ALERT_BUFF_FTAB
	SAP_ALERT_BUFF_IRBD
	SAP_ALERT_BUFF_SNTAB
	SAP_ALERT_ABAP_VB
	SAP_ALERT_ABAP_ERR
	SAP_ALERT_ABAP_SQL
	SAP_ALERT_RLPG_ROL
	SAP_ALERT_RLPG_PAG
	SAP_ALERT_TRSW_TRSW
	SAP_ALERT_TRSW_ACTIVE
	SAP_ALERT_GENP_SPO
	SAP_ALERT_GENP_ARCH
	SAP_ALERT_GENP_03
	SAP_ALERT_GENP_04
	SAP_ALERT_GENP_05
	SAP_ALERT_GENP_06
	SAP_ALERT_GENP_07
	SAP_ALERT_GENP_08
	SAP_ALERT_GENP_09
	SAP_ALERT_GENP_10

Super Class	Event Class
	SAP_ALERT_GENP_11
	SAP_ALERT_GENP_12
	SAP_ALERT_GENP_13
	SAP_ALERT_GENP_14
	SAP_ALERT_GENP_15
	SAP_ALERT_DPQU_DIA
	SAP_ALERT_DPQU_VB
	SAP_ALERT_DPQU_ENQ
	SAP_ALERT_DPQU_BTC
	SAP_ALERT_DPQU_SPO
	SAP_ALERT_DPQU_V2
	SAP_ALERT_DB_INDICES
	SAP_ALERT_DB_FREESPC
	SAP_ALERT_DB_ARCSTUCK
	SAP_ALERT_DB_BACKUP
	SAP_ALERT_DB_OPTMSTAT
SAP_Server_Monitors	AMS_R3MONITOR_ALERT
	SAP_SYSTEM_MONITOR
	ROLL_AREA_MONITOR
	PAGE_AREA_MONITOR
	MENU_BUFFER_MONITOR
	SCREEN_BUFFER_MONITOR
	TABLE_DEF_BUFFER_MONITOR
	FIELD_DESC_BUFFER_MONITOR
	SHORT_NTAB_BUFFER_MONITOR
	INITIAL_RECORDS_BUFFER_MONITOR
	GENERIC_KEY_BUFFER_MONITOR

Super Class	Event Class
	SINGLE_RECORD_BUFFER_MONITOR
	PROGRAM_BUFFER_MONITOR
	DIALOG_SERVICE_MONITOR
	UPDATE_SERVICE_MONITOR
	BATCH_SERVICE_MONITOR
	SPOOL_SERVICE_MONITOR
	OS_COLLECT_APSRVR_MONITOR
	OS_COLLECT_DBSRVR_MONITOR
	OS390_COLLECT_MONITOR
	OS390_DB2_MONITOR

Appendix C. Custom Monitor MCSL Source File

The following figures show the MCSL file for our custom SAP monitor.

```
Collection "Custom ITSO Collection" {

        OperatorGroup numeric HasOperand {
                { Label = (Sentry2_0, "(never)", 97 ); };
                { Label = (Sentry2_0, "Greater than", 98 );
                        RelOp = ">";
                        Verify = "^" "-?((\.\d+)|(\d+(\.\d*)?))"  "$" ; Failure
 = (Sentry2_0, "Must be numeric", 94 ); };
                { Label = (Sentry2_0, "Less than", 99 );
                        RelOp = "<";
                        Verify = "^" "-?((\.\d+)|(\d+(\.\d*)?))"  "$" ; Failure
= (Sentry2_0, "Must be numeric", 94 ); };
                { Label = (Sentry2_0, "Equal to", 100 );
                        RelOp = "==";
                        Verify = "^" "-?((\.\d+)|(\d+(\.\d*)?))"  "$" ; Failure
= (Sentry2_0, "Must be numeric", 94 ); };
                { Label = (Sentry2_0, "Not equal to", 101 );
                        RelOp = "!=";
                        Verify = "^" "-?((\.\d+)|(\d+(\.\d*)?))"  "$" ; Failure
= (Sentry2_0, "Must be numeric", 94 ); };
                { Label = (Sentry2_0, "Increases beyond", 102 );
                        RelOp = "->>";
= (Sentry2_0, "Must be numeric", 94 ); };
                { Label = (Sentry2_0, "Decreases below", 103 );
                        RelOp = "-<<";
                        Verify = "^" "-?((\.\d+)|(\d+(\.\d*)?))"  "$" ; Failure
= (Sentry2_0, "Must be numeric", 94 ); };
                { Label = (Sentry2_0, "Increase of", 104 );
                        Delta = "-"; RelOp  = ">=";
                        Verify = "^" "-?((\.\d+)|(\d+(\.\d*)?))"  "$" ; Failure
= (Sentry2_0, "Must be numeric", 94 ); };
                { Label = (Sentry2_0, "%% increase of", 105 );
                        Delta = "%"; RelOp = ">=";
                        Verify = "^" "-?((\.\d+)|(\d+(\.\d*)?))"  "$" ; Failure
= (Sentry2_0, "Must be numeric", 94 );  };
                { Label = (Sentry2_0, "Changes by", 117 );
                        Delta = "+"; RelOp = ">=";
                        Verify = "^" "-?((\.\d+)|(\d+(\.\d*)?))"  "$" ; Failure
```

Figure 179. Custom Monitor MCSL Source File (Part 1 of 4)

```
                        = (Sentry2_0, "Must be numeric", 94 );  };
                           { Label = (Sentry2_0, "Outside range", 106 );
                                 RelOp = "<>";
                                 Verify = "^" "-?((\.\d+)|(\d+(\.\d*)?))"  "-"
"-?((\.\d+)|(\d+(\.\d*)?))"  "$" ; Failure = (Sentry2_0, "Expected pair of numbers
separated by -", 96 ); };
                   };
             ChoiceList Work_Process_Type {
             ButtonLabel = (SAPCat, "Type", 999 );
                     {
                     { (SAPCat, "Dialog", 999 ) "DIA" }
                     { (SAPCat, "Batch", 999 ) "BTC" }
                     { (SAPCat, "Spool", 999 ) "SPO" }
                     { (SAPCat, "Update", 999 ) "UPD" }
                     { (SAPCat, "Enqueue", 999 ) "ENQ" }
                     };
             };
             OperatorGroup string HasOperand {
                     { Label = (Sentry2_0, "(never)", 97 ); };
                     { RelOp = "==";
                            Verify = "[^\":]+" ;
                            Failure = (Sentry2_0, "Invalid character in string
(double-quote or colon)", 93 );
Label = (Sentry2_0, "Equal to", 100 ); };
                     { RelOp = "!=";
                            Verify = "[^\":]+" ;
                            Failure = (Sentry2_0, "Invalid character in string
(double-quote or colon)", 93 );
                            Label = (Sentry2_0, "Not equal to", 101 ); };
                     { RelOp = "=~";
                            Verify = "[^\":]+" ;
                            Failure = (Sentry2_0, "Invalid character in string
(double-quote or colon)", 93 );
                            Label = (Sentry2_0, "Matches", 113 ); };
                     { RelOp = "!~";
                            Verify = "[^\":]+" ;
                            Failure = (Sentry2_0, "Invalid character in string
(double-quote or colon)", 93 );
                            Label = (Sentry2_0, "Mismatches", 114 ); };
                     { RelOp = "->";
                            Verify = "[^\":]+" ;
                            Failure = (Sentry2_0, "Invalid character in string
(double-quote or colon)", 93 );
                            Label = (Sentry2_0, "Changes To", 115 ); };
                     { RelOp = "-<";
                            Verify = "[^\":]+" ;
                        Failure =(Sentry2_0, "Invalid character in string (double-quote
or colon)", 93 );
                            Label = (Sentry2_0, "Changes From", 116 ); };
                   };
```

Figure 180. Custom Monitor MCSL Source File (Part 2 of 4)

```
Format = (Sentry2_0, "Sentry %6$s/%8$M on host %7$s %12$t{%c}\n\nStatus: >>> %1$s
<<<\n\n%8$M (%2$s) %10$M %9$M %11$s\n(Previous: %3$s %14$M Current: %4$s Effective:
%5$s)\n%13$s", 122 );
FormatName = (Sentry2_0, "Standard", 123 );
Format = (Sentry2_0, "%12$t{%c} %6$s %1$s %5$s %8$M(%2$s)", 124 );
FormatName = (Sentry2_0, "Brief (one line)", 125 );
Format = (Sentry2_0, "Sentry Monitor Status Report: %1$s\nFrom profile %6$s on host
%7$s, %12$t{%c}\nMonitor: %8$M(%2$s)\n\nCurrent effective monitor value: %5$s
%14$M\n(Previous value: %3$s, current raw value: %4$s)\n\nThreshold comparison: %10$M
%9$M %11$s\n\nResulting severity level: >>>%1$s<<<\n\nAdditional
information:\n%13$s\n", 126 );
FormatName = (Sentry2_0, "Long", 127 );
Format = (SentryFormats, "LOCAL FORMAT 1 CATALOG FAILURE", 1);
FormatName = (Sentry2_0, "Local format 1", 143 );
Format = (SentryFormats, "LOCAL FORMAT 2 CATALOG FAILURE", 2);
FormatName = (Sentry2_0, "Local format 2", 144 );
        CodeID = "$Id: testITSO.csl,v 1.4 1996/06/26 21:33:46 name Exp $";
        Version = "1.0";
        Require = ">2.0.2";
        EventBaseClass = "NUM_WP_MONITOR";
        HelpMessage = (SAPHelpCat, "ITSO test collections", 999);
        Monitor SapSystem Numeric Group numeric {
                EventClass = "NUM_WP_MONITOR";
                HelpMessage = (SAPHelpCat, "Work process by type", 42 );
                Description = (SAPCat, "Work Processes", 999 );
                SetID = "YES";
                Argument (SAPCat, "Work Process Type", 999 )
                        RestrictedChoice Work_Process_Type
                        DefaultValue "DIA";
                Implementation
(aix4-r1,aix3-r2,solaris2,hpux9,hpux10,osf-axp,sunos4,w32-ix86)
                        Shell("/bin/sh", "-c", Command, "SapWP")
                        .TYPE=$1
                        .if [ "$INTERP" = "w32-ix86" ] ; then
                        .   TMP=`wtemp`
                        .else
                        .   TMP=/tmp
                        .fi
                        .exec 2> ${TMP}/ITSO_WP_monitor.log
                        .set -x
                        .if [ "$INTERP" = "w32-ix86" ] ; then
                        .   . $SystemRoot/system32/drivers/etc/Tivoli/setup_env.sh
                        .else
                        .   . /etc/Tivoli/setup_env.sh
                        .fi
```

Figure 181. Custom Monitor MCSL Source File (Part 3 of 4)

```
                                    .WR3RFC=$BINDIR/TME/SAP/2.2C/wr3rfc
                                    .RFCDIR=$BINDIR/../generic_unix/TME/SAP/2.2C/rfc
                                    .cd $RFCDIR
                                    .HOST=`idlattr -t -g $ENDPOINT_OID HostName string`
                                    .HOST=`eval echo $HOST`
                                    .SAPSYSTEM=`idlattr -t -g $ENDPOINT_OID InstanceID string`
                                    .SAPSYSTEM=`eval echo $SAPSYSTEM`
                                    .SAPSYSTEMNAME=`idlattr -t -g $ENDPOINT_OID SystemID string`
                                    .SAPSYSTEMNAME=`eval echo $SAPSYSTEMNAME`
                                .OUTPUT=`$WR3RFC -h "$HOST" -d "$SAPSYSTEMNAME" -s "$SAPSYSTEM"
              SAP_WP`
                                    .WPLINE=`echo "$OUTPUT" | grep "^$TYPE ="`
                                    .WPNUM=`echo $WPLINE | awk -F= '{print $2}'`
                                    .echo $WPNUM
                                    .exit 0
                          ;
                   };
```

Figure 182. Custom Monitor MCSL Source File (Part 4 of 4)

Appendix D. Destiny Database Structure

UED

tbl_calendars		tbl_destinations		tbl_destinations (continued)	
	cal_name cal_year cal_desc jan feb mar apr may jun jul aug sep oct nov dec cal_exp_date owner_name update_datetime		dest_id dest_name locale_name res_level node_id color duplex paper input_paper output_paper persist dest_desc dest_type exec_file init_file reset_file device_info no_of_retry speed conf_flag min_bytes		max_bytes serial_num last_svs_date def_stat_domain_name def_stat_name def_banner_domain_name def_banner_name owner_name update_datetime
tbl_user_security_roles	user_name sec_name owner_name update_datetime	tbl_dist_list	dist_list_name dist_list_desc owner_name update_datetime	tbl_server	server_name server_key server_desc service
tbl_dist_list_details	dist_list_name member_name member_flag owner_name update_datetime	tbl_group_security_roles	group_name sec_name owner_name update_datetime	tbl_domains	domain_name domain_desc domain_mgr_node owner_name update_datetime
tbl_groups	group_name group_desc bus_queue_name bus_domain_name bus_node_name other_queue_name other_domain_name other_node_name owner_name update_datetime	tbl_node_communications	node_comm_id node_id remote_node_name access_deny_flag owner_name update_datetime	tbl_schema	db_name db_version db_level db_engine db_engine_vers db_engine_level db_driver db_driver_vers db_driver_level
tbl_user	user_name full_name user_password empl_num account_name title group_name def_queue_flag bus_queue_name bus_node_name bus_domain_name other_queue_name other_node_name other_domain_name def_domain def_node bus_address bus_phone_num bus_email bus_fax bus_pager	tbl_user (continued)	bus_bin other_address other_phone_num other_email other_fax other_pager other_bin owner_name update_datetime	tbl_nodes	node_id node_name domain_name network_name node_desc node_type port_num def_route_domain_name def_route_node_name exec_file owner_name update_datetime
tbl_security_roles	sec_name sec_desc domain_name node_name object_name object_type owner_access_details other_access_details owner_name update_datetime				

Figure 183. UED Database Structure (Part 1 of 8)

SCD

tbl_banners	banner_name banner_desc banner_file owner_name update_datetime	tbl_glom_detail	glom_name search_string owner_name update_datetime	tbl_mapper_calend ar	mapper_id cal_name cal_except_flag owner_name update_datetime
tbl_device_history	dest_id total_printouts total_bytes total_users no_of-loggings no_of_stat_changes owner_name update_datetime	tbl_queue_history	queue_id total_printouts total_bytes total_users no_of_loggings no_of_stat_changes owner_name update_datetime	tbl_schema	db_name db_version db_level db_engine db_engine_vers db_engine_level db_driver db_driver_vers db_driver_level
tbl_filters	filter_ser_num filter_desc filter_name user_name device_name node_name glom_name test_prog_file spl_option owner_name update_datetime	tbl_stationery	stat_name stat_desc no_of_copies form_message init_file exec_file reset_file stat_mode owner_name update_datetime	tbl_mappers	mapper_id handle_name node_name mapper_name archive_flag archive_period archive_dest archive_comp_flag mapper_desc owner_name
tbl_handles	node_name handle_name handle_desc owner_name update_datetime	tbl_queue_destinati on	queue_id dest_id owner_name update_datetime	tbl_server	server_name server_key server_desc service
tbl_glom_header	glom_name glom_desc x_min_pos y_min_pos x_max_pos y_max_pos start_page_no end_page_no handle_line_no handle_page_no handle_x_min_pos handle_x_max_pos owner_name update_datetime	tbl_queue	queue_id queue_name queue_format node-name queue-desc queue_stat_rule dev_sel_rule queue_sort_rule queue_on_from queue_on_till queue_forward_name queue_for_domain_na me queue_for_node_name language_type owner_name update_datetime	tbl_rules	rule_id node_name mapper_id send_to send_to_type queue_name queue_flag domain_name rule_conf_flag output_file no_of_copies stat_name notify_to notiry_ty[e notify_event notify_command priority owner_name update_datetime
tbl_watchers	watcher_name node_name watcher_desc exec_file owner_name update_	tbl_users_history	user_name total_printouts total_bytes no_of_devices_used no_of_loggings owner_name update_datetime		

Figure 184. SCD Database Structure (Part 2 of 8)

News_Design1

tbl_glom_detail	glom_name search_string owner_name update_datetime	tbl_dist_list	dist_list_name dist_list_desc owner_name update_datetime	tbl_group_security_roles	group_name sec_name owner_name update_datetime
tbl_active_sels	sel_id sel_state active_joe_cnt owner_name update_datetime	tbl_banners	banner_name banner_desc banner_file owner_name update_datetime	tbl_domains	domain_name domain_desc domain_mgr_node owner_name update_datetime
tbl_dist_list_details	dist_list_name member_name member_flag owner_name update_datetime	tbl_mapper_calendar	mapper_id cal_name cal_except_flag owner_name update_datetime	tbl_inactive_sels	sel_id sel_state active_joe_cnt owner_name update_datetime
tbl_configuration	config_name section_name item_name item_type item_value item_comments owner_name update_datetime	tbl_handles	node_name handle_name handle_desc owner_name update_datetime	tbl_device_history	dest_id total_printouts total_bytes total_users no_of_loggings no_of_stat_changes owner_name update_datetime
tbl_glom_header	glom_name glom_desc x_min_pos y_min_pos x_max_pos y_max_pos start_page_no end_page_no handle_line_no handle_page_no handle_x_min_pos handle_x_max_pos owner_name update_datetime	tbl_filters	filter_ser_num filter_desc filter_name file_name user_name device_name handle_name node_name glom_name test_prog_file spl_option owner_name update_datetime	tbl_calendars	cal_name cal_year cal_desc jan feb mar apr may jun jul aug sep oct nov dec cal_exp_date owner_name update_datetime
tbl_destination_status	dest_id dest_state current_banner current_stat joe_id queue_id msg_id owner_name update_datetime	tbl_DemoWeb	joe_id old_joe_id sel_id old_sel_id queue_name dest_id user_name handle_name file_name current_page joe_info joe_priority conf_flag joe_status output_file no_of_copies stat_name notify_to notify_event notify_type notify_command	tbl_DemoWeb (continued)	joe_info joe_priority conf_flag joe_status output_file no_of_copies stat_name notify_to notify_event notify_type notify_command group_name dist_list_name msg_id creation_time file_size queue_node_name orig_node_name orig_domain_name owner_name update_datetime

Figure 185. News Database Structure (Part 3 of 8)

News_Design1 (continued)

tbl_active_joes	joe_info joe_priority conf_flag joe_status output_file no_of_copies stat_name notify_to notify_event notify_type notify_command group_name dist_list_name msg_id creation_time file_size queue_node_name queue_domain_name orig_node_name orig_domain_name owner_name update_datetime	tbl_destinations	input_paper output_paper persist dest_desc dest_type exec_file init_file reset_file device_info no_of_retry speed conf_flag min_bytes max_bytes serial_num last_svs_date def_stat_domain_name def_stat_name def_banner_domain_name def_banner_name owner_name update_datetime	tbl_destinations (continued)	dest_id dest_name locale_name res_level node_id color duplex paper input_paper output_paper persist dest_desc dest_type exec_file init_file reset_file device_info no_of_retry speed conf_flag min_bytes
tbl_inactive_joes	joe_id old_joe_id sel_id old_sel_id queue_name dest_id user_name handle_name file_name current_page joe_info joe_priority conf_flag joe_status output_file no_of_copies stat_name notify_to notify_event notify_type notify_command	tbl_inactive_joes (continued)	joe_info joe_priority conf_flag joe_status output_file no_of_copies stat_name notify_to notify_event notify_type notify_command group_name dist_list_name msg_id creation_time file_size queue_node_name queue_domain_name orig_node_name orig_domain_name owner_name update_datetime	tbl_groups	group_name group_desc bus_queue_name bus_domain_name bus_node_name other_queue_name other_domain_name other_node_name owner_name update_datetime

Figure 186. News Database Structure (Part 4 of 8)

News Design2

tbl_save_sel_request		tbl_save_sels		tbl_save_sels (continued)	
	sel_id node_name send_to send_to_type queue_name queue_flag domain_name rule_conf_flag output_file no_of_copies stat_name notify_to notify_type notify_event notify_command priority owner_name update_datetime		sel_sel_id sel_old_sel_id sel_user_name sel_file_name control_file_name sel_orig_node_name sel_orig_domain_name final_node_name final_domain_name sel_file_size control_file_size file_completion_time watcher_file_date archive_dir input_dev_name archive_period archive_comp_flag total_joe_cnt spl_option archive_file_time archive_flag		sel_user_name sel_file_name control_file_name sel_orig_node_name sel_orig_domain_name final_node_name final_domain_name sel_file_size control_file_size file_completion_time watcher_file_date archive_dir input_dev_name archive_period archive_comp_flag total_joe_cnt spl_option archive_file_time archive_flag document_name sel_owner_name sel_update_datetime
tbl_queue		tbl_sels		tbl_sels (continued)	
	queue_id queue_name queue-format node_name queue_desc queue_stat_rule dev_sel_rule queue_sort_rule queue_on_from queue_on_till queue_forward_na me queue_for_domain _name queue_for_node_n ame language_type owner_name update_datetime		sel_sel_id sel_old_sel_id sel_user_name sel_file_name control_file_name sel_orig_node_name sel_orig_domain_name final_node_name final_domain_name sel_file_size control_file_size file_completion_time watcher_file_date archive_dir input_dev_name archive_period archive_comp_flag total_joe_cnt spl_option archive_period archive_comp_flag total_joe_cnt spl_option archive_file_time archive_flag		sel_user_name sel_file_name control_file_name sel_orig_node_name sel_orig_domain_name final_node_name final_domain_name sel_file_size control_file_size file_completion_time watcher_file_date archive_dir input_dev_name archive_period archive_comp_flag total_joe_cnt spl_option archive_file_time archive_flag document_name sel_owner_name sel_update_datetime
tbl_Notifications		tbl_net_joes		tbl_net_joes (continued)	
	joe_id old_joe_id sel_id old_sel_id queue_name dest_id user_name handle_name file_name current_page joe_info joe_priority conf_flag joe_status output_file no_of_copies stat_name notify_to notify_event notify_type		joe_id old_joe_id sel_id old_sel_id queue_name dest_id user_name handle_name file_name current_page joe_info joe_priority conf_flag joe_status output_file no_of_copies stat_name notify_to notify_event notify_type notify_command		joe_info joe_priority conf_flag joe_status output_file no_of_copies stat_name notify_to notify_event notify_type notify_command group_name dist_list_name msg_id creation_time file_size queue_node_name queue_domain_name orig_node_name orig_domain_name owner_name update_datetime

Figure 187. News Database Structure (Part 5 of 8)

News_Design2 (continued)

tbl_rules		tbl_sel_request		tbl_messages	
tbl_rules	rule_id node_name mapper_id send_to send_to_type queue_name queue_flag domain_name rule_conf_flag output_file no_of_copies stat_name notify_to notify_type notify_event notify_command priority owner_name update_datetime	**tbl_sel_request**	sel_id node_name send_to send_to_type queue_name queue_flag domain_name rule_conf_flag output_file no_of_copies stat_name notify_to notify_type notify_event notify_command priority owner_name update_datetime	**tbl_messages**	msg_id msg_desc msg_type user_name reply_status table_name table_id read_status final_node_name final_domain_name orig_node_name orig_domain_name owner_name update_datetime
tbl_mappers	mapper_id handle_name node_name mapper_name archive_flag archive_period archive_dest archive_comp_flag mapper_desc owner_name update_datetime	**tbl_nodes**	node_id node_name domain_name network_name node_desc node_type port_num def_route_domain_name def_route_node_name exec_file owner_name update_datetime	**tbl_security_roles**	sec_name sec_desc domain_name node_name object_name object_type owner_access_details other_access_details owner_name update_datetime
tbl_schema	db_name db_version db_level db_engine db_engine_vers db_engine_level db_driver db_driver_vers db_driver_level	**tbl_queue_history**	queue_id total_printouts total_bytes total_users no_of_loggings no_of_stat_changes owner_name update_datetime	**tbl_nqm**	nqm_id nqm_status table_id table_name domain_name node_name owner_name update_datetime
tbl_mapper_calendar	mapper_id cal_name cal_except_flag owner_name update_datetime	**tbl_queue_state**	queue_id queue_state msg_id owner_name update_datetime	**tbl_node_communications**	node_comm_id node_id remote_node_name access_deny_flag owner_name update_datetime
tbl_server	server_name server_key server_desc service	**tbl_queue_destination**	queue_id dest_id owner_name update_datetime	**tbl_node_link**	node_id link_state owner_name update_datetime

Figure 188. News Database Structure (Part 6 of 8)

News_Design3

tbl_queue		tbl_rules		tbl_save_sel_ request	
	queue_id queue_name queue-format node_name queue_desc queue_stat_rule dev_sel_rule queue_sort_rule queue_on_from queue_on_till queue_forward_name queue_for_domain_nam e queue_for_node_name language_type owner_name update_datetime		rule_id node_name mapper_id send_to send_to_type queue_name queue_flag domain_name rule_conf_flag output_file no_of_copies stat_name notify_to notify_type notify_event notify_command priority owner_name update_datetime		sel_id node_name send_to send_to_type queue_name queue_flag domain_name rule_conf_flag output_file no_of_copies stat_name notify_to notify_type notify_event notify_command priority owner_name update_datetime
tbl_save_sels	sel_sel_id sel_old_sel_id sel_user_name sel_file_name control_file_name sel_orig_node_name sel_orig_domain_name final_node_name final_domain_name sel_file_size control_file_size file_completion_time watcher_file_date archive_dir input_dev_name archive_period archive_comp_flag total_joe_cnt spl_option archive_file_time archive_flag	tbl_save_sels	sel_user_name sel_file_name control_file_name sel_orig_node_name sel_orig_domain_name final_node_name final_domain_name sel_file_size control_file_size file_completion_time watcher_file_date archive_dir input_dev_name archive_period archive_comp_flag total_joe_cnt spl_option archive_file_time archive_flag document_name sel_owner_name sel_update_datetime	tbl_unknown	joe_id old_joe_id sel_id old_sel_id queue_name dest_id user_name handle_name file_name current_page joe_info joe_priority conf_flag joe_status output_file no_of_copies stat_name notify_to notify_event notify_type
tbl_sels	sel_sel_id sel_old_sel_id sel_user_name sel_file_name control_file_name sel_orig_node_name sel_orig_domain_name final_node_name final_domain_name sel_file_size control_file_size file_completion_time watcher_file_date archive_dir input_dev_name archive_period archive_comp_flag total_joe_cnt spl_option archive_period archive_comp_flag total_joe_cnt spl_option archive_file_time archive_flag	tbl_sels (continued)	sel_user_name sel_file_name control_file_name sel_orig_node_name sel_orig_domain_name final_node_name final_domain_name sel_file_size control_file_size file_completion_time watcher_file_date archive_dir input_dev_name archive_period archive_comp_flag total_joe_cnt spl_option archive_file_time archive_flag document_name sel_owner_name sel_update_datetime	tbl_sel_request	sel_id node_name send_to send_to_type queue_name queue_flag domain_name rule_conf_flag output_file no_of_copies stat_name notify_to notify_type notify_event notify_command priority owner_name update_datetime

Figure 189. News Database Structure (Part 7 of 8)

News_Design3 (continued)

tbl_users	user_name full_name user_password empl_num account_name title group_name def_queue_flag bus_queue_name bus_node_name bus_domain_name other_queue_name other_node_name other_domain_name def_domain def_node bus_address bus_phone-num bus_email bus_fax bus_pager	tbl_users (continued)	bus_queue_name bus_node_name bus_domain_name other_queue_name other_node_name other_domain_name def_domain def_node bus_address bus_phone_num bus_email bus_fax bus_pager bus_bin other_address other_phone_num other_email other_fax other_pager other_bin owner_name update_datetime	tbl_stationary	stat_name stat_desc no_of_copies form_message init_file exec_file reset_file stat_mode owner_name update_datetime
tbl_queue_history	queue_id total_printouts total_bytes total_users no_of_loggings no_of_stat_changes owner_name update_datetime	tbl_user_ registration	user_name note_ipaddress note_dns_name note_win_name note_conn_mode note_port_number note_proc_name note_cookie	tbl_users_ history	user_name total_printouts total_bytes no_of_devices_used no_of_loggings owner_name update_datetime
tbl_queue_state	queue_id queue_state msg_id owner_name update_datetime	tbl_watcher_ state	watcher_name node_name watcher_state owner_name update_datetime	tbl_watches	watcher_name node_name watcher_desc exec_file owner_name update_datetime
tbl_queue_ destination	queue_id dest_id owner_name update_datetime	tbl_server	server_name server_key server_desc service	tbl_user_ security_roles	user_name sec_name owner_name update_datetime
tbl_security_roles	sec_name sec_desc domain_name node_name object_name object_type owner_access_details other_access_details owner_name update_datetime	tbl_schema	db_name db_version db_level db_engine db_engine_vers db_engine_level db_driver db_driver_vers db_driver_level		

Figure 190. News Database Structure (Part 8 of 8)

Appendix E. Useful SAP Transactions

The following codes are SAP R/3 transaction codes, which are useful to navigate through the SAP R/3 system:

RZ03 CCMS Control Panel
RZ06 Maintain Alert Thresholds and maintain Syslog Output
RZ10 Edit Profile
RZ20 Alert Monitor 4.X
RZ21 Monitoring: SettingS and Tool Maintaince 4.X

SM04 Overview of users
SM21 Syslog
SM28 Initial Consistency Check
SM31 Table Maintainance
SM36 Job Definition
SM37 Job Overview
SM51 Server Overview
SM50 Workprocess Overview

SE06 Workbench Entry Setting up
SE09 Workbench Organizer Entry
SE12 Dictionary Initial Screen - Check Tables
SE16 Data Browser
SE38 ABAP Editor

ST02 Tune Summary
ST04 Database Performance Analysis
ST06 OS Monitor Local
OS07 OS Monitor
ST22 Dump Analysis
STUN Performance Monitor

Appendix F. Special Notices

This publication is intended to help system designers and technical consultants to understand how to manage SAP R/3 with Tivoli. The information in this publication is not intended as the specification of any programming interfaces that are provided by Tivoli. See the PUBLICATIONS section of the IBM Programming Announcement for Tivoli for more information about what publications are considered to be product documentation.

References in this publication to IBM products, programs or services do not imply that IBM intends to make these available in all countries in which IBM operates. Any reference to an IBM product, program, or service is not intended to state or imply that only IBM's product, program, or service may be used. Any functionally equivalent program that does not infringe any of IBM's intellectual property rights may be used instead of the IBM product, program or service.

Information in this book was developed in conjunction with use of the equipment specified, and is limited in application to those specific hardware and software products and levels.

IBM may have patents or pending patent applications covering subject matter in this document. The furnishing of this document does not give you any license to these patents. You can send license inquiries, in writing, to the IBM Director of Licensing, IBM Corporation, 500 Columbus Avenue, Thornwood, NY 10594 USA.

Licensees of this program who wish to have information about it for the purpose of enabling: (i) the exchange of information between independently created programs and other programs (including this one) and (ii) the mutual use of the information which has been exchanged, should contact IBM Corporation, Dept. 600A, Mail Drop 1329, Somers, NY 10589 USA.

Such information may be available, subject to appropriate terms and conditions, including in some cases, payment of a fee.

The information contained in this document has not been submitted to any formal IBM test and is distributed AS IS. The information about non-IBM ("vendor") products in this manual has been supplied by the vendor and IBM assumes no responsibility for its accuracy or completeness. The use of this information or the implementation of any of these techniques is a customer responsibility and depends on the customer's ability to evaluate and integrate them into the customer's operational environment. While each item may have been reviewed by IBM for accuracy in a specific situation, there is no guarantee that the same or similar results will be obtained elsewhere. Customers attempting to adapt these techniques to their own environments do so at their own risk.

Any pointers in this publication to external Web sites are provided for convenience only and do not in any manner serve as an endorsement of these Web sites.

Any performance data contained in this document was determined in a controlled environment, and therefore, the results that may be obtained in other operating environments may vary significantly. Users of this document should verify the applicable data for their specific environment.

The following document contains examples of data and reports used in daily business operations. To illustrate them as completely as possible, the examples contain the names of individuals, companies, brands, and products. All of these names are fictitious and any similarity to the names and addresses used by an actual business enterprise is entirely coincidental.

The following terms are trademarks of the International Business Machines Corporation in the United States and/or other countries:

AIX	DB2
CICS	IBM
NetView	MQSeries
OS/390	OS/2
ADSTAR	PROFS
RS/6000	

The following terms are trademarks of Tivoli Systems, Inc., an IBM Company:

Tivoli, Tivoli Enterprise Console, Tivoli Management Framework, Tivoli Global Enterprise Manager, Tivoli Reporter, Tivoli Plus, Tivoli Manager, Tivoli ADSM, Tivoli OPC, Tivoli Maestro, Tivoli Destiny, Tivoli Cross-Site, Cross-Site, Tivoli IT Director, Tivoli Partner Association, Tivoli Professional Services, Tivoli Ready, Planet Tivoli.

The following terms are trademarks of other companies:

C-bus is a trademark of Corollary, Inc.

Java and HotJava are trademarks of Sun Microsystems, Incorporated.

Microsoft, Windows, Windows NT, and the Windows 95 logo are trademarks or registered trademarks of Microsoft Corporation.

PC Direct is a trademark of Ziff Communications Company and is used by IBM Corporation under license.

Pentium, MMX, ProShare, LANDesk, and ActionMedia are trademarks or registered trademarks of Intel Corporation in the U.S. and other countries.

UNIX is a registered trademark in the United States and other countries licensed exclusively through X/Open Company Limited.

Other company, product, and service names may be trademarks or service marks of others.

Appendix G. Related Publications

Tho publications listed in this section are considered particularly suitable for a more detailed discussion of the topics covered in this book.

- *Managing RDBMS Servers With Tivoli,* IBM Corporation, ISBN 0-7384-0062-9

- *Deploying a Tivoli Infrastructure in Large-Scale Environments,* IBM Corporation, ISBN 0-7384-0018-X.

- *New Features in Tivoli Software Distribution 3.6,* IBM Corporation, ISBN 0-7384-0109-9

- *Problem Management Using Tivoli Service Desk and the TEC,* IBM Corporation, ISBN 0-7384-1204-X

- *An Introduction to Tivoli's TME 10,* Prentice Hall, ISBN 0-13-899717-9

- *The SAP R/3 Handbook,* McGraw-Hill, ISBN 0-07-033121-9

- *Introduction to ABAP/4 Programming for SAP,* Prima Publishing, ISBN 0-7615-1392-2

- *Network Resource Planning for SAP R/3, Baan IV and Peoplesoft,* McGraw-Hill, ISBN 0-07-913674-8

- *Writing SAP ABAP/4 Programs,* McGraw-Hill, ISBN 0-07-913743-1

- *Sybase SQL Server 11 Unleashed,* SAMS Publishing, ISBN 0-672-30909-2

Index

Symbols
$BINDIR 56
%BINDIR% 59
%DBDIR%mp 144
/tmp 144
/usr/lib/maestro 86
/usr/sap/trans/bin 92
_sap_alert_control.log 144

Numerics
32-bit option 76
8.3 DOS format file names 113

A
ABAP 46
ABAP/4 Development Workbench 94
abstraction 23
Accountability 6
accounting 16
ack_sap_alert rule 153
ack_sap_sentry_alert rule 155
ADABAS 17
Administrator 80, 114
AIX 33
AMS Module for R/3 43
AMS Module for R/3 policy region 159
AMS_WR3MIB_PROCESS_ALERT 142, 151
application components 6, 13
application server 17, 92, 174
archive/retrieve 15
authorization profile 89
automation 23
Availability 6
availability management 10

B
backup/restore 15
bandwidth optimization 13
Banners 40
baroc files 149
batch job 80
BATCH_SERVICE_MONITOR 151
Batchman 84
buffer information 131, 146

business design 29
business logic 5
business processes 16
business rules 14

C
Calendars 40
catalyst for change 16
CCMS 10, 19, 138
CCMS Alert Monitor 19
CD-ROM 65, 72, 90, 105, 114, 137
central administration 86
central event display 13
central instance 18, 30
central monitors 61, 145
centralized administration 79
channels 116
classes 61
clone profile 135
close_sap_alert rule 153
close_sap_sentry_alert rule 155
cofiles 92
communications 15
communications protocol 17
Composer 39, 41, 123
composer command 84
Computing Center Management System 19
Conductor 39, 41, 113, 123
conman command 112
convert_mib_to_internal_alert rule 142, 153
core applications 9
correlation 13, 16
correlation rule 16
CPIC 89, 147
CPIC-only 50
CPU 81
critical system parameters 20
CUA buffer quality 142
customize script 86

D
data files 92
database server 17, 174
dataless endpoint mode 135
dataless profile manager 135
DB2 15, 17

network management system   7
network nodes   16
network topology   16
NEWS   40, 113
node down event   7
Nodes   40
notepad command   124
notification   20
NT path environment   82

O

operating system   7, 174
operations management   7
Oracle   15, 17
Oracle 7   79
Oracle 7.3   35
Oracle 8   79
Oracle 8.1   36
ordering system   5
OS collect   131
OS Collect - Application Server   174
OS Collect - Database Server   174
OS Collect Application Server   146
OS database collection   146
OS/390   17, 146, 174
OS/390 DB2   174
OS/390 DB2 collection   146
OS/390 OS collection   146
output channels   14
output environment   14
output management   14
output network   39
output resources   14
Output Server   39, 113
Output Server database   113

P

Page Area   146, 174
paging space   6
password   58
PC Managed Nodes   135
PCL   14
Performance   6, 174
Performance Monitor   146
planning considerations   5
planning process   5
policy region   11, 43, 51
port 31111   81

port 32222   119
PostScript   14
presentation   15
Presentation Clients   17
printing devices   14
priority   102
process token   80
processes   17
Product Group   81
profile manager   51, 71, 130, 155
PROFS   14
proposed management solution   21
psetcode command   81
PXA Program buffer   174

Q

Queues   40

R

R/3 architecture   5
R/3 authorization   88
R/3 Maintain Profiles transaction   88
R/3 MIB   10
R/3 monitoring collections   11
R/3 user profile   88
r3batch   99
r3options file   90
r3setup script   90
R900031.IXK   90
R900057.TV1   47
R900095.TV1   47
RDBMS   14, 17, 79
RDBMS servers   14
reference client   65
reference installation   65, 137
Relational Database Management System   17
Reliability   6
Remote Function Call   140
remote monitors   61, 145
reports   14
requirements   5
reset_certain_events_on_statechange rule   153
reset_syslog_alert rule   153
resource roles   11
response time   173
RFC   57, 145
RFC interface   50, 145
RFC user   57

transport system   92
TST   18
TTAB Table Description buffer   174
two-way connection   34

U
UED   40, 113
unauthorized access   147
Universal Monitoring Collection   36
UNIX   17, 65, 105
UNIX database server   134
UPDATE_SERVICE_MONITOR   151
Users   40

W
WAN link   35
watcher   122
Watchers   40
Web servers   14
Windows 95   18, 65, 135
Windows NT   17, 135
Windows NT 4.0   120
Windows NT 4.0 with Service Pack 3   36
Windows NT long file names   113
WR3MIB   63
wr3mib   139, 145
wr3rfc   58, 140, 145

X
X400   14

Y
YMA3 development class   92

Z
Z_TV1_ALERT_CONTROL   149
Z_TV1_ALERT_READER   142, 149
Z_TV1_BUFFER_INFO   149
Z_TV1_BUFFER_NAMES   58, 149
Z_TV1_OS_COLLECT   149
Z_TV1_OS390_COLLECT   149
Z_TV1_OS390_DB2   149
Z_TV1_ROLL_PAGES_SIZES   149
ZMAESTRO   88
ZTIV1INC   46
ZTIVOLI   46
ZTTC180   46

ZTV1   46
ZTV2   46
ZTVDATA   46

Back	Forward	Home	Reload	Images	Open	Print	Find	Stop

http://www.phptr.com/

What's New?	What's Cool?	Destinations	Net Search	People	Software

PRENTICE HALL

Professional Technical Reference
Tomorrow's Solutions for Today's Professionals.

Keep Up-to-Date with

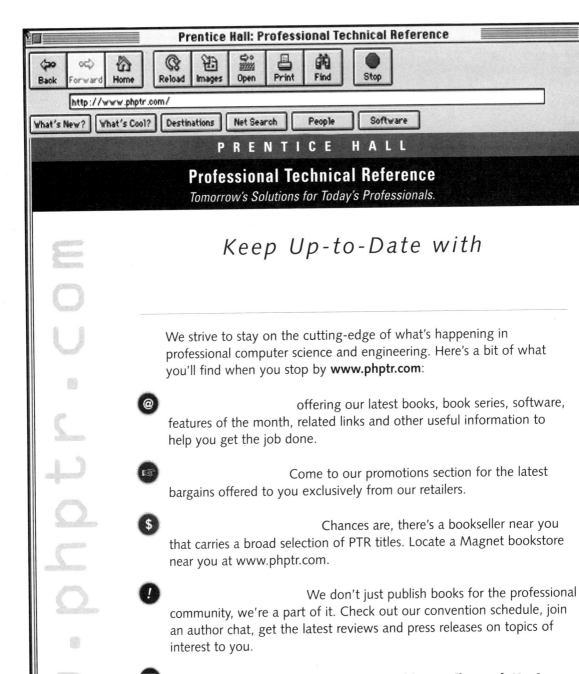

We strive to stay on the cutting-edge of what's happening in professional computer science and engineering. Here's a bit of what you'll find when you stop by **www.phptr.com**:

@ offering our latest books, book series, software, features of the month, related links and other useful information to help you get the job done.

Come to our promotions section for the latest bargains offered to you exclusively from our retailers.

$ Chances are, there's a bookseller near you that carries a broad selection of PTR titles. Locate a Magnet bookstore near you at www.phptr.com.

! We don't just publish books for the professional community, we're a part of it. Check out our convention schedule, join an author chat, get the latest reviews and press releases on topics of interest to you.

Join PH PTR's monthly email newsletter!

Want to be kept up-to-date on your area of interest? Choose a targeted category on our website, and we'll keep you informed of the latest PH PTR products, author events, reviews and conferences in your interest area.

Visit our mailroom to subscribe today! **http://www.phptr.com/mail_lists**